TSAVO

Oddball Reseachers Use Data and Guns to Save African Elephants

A Novel

DANIEL B. BOTKIN
With JOAN MELCHER

Library of Congress Control Number		2018954405
ISBN	Softcover	978-1-949574-03-6
	Hardcover	978-1-949574-04-3
	eBook	978-1-949574-05-0

Printed in the United States of America.

Book Vine Press
505 W. Lancaster Court
Inverness, IL 60010

CONTENTS

TSAVO'S GENESIS

This is a tale of what men can and cannot do when they must do something or die.

Attributed to the 16th century Spanish explorer of North America, Cabeza de Vaca, by H. Long.

*T*he British Government established Tsavo National Park in 1948, when Kenya was still one of its colonies. The new park covered 5,000 square miles of mostly flat and dry countryside to the south of Nairobi, the capitol city. What it lacked in scenic beauty it contained, at least in potential, its once abundant wildlife. Thickly vegetated by dry-land trees, shrubs and grasses, it was home to tens of thousands of elephants. Its first warden, David Sheldrick, sought to develop Tsavo into a park so that tourists could see the elephants, and he took actions to build up the elephant populations. The elephants attracted poachers who killed the animals for their ivory.

Sheldrick mounted a minor war against the poachers, temporarily eliminating them. He built roads. He dammed the park's major river and dug artesian wells to provide year-round water for the wildlife. But he succeeded too well. By the late 1950s much of the dense vegetation was gone, eaten by wildlife, mainly by elephants. By the early 1960s, worldwide concern grew that Tsavo's elephants had undergone a dangerous population explosion and were destroying the park. Tsavo became an international cause célèbre. Some experts proposed shooting excess elephants, but Sheldrick decided to hold back and let nature take

1

its course. In 1968 and 1969 a major drought struck, and 6,000 of the park's estimated 30,000 elephants died. As they died, they knocked down trees to eat the bark and upper leaves, destroying most of the vegetation. Tsavo became a wasteland, empty of all but a few wildlife, a desert for vegetation, rarely visited by tourists.

Then, a decade later, in 1979, wildlife experts piloting small aircraft began once again to see elephants moving through the park. An American philanthropic foundation, the International Ecological Fund, decided to send a small team of wildlife experts and other scientists into the park to find out how many elephants there were, learn of their condition, and determine if the park could recover and once again become a major wildlife preserve for the threatened elephants. But large numbers of elephants would attract poachers as well as scientists. And the African elephant, unlike its Indian relative, has never been tamed. It remains one of the world's most powerful and dangerous — as well as one of its most intelligent — mammals. Into this vast dry country ten people came at the request of the foundation, to find out what had happened to nature in Tsavo, to deal with wildlife and, if necessary, deal with any poachers who sought to kill elephants for profit. Here is their story.

CHAPTER 1

Within the Plains

September 1979

Here was no man's garden, but the unhandseled globe. It w as not lawn, nor pasture, nor mead, nor woodland, nor lea, nor arable, nor waste land. It was the fresh and natural surface of the planet Earth.

Henry David Thoreau, 1846.

The elephant herd moved slowly across Tsavo's dry plains, searching for plants to eat, meandering generally southward toward a river basin whose dampness, even in this drought season, the animals could scent. Dust swirled from the parched soil as the elephants walked along, but their soft, careful steps made no sound. They moved like silent pilgrims over the pages of Tsavo, following, more or less, the great matriarch, the herd's leader and the mother, grandmother, or great-grandmother of the other elephants. A few bulls, pushed out of the herd when they had reached puberty, strayed nearby, paying only slight attention to the herd of females and their young. Two bulls rubbed their trunks together as they grazed and browsed peacefully in the silent sunlight. One blew dust over its back.

The great matriarch stepped carefully over a fallen log and stopped at a graying, dying bush to pull dry leaves from it with her trunk. A secretary bird rushed away from the bush, scurrying busily along the ground as if on the way to an important meeting. The matriarch turned toward it briefly, then brought her head back to the vegetation and pushed leaves into her mouth, chewing slowly, as if thoughtfully. She raised her trunk high, sniffing the air, her huge ears out, listening, listening. Her descendants slowed their meanderings, waiting for her, some searched for a leaf or twig.

A young bull, barely a teenager, rushed past her, scattering dust, and attacked a small tree, pushing with his head, then backed away and charged it again. The tree bent, snapped, and fell. A crowned hornbill that had been considering a hollow in the tree for its nest flew before the tree struck the ground. It emitted its mournful call as if in lament and landed in a smaller tree east of the herd. A pair of weaverbirds rose from the downed tree, their elaborate woven nest cut open in the fall. They joined the hornbill on its perch, then rose and circled away. Dust rose around the fallen tree, a column of yellow smoke rose high into the air. The silent herd had signed its presence to any wishing to know.

Several large females joined the young bull, pulling what remained of the tree's sparse foliage with their trunks, stuffing the leaves into their mouths. Their chewing made a dry, crackling sound, like a small fire sparking. But the matriarch remained still, reaching her trunk out and moving it as if to locate some scent, fanning her ears and turning them this way and that, listening, listening.

One of her daughters, also a huge animal, stepped over a small, rocky rise and stopped at a standing dead tree, searching it for something to eat. A small gray mammal, a tree hyrax, colored much the same as the elephant, came out of a hollow in that tree and climbed down. The elephant ignored it. High above, unseen by the elephants, vultures soared in the searing sunlight, coasting on updrafts of the sun-heated air, watching, waiting.

The tip of the matriarch's trunk shifted to her right. Her ears had picked up the distant sound of a motor vehicle. After some minutes, two vehicles came over a rise and stopped. Men got out,

4

and the matriarch turned toward them, her eyes trying to focus on them. One lifted a large automatic rifle and began firing at the herd. Bullets struck one of the matriarch's daughters, and she sank down slowly, noiselessly. The matriarch trumpeted and began to charge, but one of the men threw a small object, like a rounded stone, at her. It exploded, blowing a large hole in her stomach. Blood cascaded onto the parched ground. She reached her attacker and tossed him into the air. He tumbled, twisted, to the ground. She settled slowly.

Another man rushed out of one of the vehicles and dragged the injured man away. Other men came out of the two vehicles, shooting into the herd and driving them back, away from the matriarch's body. Several of the men started power saws. They pulled on starter-chains and the small machines responded, calling out a harsh roar like an angry animal in danger. The sawyers cut tusks from the downed matriarch, ivory dust dropping like tears of stone. They loaded the ivory into their vehicles, and were just beginning to attack the tusks from the dying daughter when a huge bull elephant crashed out of the bush, charging.

The men jumped into their vehicles and stepped on the gas to flee, scattering dust into the bull's face. He dug his tusks into one vehicle's sheet metal skin, sending the machine skidding and sliding before it escaped, bouncing over low bush, a column of yellow dust rising behind it. He chased it into its tail of dust, then stopped, turned, and came back to the two downed animals. He tried to push each elephant up, using his trunk, tusks, and head. The scattered and confused crowd of the herd returned to watch. Then one of the matriarch's daughters raised her trunk and called and led the others away, once again on a meandering path toward the riverbed. The big bull walked slowly northward into Tsavo's silence.

CHAPTER 2

An Old Man on Horseback

A month later

A silent wilderness . . . something great and invincible, like evil or truth, waiting patiently.

Joseph Conrad in Lord Jim

An old man on horseback rode just inside the highway, the railroad, and a dirt track that marked the border of Tsavo National Park. He was dressed in leather and had a long rifle mounted on one side of his saddle, an old sword from a nineteenth-century military officer on the other. He rode stiffly, as if on military parade, then stopped just off the dirt track, where the deep shaded green of dense forests gave way to the arid yellow of Tsavo's dry soil, its barrenness marked by a seemingly ordered scattering of dead trees, silent symbols of the land's destruction, like wooden branching tombstones of that dying land. It was a transition from living to death that always caused him to pause and ponder. Off in the distance he saw a small cloud of dust traveling slowly toward him in the bright sunlight.

There was a shadow within, some kind of animal, moving slowly. From his old and wrinkled leather saddlebag he took a large, ancient

6

pair of field glasses. Through them he saw that the darkness within the dust was a person, struggling, falling down and rising, again and again. He put away the field glasses and spurred his horse toward the person, then slowed to a trot and stopped. A dirty, dusty man appeared, with long scraggly hair. A strong smell emanated from him. The old man held his horse's reins tight.

The ragged man approached and leaned, almost falling, against the horse, who whinnied and shied, shifting sideways. The man fell to the ground. The rider stared at the man, waiting. The wanderer mouthed something the old man could not understand, and pointed at his lips, then sank to the ground. Reaching into a saddlebag, the old man pulled out a canvas canteen and tossed it to the ground. The younger man crawled to it and drank greedily.

"They're out there. Lost. Maybe dyin'. Help Mary. . . ." He rolled over and rested, saying nothing more for a few minutes, then struggled up and began walking. "Maybe I can hitch a goddam ride. Please, go help 'em. Some of 'em could be dead by now, others dyin'. Save 'em ... Mary. And Bruce. Him too. They'll want him dead especially." He spat and took another drink of water.

He stumbled toward the dirt track and the railroad, then to the paved highway and north toward Nairobi without looking back. The man on horseback shook his head, thinking another fool who thought he could play in Tsavo and come out alive. He'll probably make it. But those he spoke about leaving behind. Not likely. Curious. He would have to find them, within this unrelenting unyielding vastness whose pale ghostly soil marked a place of death as clearly as any devastated landscape could. He spurred his horse, and rode into the Tsavo plains in the direction the dirty, stumbling man had pointed. Help them. But who and what are they doing? He flashed his whip and his horse galloped into the sun-drenched plains, mouth foaming in the dry heat, as if he were carrying not a man but death himself.

CHAPTER 3

Davie and the Elephants

The month before

Who speaks in primordial images speaks to us as with a thousand trumpets.

C.G. Jung

Three old and dusty Land Rovers, two pulling trailers, turned off Route 109, the paved road south from Nairobi, Kenya, and drove east into the dry lands of Tsavo National Park. To Joseph Kenjoy the man watching them from the Manyani Gate that led into the park, the vehicles and their trailers appeared as beads sliding silently on an invisible and flexible string across mauvish plains. He stared intently, listening, but heard no sound. Sunlit dust rose as they moved, surrounding each with a sepia tone as if in an old photograph. He shouldered a sniper's rifle and aimed it at the lead Land Rover, but sunlight reflected off something metallic in the distance, blinding him, and the dust deflected details. He wiped his eyes and looked again.

He saw a lumpy, roundish spot appear on the horizon — an elephant, he believed. It approached the lead vehicle, which slowed and stopped, while the two other Land Rovers turned southeastward.

He expected the lead vehicle to do the same, but instead it started up and continued toward the elephant, if that was what it was — it was still too far to tell. He let his gun hang loosely toward the ground, took out a cigarette, and smoked as he watched the meandering dots and dashes. The elephant and lead vehicle were like two magnets drawn together. The other vehicles wandered away toward the Galana River.

From a backpack he took out a pair of binoculars and focused on the elephant. That's what it was, all right, and it had stopped, facing the Land Rover. The Land Rover stopped too. This was getting interesting. If that group was being led by the person he thought it would be, Bruce Airley, a man Joseph had known since schooldays, they would have stopped only if that were some amazing elephant. Maybe it was the big tusker that everyone talked about — the biggest of the big, the oldest of the old. His ivory would be worth a fortune. It made him take a deep breath. During all the ivory poaching he had done, years now, he had never killed an elephant with tusks so huge, worth a fortune.

Nice of Bruce to decide just now to come back to Tsavo and show him where the grand old elephant was, the elephant all the poachers talked about, but few had ever seen. Now was Joseph's big chance to get its ivory. What a story that would make! And it would also be a chance for a little revenge against Bruce, who he had tried to befriend for all the years when both of them went to a church-led primary school. Perhaps that Maasai was with them too, Michael, another school chum, the only Maasai at that school. With Bruce gone, poaching had been much easier. In fact, it had made Joseph rich. He should be sorry to see Bruce back, but strange to say he was happy to know it; there were old scores to settle, and with Michael.

A wind blew a dusty cloud between Joseph and the distant scene, obscuring the elephant, the Land Rover, and its driver. He stamped out his cigarette and pulled a grenade from his military belt, tossed it into the air, caught it, and tossed it again, then put it back. He walked over to his shiny new Toyota Land Cruiser He was proud of his vehicle. It represented his success. Not many people in Kenya could afford a Land Cruiser. He wiped dust from its door panel, polished away a spot of dirt, placed his gun in a rack and his pack in the back seat. He started the engine, and drove through the gate into the park, following the path of the Land Rovers.

* * *

When they first saw the big bull elephant, Davie was driving their Land Rover, Mary was in the front seat next to him and Paul, Howie, and Elizabeth in back. They had entered Tsavo National Park and driven through dry lands with little vegetation, a flat, barren landscape, seeming flatter in the harsh morning sun.

"This here's the Yatta Plateau," Davie told them. "We're near Lugard Falls on the Galana River — they call it the Athi River here." He rubbed a hand through his black, greasy-looking beard and glanced over at Mary, who was looking intently out her side window.

"The vegetation's a little denser than any we've seen since we entered the park," she said. "More like what I expected in the Serengeti, more like prairie and savanna."

"Yeah. That's it. All the water, I guess," Davie said. She can talk about anything she wants to and I'll answer, he thought. Don't see many chicks like her out here, 'cept some tourist babes ya can't get near. Out of the corner of his eye he admired her blond hair — its ends curled inward, caressing her neck. She had the damnedest freckles on her nose and cheeks, like little decorations, sprinkles on peaches and cream. He turned his attention to the elephant, slowing the Land Rover and stretching his long, birdlike neck to peer at the huge animal.

Although the bull elephant was fully a hundred yards away, he appeared to Elizabeth, watching from the backseat, the biggest thing she had ever seen. The thicket of small shrubs on each side of the dirt track where he emerged made him look even bigger. Not only was he tall, his head was massive and lumpy. The tip of one tusk was broken off, and one ear was torn. The defects only made him look more ominous. When he came out into the clearing — a long grassy swath the length of a football field — he stopped and stared at the Land Rover. Elizabeth was sure he could overturn the vehicle with ease and kill all of them in an instant. She assumed that Davie would pull off the track and let the big bull pass. But he didn't. He stopped on the path and turned off the engine.

"Show you what a jumbo's like when he gets mad," Davie said.

"I don't think I want to know," Mary replied meekly.

"Me either," Elizabeth said. She glanced at her watch. Ten o'clock.

Paul and Howie, next to her, stared silently. They might say something too, to get us out of here, she thought.

"They're int'restin'. Fascinatin'," Davie said. "Watch this old guy carefully." The big bull turned his body perpendicular to the line between himself and the Land Rover and walked at right angles to that line, moving his head vigorously up and down.

"Oh, good," Mary said. "He's going away."

Davie laughed. "Oh, no he ain't. That's just the start, his first warning."

"Can't wait for his second warning," Elizabeth said drily.

The elephant paced about thirty yards and then stopped. He turned, now off the track, and stared at the Land Rover.

"He's tellin' us he don't want us around and we should get outta the way," said Davie. "*Loxodonta africana.* Yeah. *Loxodonta africana maximus.* Big fucker!"

The elephant watched silently. Elizabeth and the others sat riveted to their seats, partly in fear, partly in fascination.

"Pretty well-known behavior, is it?" Paul asked. "Seen it before?"

Davie nodded. "Big motherfucker. Y'see," he whispered over his shoulder to the three in the back, "if he came straight at us, now that'd be a direct threat. This way, he's showin' us his threat, but it ain't directly aggressive."

Paul, Howie, and Elizabeth, squeezed in the backseat, shifted against each other, trying to see out. The brim of Howie's baseball cap pushed against Elizabeth's forehead and slid down against her eye. "Howie, for God's sake," she whispered. Howie grinned.

"You can *feel* that elephant's mood," Paul said,

In spite of herself, and in spite of Davie, Elizabeth was finding the elephant fascinating; as a geologist she had had little experience with these big game animals. Paul and Howie probably are more familiar with them, she thought.

The big bull took a step back and stared at them again. There was a silent pause. To Elizabeth it seemed that all of nature was holding its breath. Then an African dove began a steady, monotonous call somewhere off to the right. The bull turned his head and began to pull at the leaves on a nearby shrub with his trunk. He pushed the leaves into his mouth and chewed slowly, still watching them, as if in contemplation.

"He seems undecided," Paul said from the backseat, squirming.

"Kee-rect," Davie said. "That's your elephant. Seems undecided, but fuckin' dangerous and aggressive as hell when he makes up his mind. Six and a half tons of mind-made-up. Thirteen feet high, so they say. Betcha he's fourteen!"

"Wow! Story and a half tall," Howie said, "Yeah. More than one story, that elephant, for sure."

"While he's making up his mind, let's get off the path and let him pass," Elizabeth said.

There was no answer. The big bull looked up and stared at the Land Rover. Then he came directly toward them, moving his head up and down the same way as before, but approaching directly this time. He came on and on.

"That's his next level of threat," Davie whispered.

The elephant came within thirty yards of the Land Rover, moving with the momentum of a locomotive on a track, slow but all power and no braking. Then he stopped and stared silently at the Land Rover. The windshield framed his large head, the only part of him really visible, much like a view in a television program about wildlife.

"Nature in the raw," Howie whispered. Elizabeth bit her lip.

"Now he's beginnin' to get upset," Davie said. "He really wants us to get the hell away."

"Let's do it, then," Mary said. "Let's go. Please!"

"Nah. I gotta show you guys what you're out here studyin', don't I?" Davie turned his long neck to look at those in the backseat. Elizabeth sat in wonderment, as much at Davie's bald machismo as at the ominous presence of the elephant. It was unclear who was the more rational, the elephant or Davie, and who was the more patient.

The elephant approached closer, now within twenty yards, and raised his huge head as if looking at them over bifocals. He trumpeted for the first time, so loudly that it seemed to shake the Land Rover. Mary involuntarily put her hands over her ears. Davie saw her do this and smiled. He rarely got this close to such a good-looking woman. The bull lowered his head and stared at them for what felt like minutes but was only a few seconds, as if trying to make up his mind whether to charge. At last he backed slowly away, still staring at them.

"Might charge next," Davie said. He started the engine, pushed in the clutch, and put the Land Rover into first gear, but he still did not move the vehicle. "Ever see a charge by a bull elephant? Somethin' you'll never forget," he said. Mary put her hand on the gearshift — and thereby inadvertently on Davie's hand. He'd been waiting for that. "I — I don't know that I want to see that," she said.

"Ya gotta see it. Far out. That's the biggest bull I ever seen. He's worth as much as this Land Rover, at least his ivory is. What them poachers wouldn't do to get his ivory," Davie said, whistling softly and once again stretching his long, birdlike neck to get a better view.

The bull continued to back away carefully, maintaining a direct view of the Land Rover. When he had retreated about forty yards, he stopped and stared once again at the vehicle.

"Come on, you bastard," Davie said under his breath. Nobody else said a word. The bull raised his trunk and put his ears straight out, seeming to grow even larger.

"That's his charge mode," Davie whispered.

"Please move away," Mary said, unthinkingly tightening her hand on Davie's. Davie felt a thrill. The bull trumpeted again, raising his head and shaking it violently from side to side, his ears straight out, flapping slightly, his yellow-white tusks flashing. It was an incredibly violent and aggressive gesture to the four newcomers to Tsavo. Once again the elephant seemed to shake the vehicle with his trumpeting. But then he lowered his head, turned, and began to walk away, following an arc that led him onto the grassy field. When he reached a point opposite them and about a hundred yards distant, he stopped, turned to face them, and twisted his head to the left and then to the right in a figure eight.

"It's as if he's saying, 'that's what I could've done to you, you sons of bitches,'" Paul said.

"You bastard," Elizabeth said, leaning forward to Davie. "That elephant's got more sense than you. Why the hell didn't you move?" The big bull stood still, staring them down.

"I wanted you guys to see nature in the raw. Most powerful animal walkin' the earth. Nothin' else like it. Someday you'll thank me and tell your grandkids about this."

The bull turned abruptly and marched away, circling the Land Rover and returning to the dirt track about a hundred yards behind them. Once back on the track, he turned again, twisted his head from side to side one last time, then moved on.

"Yep. Just showed us what he coulda done to us if he wanted to," Davie said. Elizabeth shifted and stretched and shook her black hair back f rom her face. Why hadn't Paul or Howie spoken up more and urged Davie to move? she wondered. What were they thinking? She turned and watched the elephant marching off into the distance. For herself, it was not a good beginning with Davie, but it sure was an impressive first meeting with elephants.

* * *

Bruce Airley had passed Davie's Land Rover as it turned toward the big bull. He was torn about what to do. He wanted to do the same as Davie — that old bull fascinated him — but he had been hired to lead this group of scientists into Tsavo and, as usual, felt obliged to do things right, so he should continue on directly to the camp. But he had come back to Tsavo and taken this job — probably his last, he thought, as a wildlife guide — to bring himself once more, one last time, among the elephants and, of all the elephants, to that one. The oldest of the old, the ancient bull of Tsavo represented all of nature to Bruce, the epitome of it, he thought. His friend and colleague, Johnny Mackenzie, who would be joining them soon, said elephants were fascinating because they seemed so intelligent, but there was something more to them for Bruce — a kind of intelligent contentment, a comfortable confidence. He wished that for himself. And a robustness that he envied and planned to study. He had brought along a newly developed kit for tranquilizing animals — tranquilizer-containing pellets that could be shot from his rifle. Bruce was planning to put the big bull to sleep long enough for him to make some measurements, to record the details of this biggest of the big. But he knew he wanted to reach out and touch the big elephant, some kind of emotional contact with him. What he was wishing for deep inside himself he couldn't put it into words. He hoped would reveal secrets to the bull's vigor, longevity, and contentment. But it was something more. Contact with the essence of nature, or something like that. He couldn't quite explain it even to himself. Maybe he would use the kit, maybe he wouldn't.

Bruce drove his Land Rover on, weaving among acacia trees, unaware that he was slowing down, aware only of his own discomfort, an inner turmoil that had always driven him through life.

Pushing those thoughts away as best he could, Bruce continued toward the camp, hoping Davie had shown the newcomers the elephant quickly and had then moved on. Bruce could save his own search for that bull for another day. But after Bruce had gone a half mile or more Davie was still not visible in Bruce's rearview mirror. Against his better judgment, he turned his Land Rover and its trailer around and drove back to find Davie. Or rather the Land Rover seemed to turn itself. It wasn't easy hauling that trailer. He rarely used one — few did out here. His big-game guide buddies would laugh at him for doing so, but this group of scientists just had too much equipment. Michael was pulling one, too. But Davie wasn't, so he would be hard to follow over the rough terrain.

"What are we doing?" a voice asked from the back.

"Davie's just spotted the biggest and oldest bull elephant in Tsavo," Bruce explained. "Famous all over East Africa, known to the Brits as Old Ragged Ears. In Swahili, he's called 'Zamani Baba,' which means long ago, but I guess with this elephant it means something closer to 'born long ago,' so literally 'old father.' We'll just take a quick look ourselves."

Before the big elephant die-off, when there were still plenty of tourists coming to Tsavo, that big bull even had his own police guards, around the clock, to protect him from poachers. Not anymore. He was on his own, just like Bruce. He began to wonder if the elephant ever had to lead a crowd of his own kind around Tsavo, a kind of elephant wildlife guide, and suffer things like Bruce suffered.

"Not like you, Bruce." It was Horst Grobben, his old nemesis, riding in the backseat. Horst had invited himself on this trip and there had been no way for Bruce to say no to the old son-of-a-bitch. Why, he wondered, had he accepted this job once he knew that Horst would be one of his charges?

"I thought you always stuck to plans — old reliable Bruce. But just a short time inside Tsavo and look at you, you're acting on a whim. Don't we have to get settled in camp?"

Horst was succeeding again in his ability to put Bruce on edge. Bruce found it unsettling, annoying at best and sometimes it seemed to push him to do things he wouldn't have done without the man's influence.

"I don't want Davie going off by himself," Bruce answered, but he knew Horst was right. This was not a good way to start the expedition. Bruce had planned this trip carefully and wanted it to go smoothly. Damn Davie and damn Horst, he thought.

"Still plenty of time, but best to get things set up early. You're right. Just be a short side-trip."

It was true. Well, it was *partially* true. Davie did not have a walkie-talkie, so Bruce could not just call him and order him to turn around. Besides, Davie was not likely to do what he was asked over a radio. You had to confront Davie, stare him down to get him to do anything he wasn't keen to do.

"I for one would love to see this great animal, if he's all that Bruce says he is," came a British accent from the front passenger seat. Thank God for once for Cecile, Bruce thought. Cecile Carr was a leader in the British animal welfare movement, and Bruce had come across him many times over the years, but, away from Tsavo now for almost five years, he had lost touch with Cecile and so many of the old hands. The big fat Brit was usually a pain in the rear, but he and Bruce had always managed to get along over the years, even though Bruce disagreed strongly with Cecile's insistence that you should never shoot any wildlife, even for scientific research or even to keep a population in check. Mushy-headed sentimentalist, that's what he was, Bruce thought.

Bruce picked up his walkie-talkie and called Michael, who was driving the third Land Rover. Michael said he would follow Bruce as well.

"You know this guy Davie very well?" Cecile asked.

"Not very. Run across him once in a while. I had to get a third driver who knew Tsavo, and I didn't have much time to look," Bruce answered. "Davie was available, and few know Tsavo as well as he does. Heard stories about him though. Oddball. Self-taught, no degrees. They say he was a grave digger in the States, somehow got interested in vultures. He's known for it all over East Africa — the States too — as *the* vulture expert. They brought him to California to help with condors, some organization did. Erratic, though, some say."

"Weird."

"The kind you often meet in the bush. Expatriate who probably couldn't succeed in a regular job back home."

Bruce caught up with Davie just as the bull was passing Davie's vehicle and corkscrewing his head and tusks. Bruce stopped and watched. Yes, if any living thing can take care of itself, it's that old bull, he thought. Controlled intelligence. Funny thing for a so-called wildlife scientist like me to be caught thinking. He watched the bull's every move, forgetting everything else, including the human charges in his vehicle and the very purpose of the expedition into Tsavo. There was just himself and the elephant.

Bruce had planned to walk over to Davie and tell him to turn around immediately and head for camp. But before he could, Davie's Land Rover sped off toward Lugard Falls. "Damn him," Bruce muttered again, half to himself, realizing that he had gotten so distracted that he had fallen down on his job.

CHAPTER 4

At Lugard Falls

You cannot understand science and its relation to anything else unless you understand and appreciate that it is the great adventure of our time. You do not live in your time unless you understand that this is a tremendous adventure and a wild and exciting thing.

Richard Feynman

Worn engine running roughly, the Land Rover wrenched low shrubs, plowed the sandy soil, four-wheel drive grinding downed branches, scraping old logs, sheet metal screeching. No game, no wildlife at all. Empty plains. Bruce drove northwest and soon saw Davie's Land Rover up ahead, stopped at Lugard Falls, a scenic overlook on the edge of a plateau.

Bruce pulled up about twenty yards from Davie's Land Rover and got out, appreciating the scent of the bush and even the incessant sound of the Africa doves, the old scents and sounds that he loved so much. He had missed Tsavo, had felt adrift ever since the big elephant die-off a decade before and the terrible things that had happened to him since. Terrible for his career, for his personal life, for his feelings about himself, terrible for the elephants — terrible for everything.

Ten years ago he thought the solution for him was simple: It was time for him to leave Africa and do something different. What was that he had heard? You had to reinvent yourself every seven years in this modern world? Then he was just thirty-six, not even at the prime of his life. Well, he would go off and do that. But it hadn't worked out. He never could shake the peculiar feelings that had taken over him after things had gone so badly, and just when he had thought he was doing what was right. His life had become worse, not better, as soon as he had left the great savannas and plains and the wildlife of East Africa. On top of all his other feelings, his time away from Africa had left him with a special emptiness. And now he was back, with the old familiar scents of the plains refreshing, renewing him.

Years before — before the worst had happened — he had thought of himself as the complete rationalist, able to take on any challenge, outthink and outsmart any opponent, because, in particular, he was so rational. A child of Descartes is the way he had thought about himself. And here he was back in Tsavo, with the feeling that Tsavo itself was challenging him, a most irrational, or perhaps more to the point, most nonrational, feeling.

Davie and his passengers were not yet out of their vehicle, so Bruce walked over to the falls and searched the rainless vista for wildlife, people, anything unusual, staring at the occasional shrub and fever tree in the distance to see whether any animal — or poacher — might be trying to hide behind one. Years of working as a big-game hunter, photographer's guide, and as a wildlife scientist, had made this second nature to him, at least when he was not distracted by something that especially fascinated him, or something that deeply troubled him.

Heat rose from the hot, desiccated land, making the distant scene seem to rise and fall in waves. He stretched his long legs, adjusted his hat, wiped dust from around his eyes, and put his sunglasses back on. Always the professional when out in the bush, he wore a starched tan khaki shirt and shorts. Attached to his belt in a leather sheath was a long, sharp knife that he used to skin and clean game. His thirty-ought-six rifle — his elephant gun — and his two

German-made pistols were in the Land Rover. Everything recently cleaned and polished, restored to perfect working order.

He walked over to Davie's Land Rover just as Paul Peterson, whom he had met briefly a few months before in New York City to plan this trip, climbed out. Six foot, light brown hair — longish, like a Beatle haircut from the Sixties — blue-violet eyes, rugged build. A Ph. D. ecologist from the States, but not the usual wimp scientist, Bruce thought. Paul had been hired by the International Ecological Fund to do much of the work of this expedition and seemed earnest, academic, and naive, but probably pretty good at what he did.

As Paul approached, Bruce noticed that he walked with a limp — very slight, but something that Bruce, always watchful of animals of all kinds, noticed. He had missed it in their brief encounter in the States. He guessed Paul was in his thirties. Young guy. Too bad, Bruce thought to himself. Wonder how it happened. They greeted each other, shaking hands warmly. Perhaps Paul needed a mentor, a father figure, and perhaps it might be himself.

Climbing awkwardly from Davie's Land Rover and grinning broadly, another young man emerged who seemed all arms and legs, with eyes out of focus behind big glasses, a wide smile, and big ears. He stretched and stood blinking in the sun, wiping dust from his glasses. Paul introduced him as Howie — "actually Howard Elwin Clark, if you want to know his full name. Howie's an expert on soils."

Howie walked over to Bruce and vigorously shook his hand. "Yep, Howard Elwin Clark — my friends call me 'Heck'."

Bruce had little experience with this kind of expert and thought Howie suitably strange for what he did for a profession. His attire was equally bizarre: a short-sleeved sport shirt in a patchwork pattern of orange and blue hanging out over faded and patched blue jeans, a baseball cap with alternating triangles of red and white, and lightweight black-and-white basketball sneakers. Howie put his glasses back on and stared to the eastward plains of Tsavo.

God, have American scientists gotten as bad as that? Bruce thought. He had spent most of the last few years in Bermuda, trying to find peace and quiet for himself, with an occasional trip to London or New York when asked to consult on some endangered species, and he hadn't seen anybody like Howie in his brief New York visits. For a moment, he pictured his mother, a beautiful American, and his father, a stiff upper-class Englishman. He looked again at the two American men. What a contrast between Howie and Paul. Then a rising column of dust in the distance caught his eye.

"What's that?" Paul asked. "Dust devil? We have those sometimes back home in Oregon, in the eastern grasslands — do you call them that here? Miniature tornadoes spun up during the heat of the day."

The dust cloud continued moving steadily away from them, like a truck hauling grain on a dirt road. "Most likely a vehicle," Bruce said. "Hmm — not many people come to the park anymore. Not since the big elephant die-off. It was elephants the park was made for, and that attracted tourists."

"Poachers. I knew it," Howie said. "'Come along for a good time. See lots of wildlife.' That's what *you* told me, Paul. 'Perfectly safe. Free of poachers for years.' Well, they must be back." He hunkered down and stared across the falls down into the dry plains below. "Oh, God, why me?" he said loudly to no one in particular as he wiped his forehead.

Paul laughed softly. Bruce smiled but said nothing. Paul had told him in New York that Howie had insisted on being allowed to come along, and Paul had warned that Bruce would have to put up with a rather strange character, but assured him that it was worth it because Howie knew so much. Much about what? Bruce wondered. Sometimes a fool, sometimes a wise man, was that what Paul had said about him? And what could be the problem with another difficult character out here in a wildlife park? Tsavo seemed to attract them — expatriates of many nations who could never have made it back home.

Howie reached into a pocket of his backpack, took out a yo-yo, and began to play with it. Bruce watched, fascinated. Howie had the yo-yo doing loops and arcs, moving so quickly that even Bruce's keen eyes could not quite follow it. Well, maybe Howie would be a unique character in Bruce's experience.

"Where'd you get that thing?" Bruce asked.

"It's a long story. Paul's fault. I'll tell you later."

"So you've worked together before?"

"Yes. The four of us — Mary, Liz, Paul, and me." He palmed the yo-yo for a moment and changed the subject. "So this is Tsavo. World's largest wildlife sanctuary. Fodor's Guidebook says it's bigger than Connecticut, two-thirds the size of Belgium." He spun the yo-yo a couple more times. "I'd say it's a Connecticut turned dustbowl. What'd I read? Six thousand elephants died here in that drought ten years ago — in 'sixty-eight or 'sixty-nine. A sanctuary of elephant skeletons. Dead wildlife. Dust and shrubs. Maybe a few live elephants left. Parsimonious Park."

He squatted in the shade cast by the Land Rover and picked up some sandy soil. He sifted the soil through his hands, rubbing a little of it between his right thumb and index finger.

Bruce watched. So that's what an expert on dirt does when he's uncomfortable, he thought. Uncomfortable until he touches the ground and sifts the soil through his fingers. Hmm . . . strange, but not so strange. Bruce was suddenly fascinated, and knelt down beside Howie. "Paul tells me you're one of the world's experts on this stuff," he said, picking up some soil and rubbing some between his thumb and forefinger.

"Did he? Well, you know, if you learn fifty terms in any profession, you can pass yourself off as an expert. So don't be too sure." Howie grinned a wide, toothy, foolish sort of grin and licked his lips. Then he took a tiny magnifying lens out of his shirt pocket and peered through it at some of the soil he had in his palm. He looked like a watchmaker fixing a timepiece, Bruce thought. Howie motioned him to squat down and look, and he did, finding in the lens sparkling grains like little jewels mixed in with some fine-grained organic duff, out of which a tiny, brightly colored insect crawled.

A new feeling came over Bruce, a kind of relief. Was this where the truth lay, the secrets of nature in a handful of dust microscopically, in the very soil over which he had walked and searched, searched and walked, for decades? It was almost an overwhelming thought, at least for a second or two.

"Aha! Another seeker," Howie said, nodding his head up and down, toothy grin in motion. Bruce asked him what he meant, but Howie did not answer, only saying, "It's the dilemma of our time, isn't it? The meaning of it all, what this nature stuff really is. Back home, it's the latest fad, environmentalism. But fad or no, who understands how we moderns fit into nature? Strange time we're living in."

"It didn't always look this way," Bruce said, standing up beside Howie. "When my grandfather came out to Africa from England, around the turn of the century, this was miles of wooded country, or so he described it in his letters home. It would have looked dark green as far as you could see."

"You mean all that brown — that land all the way to the horizon that's almost empty of vegetation — that's what the elephants did?" Howie asked.

"Yes. And they did it in a shockingly short time. In one of his letters — we have a trunk full of them — my grandfather wrote that he felt hemmed in by an 'impenetrable jungle' on all sides when he first stepped out of the hut where he had camped his first night here. He wrote about low, stunted trees and thick undergrowth, full of thorns. He said it was so thick you could get through it only by crawling."

"Full of wildlife you couldn't see," Howie said.

"British grandfather? I thought you were American," Paul said.

"Half and half. My mother was from the States." Bruce looked again into Tsavo, and saw a small dot moving across the plains. He was sure it was the big bull that Davie had affronted and Bruce had wanted to approach, moving away from them, deeper into the wilderness. For a moment his heart sank. What was it about that elephant? He wanted to follow it, leaving everything else behind. But then he was back, pushing his hat firmly on his head, back to the reality of the here and now and his task to lead these people into and out of Tsavo.

Davie finally got out of his Land Rover, wiping his dusty hands across his black beard as if it were a towel, then through his greasy black hair. Bruce wasn't sure whether he was using his hair to clean his hands or his hands to clean his hair. Neither seemed especially clean. The guy was just as weird as he had seemed several years before, but truth to tell, his beard was trimmed neatly. If he were shaved and clean he would look like that American musician — Cat Stevens, that was it. Yes, same straight nose, actually nice features. He just dirties it up, Bruce thought.

He ushered Davie off to the side, away from the others, as if to show him something. "Glad you're along, Davie. We need all the help we can get on this bloody safari, especially an experienced person like you." He looked Davie in the eye, Davie a little shorter than he was. "No time to lose, though. So, if you don't mind my asking, what did you stop for?" He put an arm casually on Davie's shoulder. Bruce felt a little hypocritical for asking, considering his own fascination with the big bull, but he had to speak this way to Davie so he could maintain control over the group.

"Showed them that big bull ya saw."

"Well, a quick stop would be okay. But I started to get concerned about you. We don't really have time for a tourist show. We've got to get to First Camp, get settled before dark. I don't know what they told you, but we're being paid by some big American foundation to do a quick job, find out how the elephants are doing a decade after the great drought. They're fussy about time and money — you know that kind of foundation. They said something about immediate congressional action, so they want expert opinion fast. They — all those bureaucrats and congressmen and so forth — think these are simple questions. Sorry to rush you, but just between you and me, I'm feeling a bit pressured."

"Six thousand elephants died in that drought. Yep. Big time at the elephant graveyard," Davie said, shaking his head. "Destroyin' all them trees and shrubs as they starved to death, turnin' this whole place into a desert. Man! Sad time for them jumbos."

"For us as well. But the point is, my friend, we've got to stick to the job."

"Yeah, sure." Davie shrugged. "But, Bruce, you must be as interested in that big bull as me.

Come on, man, be honest. I heard about all the thing s you've done out here, years ago. Tryin' to save the elephants, tryin' to help 'em and at the same time shootin' a lot of them. You of all people got to understand — I just figured they're here to study elephants, and that sure *was* an elephant, biggest I ever seen. I'm sure it's the oldest and biggest bull, the one everybody's always talkin' about. They call him the old grandfather elephant or somethin' like that."

"Zamani Baba," Bruce said. "That's his Swahili name. Sort of Swahili, anyway."

"I betcha that was him," Davie said. "The locals tell strange stories about him. I just thought I'd take advantage of the opportunity, y'know. Loosen up, Bruce. The elephants that survived been in bad shape for years. A few more minutes ain't gonna make no difference. We'll find out what we're s'posed to find out."

"All right. Nothing wrong with a brief stop. But next time, no distractions and no going off on your own — that's my way, buddy. My safari. I'm sure you understand." Davie shrugged again. "You got it."

* * *

Joseph drove his Toyota Land Cruiser into Tsavo and took the route to Lugard Falls, guessing that his former school chum, Bruce, would take his group there for a look into the park. He wanted to make sure that it was actually Bruce and that Michael was there too. He wanted to watch them, but did not want them to see him. He picked up their tire tracks a few miles before the falls. As he neared the falls, he slowed down, stopped, turned off his engine, and listened. Doves called. A pair of crowned hornbills flew over him toward the falls, circling and rising as they passed him. He liked the crowned hornbill, one of Africa's many exotic and intriguing birds. It reminded him of a scruffy sort of parrot, but it had that extra "crown" paralleling the top of its red bill, giving it a more sober and domineering look.

He left his Land Cruiser and walked toward the falls, carrying his rifle and binoculars. He moved in close enough to see the safari vehicles, keeping out of sight — not easy to do in the open plains. He crouched behind the largest tree he could find and watched from a hundred yards or so. A bat-eared f ox ambled by, stopped, and looked at him. He beckoned to it to come over to him; he liked this small carnivore. Truth to tell, he identified with them — quiet, sneaky, hard to discover unless they wanted to be. Clever killers. The fox ambled away, stopping near the edge of the escarpment, and looked toward the people and their vehicles.

Through his binoculars Joseph was certain that he saw Bruce and, of course, there was no missing Michael, the very tall and thin Maasai, the only one to become a park ranger and to be British educated. There were women as well, which surprised Joseph. He could not make out much about them from this distance. What kind of group was Bruce guiding this time? Clearly not the usual tourist group. This was likely some kind of scientific team sent to check on poaching. Michael might be there in an official ranger capacity. He had better watch out. And Joseph certainly did not like them coming into Tsavo and upsetting his carefully made plans, to poach a few elephants when nobody else was around and leave no trace.

He watched the comings and goings for a while, surprised to see that one of the women went down over the edge of the escarpment. What was she, some kind of police or auxiliary park ranger, or one of those representatives from an international conservation organization? Whatever she was, she only spelled trouble. He wanted these people out of the park, and certainly out of his way. He put down his binoculars and picked up his rifle and aimed at Bruce, smiling to himself, then put the rifle down. Not now. Best to be the bat-eared fox, quiet, stealthy. After a half hour's viewing through the binoculars, he returned to his vehicle and drove as quietly as he could back to the Manyari Gate. With all the equipment they had in those trailers, they were clearly planning to stay a while in the park, so he had plenty of time to think over what to do.

He would call his contacts later.

CHAPTER 5

Elizabeth

---

*. . . insufficient data comin' through . . . Don't know what
I'm gonna do . . . Slow down, sweet talkin' woman . . . You've
got me runnin' . . . . . . You've got me searching.*

Electric Light Orchestra

After their little talk, Bruce ushered Davie back to the others just as the two American women emerged from Davie's Land Rover. Bruce hadn't met them yet — Davie had driven them up from the coastal city of Mombasa.

"This is Elizabeth Esker Moraine, our expert on landforms and erosion and how water shapes the land and the land shapes the water," Paul said, then hesitated for a moment, "and this is Mary Weaver, who studies the effects of large animals on vegetation," Paul said rather stiffly. He seems uncomfortable in the role as leader of the American group, Bruce thought.

Bruce took a good look at the women. Neither fit his idea of a typical American female scientist, most of whom made themselves look as unattractive and unfeminine as possible, since there was plenty of prejudice against women in these tough field sciences. Mary was one of the most beautiful women he had ever seen, a petite blonde with a delicate but perfect figure even in field clothes. When she looked at him, he saw large blue eyes, long brown eyelashes, high cheekbones beneath smooth skin. His view was suddenly only of her, the rest of the world cut off. He backed away slightly, took a deep breath, and turned to conceal his surprise, but as he did so, he noticed Elizabeth watching him coolly. Taller than the other, with shoulder-length black hair against very white skin, she was attractive, too, but she seemed to be reading his every thought.

"I hear you're the best guide in all East Africa," he heard her say to him. "I've been looking forward to meeting you." She offered her hand. "Elizabeth Esker Moraine. My friends call me Double-E or Liz." She had a firm grip, strong.

He felt — what was it? Intimidated by this slight, black-haired woman. The great white hunter, the one sent in to deal with a wounded leopard, a rogue elephant, a croc that killed women washing clothes along a river, was intimidated by a woman who was simply smiling at him.

"Glad to have you along, Double-E," he said, withdrawing his hand and taking his broad-brimmed hat off and putting it back on, as if to give a reason for separating himself from the handshake. He looked at the f our Americans more carefully. Just how competent are they? he wondered. He had been on more than one field expedition where people who made foolhardy decisions, or simply met with bad luck, ended up dead. He was confident, as usual, that he would survive no matter what happened. But given the elephants and perhaps poachers, he'd have preferred an all-male group. These women had better be able to look after themselves.

Paul and Mary meandered away to the edge of the escarpment. Paul was delighted. He had dreamed of coming to the great parks of East Africa, places often described as the perfect and original nature, a nature in balance, where the predators and prey each played their roles, each important to the other. And here he was, and with Mary, who stood now just off to one side so that he could see into the plains and see her. To him, it was the perfect view.

Mary looked out over the plains too. She saw a vastness that was desolate and alarming, a space that she hoped she was up to visiting. She was glad Paul was there with her; his familiarity and inner strength gave her a feeling of security.

Bruce, off to one side of Paul and Mary, at first watched them and then he too looked into Tsavo; Elizabeth looked with him. The land to the horizon was the golden brown of a lion's fur stretched out to dry. At the end, the horizon formed a straight line like a part cut by a knife blade into the lion's skin. In the bright midmorning sun, the sky was a blinding blue, too bright to seem real, whitened by dust blown up from the almost treeless terrain, a languishing, lost landscape, looking out of time, ancient, altered. For a moment he felt almost a sense of peace. Why was it that he had to come here for that sense of inner peace? And why was it that so many feelings churned within him so much of the time? Outwardly, he knew, he appeared the confident wildlife guide, and once in a while he actually felt that way, now for instance, but not when he was chasing Davie, not when Horst was talking to him in the Land Rover, not earlier this morning when he woke up alone with an empty feeling inside.

Elizabeth interrupted his thoughts. "I guess you would call this the perfect wilderness, nature at its best,"

"Sometimes, yes. Like an old friend. Always there," Bruce answered.

She found him immediately appealing. He seemed to be what she would have expected of such a guide, the strong, silent type. But she sensed something else, not so easy to understand; under that great-white-hunter's surface, there was turbulence.

Elizabeth turned and watched a large, overweight man with heavy jowls pull himself out of Bruce's Land Rover. He reached down and picked up a white Panama fedora hat that had fallen on the ground, and tried to brush the dust of f it. He made an attempt to push his shirt into his pants, but his large belly interfered.

"Good morning. How do you do. Name's Cecile," he said to Elizabeth.

She smiled and nodded back, sticking out her hand. Cecile's grip was soft and limp, like a wet fish, she thought.

"I'm here representing the British American Animal Welfare Society. Delighted you've come to help save the jumbos. Do like elephants, oh, yes, most certainly, and, well, all of God's creatures, you know." He bobbed his head up and down affirmatively as he talked, and tried once more to tuck in his shirt, failing again. He raised his Panama hat, rubbed his partially bald head, and put the hat back on, still nodding, as if approving of his own actions.

"So you're the geologist, if I understand correctly," Cecile said as Bruce walked away. "You know, I'm glad you're along. I think perhaps you'll be a little more neutral about things than the rest of this group."

"How do you mean?"

"Well, conservationists and naturalists" — he leaned over to her, speaking low and conspiratorially while looking at Bruce — "they tend to get passionate about some things they like to give big words to, but I don't think they understand animals much at all, and sometimes they think the big picture — as they call it — is more important than this wonderful wildlife. And the biologists, like that young American who came over with you" — he looked at Paul — "think they can control populations. Manage nature. As if they could do it. As if they knew what they were doing."

"You think it's too complicated for that?"

"Yes. And they don't know much. But even more — perhaps I shouldn't be saying this, but they *believe* they're right, you know, when they're not."

"How so?"

"You see, some of them — well, take our leader, Bruce, for example. He has always wanted to shoot elephants when he thought there were too many, rather than rely on nature to take her own course and restore her natural balance." He leaned so close to Elizabeth's ear that his belly pushed against her and she could smell his breath, a combination of mouthwash and garlic. "He takes people out hunting, you know. Shoots game himself," he whispered.

"It got him in trouble, you know, all that shooting of elephants. That's why he left Africa. Surprised he's back, I am, yes." His head went up and down.

"And what is your role here?"

"To try to make sure that your leader, Bruce, and the rest of you do not sacrifice the well-being of the elephant and its friends for the well-being of your ecosystem, as you scientists like to say. And to make sure that his team doesn't add to the killing of our fellow creatures when they claim they are here to try to prevent poaching, as they call it."

"I didn't know. I thought we were all on the same side."

"You see, each creature has a moral right to exist. It's our obligation, our religious duty, to help every one of them. Our goal should be, as it says in Isaiah, to make a world where 'the wolf will live with the lamb, the leopard will lie down with the goat, the calf and the lion and the yearling.' Yes." Tipping his hat to her, he wandered away.

Amused, Elizabeth walked over to the ledge and looked into the distance. From the Yatta Plateau down into Tsavo, the land sloped steeply away from her, and she saw bedrock exposed among the scrubby vegetation. She could not resist her geologist's instincts. Before Bruce, who was approaching her, could say anything, she was scrambling down the slope, rock hammer in hand.

What the — ? Bruce thought. First Davie, now this woman off on her own. He hurried to the edge of the slope and looked down to see what had happened to her. Dam n! In spite of himself, he was irritated. Maybe he was getting too old for this job. Maybe it was a mistake for him to come back. He kicked at a boulder. Geologist, eh. Pain in the ass more like it.

CHAPTER 6

A Lava Flow

The more one understands one's own reactions the less one is at their mercy.

William Empson, *Seven Types of Ambiguity.*

After scrambling down a ways, Elizabeth found a fairly level place to stand below an exposed rock and started chipping away with her small geologist's hammer. This was one of the largest lava flows in the world and it intrigued her. She didn't know when or if they would get back to it, so she took advantage of the moment. Might get bitten by a snake or spider or who knows what, she thought, but what the hell.

A small furry animal, about the size of a rabbit but with small ears, let out a piercing whistle and then a shriek that startled her, almost making her lose her grip on the rocks. It seemed to have been sunning itself, and her hammering woke it up. It stood up on tiny, big-toed feet and yawned, revealing a few large molar-like teeth. She smiled, amused by its behavior, and returned to chipping away at the rock. She would have to ask Bruce what the cute little critter was. As soon as she started to hammer, though, it let out another piercing whistle.

Startled again, she looked out over the valley and saw a pair of birds with large red bills fly past just above her, and as if in response to the little four-legged creature's whistle, one of the birds let out a mournful call that made her shiver. What on earth? Some kind of parrot? If nothing else, the noises in this Tsavo place were exotic and alarming.

She cut short her exploration and put some samples in her backpack. She was about to scramble up and out when she noticed a large curved piece of — what was it? She picked it up. It was ivory, part of an elephant tusk. Heavy. She looked carefully at the ground near where it had been and she saw a small grayish-black object that she had missed before. It blended in with the bedrock. Picking it up, she saw that it was a bullet. Somebody had shot the elephant?

Putting these in her pack along with her pieces of rock, she climbed back up with the intention of showing the ivory and bullet to Bruce, but when she put her head over the top she saw a startlingly tall and imposing African staring down at her. He was holding a huge rifle in his right hand and a spear in his left. The spear had a wooden shaft with two blades — a long metal blade at one end and a sharp, short metal point at the other. She thought he looked scary as hell, and her immediate reaction was that perhaps he was a poacher and they were under attack. She tried to slink down and make herself small.

CHAPTER 7

Michael

There is a streak of wildness in her; fortunately it's never had a chance to get out.

                    Charles Williams, The Greater Trumps.

S witching the rifle from his right to his left hand, so that he held both weapons in one hand, the very tall, very thin black man bent down over the edge of the ledge and spoke to Elizabeth in a clipped British accent. "May I help you?" he asked. Without waiting for a reply, he extended a long, thin arm, grasped her firmly around the waist, lifted her and her backpack up over the edge and set her on the ground.

Bruce rushed over and, seeing the look on her face, said, "This is Michael, the Maasai game warden I told Paul about, and my partner."

She guessed Michael was seven feet tall, and he seemed impossibly thin, all arms and legs. His muscles didn't look thick enough to hold up that tall skeleton. Now she could see clearly that he was a Maasai warrior like those in guidebook pictures, but instead of the traditional brightly colored Maasai clothes, he wore a regulation Kenyan game warden's uniform: khaki shirt with button-down pockets, khaki shorts, knee socks, and black boots.

"Michael's the only Maasai game warden working outside of Maasai homelands," Bruce said, responding to the look of surprise on her face.

Elizabeth recovered quickly and was fascinated. She immediately offered her hand to Michael, who shook it warmly. Her curiosity was raised considerably. This was certainly an interesting person. Why was he the only Maasai to move out of his traditional way of life to do this? There must be quite a story behind it, she thought.

"You okay?" Bruce asked. "You just disappeared."

"Sorry. I couldn't resist having a look around. I love being out in the field." She stared at
him unblinking.

"I understand, but we're going to have to become a team here and stay together," Bruce said. She felt scolded.

"What did you find down there?" Michael asked, again it in a rather formal British accent. "I understand you're our geologist."

She opened her pack and took out the piece of ivory and the bullet and passed them to Michael, who shared it with Bruce. She described the small animal she had seen and its screech.

"Rock hyrax," Bruce said, "the elephant's closest relative. Harmless, and not so smart as his bigger cousins."

That little critter is the closest relative of the elephants? Elizabeth smiled to herself. This Tsavo sure is a strange place.

Then she described the birds and their mournful call. "Crowned hornbill. Red bill, right? The epitome of sadness in flight. A true sound of the wild," Bruce answered.

They looked at the piece of ivory and the bullet. "Think it's poachers?" she asked.

"It might be poachers who shot the elephant, but who knows?" Michael answered. "The ivory looks somewhat old and weathered, but the bullet doesn't. Those two things may have just fallen there at different times, and one may have nothing to do with the other."

Bruce turned the ivory over. He wasn't so sure. "Let's let it lie, shall we?" He said. "No need to upset the others yet. Don't worry, though. I'll keep an eye out." He smiled at her.

Elizabeth smiled back, forcing herself to remain calm. They were just an innocent group of scientists who wouldn't harm a fly, weren't they? She hoped everybody else in the park would think the same thing.

Elizabeth followed discreetly behind, watching Michael carefully. When Bruce and Michael reached the group Bruce introduced Michael, telling them how glad he was that Michael had been willing to join him once again after such a long hiatus. Michael nodded regally and smiled, drawing himself up even straighter and planting the point of his spear in the ground to his right.

It was about as tall as he was. Howie stuck out his right hand. His head reached to Michael's chest. "Glad to meet you," Howie said, grinning and looking briefly at Bruce. "How'd you two get together?"

Michael looked down at Howie and smiled, like a king looking at a mouse, Elizabeth thought. She was certain she saw an amused glint in his eyes as Michael turned to look out over the plains. He stood as if the entire countryside belonged to him, and, Elizabeth thought, it probably did, in one sense or another.

"We've worked together for years — I wouldn't do this job without him. I got to know Michael when we were kids. We met at an English school here in Kenya."

"Then my British teachers sent me to school in England," Michael said, "to an English public school. Can you imagine that? They tried to turn me into an English gentleman. Bruce encouraged them, as well."

In her typical bold way, Elizabeth went over to Michael and asked him many questions, trying to be as polite as she could. As they talked, Elizabeth became more intrigued.

"Aren't you afraid that you will lose touch with your own people and your own culture?" she asked.

Michael listened quietly, not indicating any frustration with Elizabeth's intense questioning. She watched him carefully, hoping she was being polite, but unable to contain her curiosity.

"You're right, I am concerned about that." His perfect English, with its hint of an upper-class British accent, unnerved her. He wasn't the native she had expected.

"A Maasai without his culture is like a zebra without stripes. If my people abandon our way of life, our next step could be our extinction — gone like one of the rare birds of Kenya. I'm trying to help my people learn to live in the modern world — to integrate our way of life with yours. So I'm taking a risk, living partly in your world and partly in mine."

"So you're sort of studying us," Elizabeth said. "You're the reverse anthropologist. Usually it's some Westerner studying you, but you're switching things on us."

Michael nodded, smiled slightly.

"I wonder what you have found out about us," Elizabeth continued.

Michael was about to reply, but he saw another man he had not yet met approaching Elizabeth. As she turned toward the new person, Michael moved away to look out over the plains and to think about what had happened this morning. His first impression of the black-haired American woman was good. Like most Americans he had met, she was easygoing but bold and very outspoken. But unlike so many of her countrymen, she wasn't arrogant, and she didn't seem focused on money. He thought she was pretty as well, unusually so for a white person, much more so than the other woman, the very pale one whose features seemed to fade away in the sunlight, like distant hills at noon when there were no shadows. Not that white women were completely foreign to him; he had had a number of girlfriends in England and lived with one for several years while he was studying at Cambridge. Elizabeth reminded him of that wonderful, beautiful woman. Yes, she had stirred up feelings in him that he believed he had forgotten.

Elizabeth had figured it out immediately, Michael thought. He was caught between two worlds, the traditional Maasai life and this modern Western way of doing things. Deep inside he still felt a part of the Maasai herding life. How could he not, when he had spent so many days, months, years, as a child and then as an adult, following the herds of cattle, finding water for them, protecting them from predators? How could he not feel part of that life when he had killed his lion and become a Maasai warrior? And yet he had also come to like the modern world, the one he had experienced in Britain and was feeling once more now that he was working again with Bruce and with this group of American and British scientists.

Bruce's return to Tsavo, which Michael had looked forward to, was beginning to confuse him. When he and Bruce had worked together years ago, everything had seemed clear. He and Bruce had seemed to be a part of the same world. Then Bruce had left Africa. Michael had returned to his life as a Maasai warrior, but he did not fit in there anymore, and he had welcomed Bruce's invitation to rejoin him on this expedition with scientists.

Poachers, if they were back in Tsavo, did not frighten Michael. He had dealt with them before as a warden for the Kenyan Parks Department. It was his own feelings about himself that bothered him. His brothers, who had not been given a European education and had not lived in Britain, had no such problems. They were still of the land. But their way of life was threatened by the modern world, and he felt that it was his obligation, as the one educated in that world, to understand it and to help his people. And what could be more useful to himself than to spend time with these scientists who were studying Tsavo? Weren't they the best of the modern Western world? Didn't he have the most to gain from them? He had thought so yesterday, but today he wasn't so sure. Watching the group that Bruce had brought together cast doubt into Michael's mind. Of the ones he had seen so far, he liked Elizabeth the best, but he was curious about the very strange Howie, who might have some kind of direct, perhaps spiritual, contact with Tsavo, through its soil, that might help him. As to the rest, he had to come to know them better.

He looked forward to talking with Elizabeth again.

CHAPTER 8

Horst

All science involves what we might call "art" in the sense of requiring intuition, creativity, and inspiration (whether to graph the underlying causal connection between seemingly unrelated observations or to construct an elegant experimental design).

Lawrence M. Witmer, *Science Magazine*

The man who interrupted Elizabeth's conversation with Michael was of moderate height, trim, and dressed with casual elegance: blue Oxford button-down shirt, khaki trousers, moccasins, and a narrow-brimmed brown felt hat. He carried a faded tan corduroy sports jacket. The result, Elizabeth thought, is that he looked ready for a cocktail hour on a summer's evening in New York or Chicago, rather than outfitted for a wilderness expedition. But then she noticed a banged-up pair of binoculars hung from straps around his neck. He had a relaxed, pleasing smile, full of crinkles, as if he had spent a lifetime in that smile. It was appealing, she had to admit, but she had heard the stories and she was inclined to believe what the young PhD candidates had said about him. He was a womanizer – and manipulator. Not likely to work with her.

Introducing himself with his full name, George Horst Grobbin, he told her that he was on the trip representing the International Endangered Species Consortium and was here to protect the wilderness.

"We hear there may be some major elephant poaching going on in Tsavo — maybe linked to the government, just between you and me," he added, moving close to her and making her more uncomfortable. "I'm here to check that out, as well as help your science team when you need some. Don't want any of you to get hurt or in trouble."

"I thought we were pretty well protected, with Bruce and Michael — all the experience they've had here — they've dealt with poachers and worse, I believe," she said.

"Yes, well, can't have too much help that way," Horst answered. He moved closer into Elizabeth's space, a seemingly knowing smile continuing on his face. Weirdo, she was thinking to herself, or worse.

"Going to bring in the troops or something to deal with the poachers and protect us?" she asked as she moved away from him.

"Do what's necessary, if Bruce has some troubles," he said, then he guided her over to the ledge, steering her by holding her right arm with both of his hands, a sort of intimacy that startled Elizabeth. She pulled away and they walked on. He didn't miss a beat.

"Good to be back in God's country," he said, squinting into the brilliance, sweeping his arms out wide, as if giving a speech to a large crowd. "Pure nature. Save Tsavo from people. That's what we're here for." He held up his binoculars to his eyes, as if searching for a bird or something. Then he let the binoculars fall against his chest and, looking into her eyes, asked her about herself. She was relieved when Mary walked to the edge and joined them. Elizabeth introduced them. Horst smoothed his shirt as he turned toward Mary.

"Are you a birdwatcher?" Mary asked, looking at his dangling, dusty binoculars.

He said he was and that he never went anywhere without his binoculars, and asked if she was too. It was a lie. He always carried binoculars to make sure people would realize he was an ecologist, and a great one at that. Actually, he had little interest in birds and not all that much interest in the details of nature. The field glasses were as much a part of his dress as his sport jacket, to separate himself from the naturalists with their weird outfits, most of the time with dirty hands from digging down for something or other or pulling leaves off trees.

"Since I was a little girl. I can't wait to see a martial eagle. Have you seen one?"

Horst wasn't sure what bird she was talking about. His sons were birdwatchers, and the few birds he knew from them were in America. He changed the subject and asked her what she would be doing as part of the team, all the while holding her in his gaze, as if Elizabeth had never existed.

Mary explained that she was an ecologist---actually a botanist, botanical ecologist, I guess you'd call me,--- here to help Paul decide how heavily elephants and other wildlife have been feeding on the trees and grasses.

"We're glad you're along!" Horst said with his winning smile. He patted her on the back, getting close enough to catch the sweet scent of perfumed shampoo. He let his hand rest on her shoulder as if testing her response. She stiffened. The kind to go slow with, then, he thought, and removed his hand.

"I can't wait to get started measuring things," she said.

This caused Horst to give her a surprised look, but he covered it quickly by commenting on her necklace, a thin gold strand with a small heart-shaped locket. "Pretty necklace, that," he said casually.

She thanked him, blushing, admitting that it was not exactly fieldwork gear, but had been a gift from her favorite aunt who asked her to wear it always. "It's a pretty keepsake, but I — I feel it's sort of out of place when I do research."

"Not at all. It's nice to meet a woman who is feminine and capable of fieldwork, too."

Ignored now by Horst, Elizabeth wandered over to Howie, and felt immediately much more comfortable. She told him Michael's comment about a zebra without stripes.

"And what color would that zebra be?" Howie asked, "White or black?"

"There you go again with your silly comments, Heck." She thought for a minute. "What color would it be?"

"No color, that's obvious," Howie answered, looking at Michael.

Meanwhile, Bruce had moved away from the group. He counted them again. Eight here not counting myself, makes nine. Johnny flying in makes ten. But what a crew. Those four Americans have never been to Tsavo: Paul, Howie, and the two women. Then there's weird Davie and Cecile, the fat Brit from the animal-welfare group, and Horst, his old enemy. He noticed that Horst, standing near the edge of the escarpment, had taken a small vial out of his sport jacket pocket and was rolling it back and forth, back and forth, in his hands. Bruce remembered that Ahab, in *Moby Dick*, always carried a vial of Nantucket beach sand with him. And Horst was a New Englander. It sure was an odd connection, Bruce thought. Bruce saw it was white beach sand, and realized Horst was carrying it as a token, probably to remind him of his home on Nantucket. *Christ what a team.* Michael, his partner, was the only one he could really trust, having worked with him for years. Well, the four new Americans had worked together — that's a plus. Ten. Why did that bother him? He'd taken many a group that size, but not this large a group of scientists — oddball scientists at that. He tried to concentrate on each of them. Always tried to know his customers. Which could he trust in a showdown? If they met up with poachers with machine guns? Rowdy elephants? An accident?

Crossing into Tsavo was like boarding an ocean liner, he mused. They would go from being immersed in their normal world to being on a kind of island. Isolated. This had strange effects on people. It often made women very romantic. That could be a plus. It also helped to mold people into a team. Strange how groups like this, isolated in the bush a week, would tell each other secrets that they would not tell their oldest friends. Well, in two or three days he would have them sorted out — who was strong, who had the willpower to survive.

As he was musing about this, he heard the sound of an airplane, a sudden loud roar like motorcycle turning a corner and accelerating. Only Bruce seemed to hear it.

What now? Friend or foe?

CHAPTER 9

Johnny

Glamour urged him on, glamour kept him unscathed. He surely wanted nothing from the wilderness but space to breathe in and to push on through. His need was to exist, and to move onwards at the greatest possible risk.

Joseph Conrad, *Heart of Darkness*

The roaring airplane startled them all. It came at them just over the treetops, exploding from acacia trees, looking as if its wheels would hit the ground and the plane would crash into one of the Land Rovers. But then, passing quickly overhead, the plane angled up steeply and, roaring even louder, rose abruptly up and up, did a tight figure eight over their heads and came back down, buzzing them again. Then the high-winged plane made a wide circle out into the plains, far enough away to appear as a small dragonfly, and then, wings rocking in a kind of hello, roared back, skiing over the terrain. A grinning face appeared in the cockpit as it passed over their heads a second time, the pilot's hand raised up in a victory V and then a wave, and the plane soared off into the valley and was gone. Silence. Mourning doves calling. Rustling in the rocks.

Elizabeth looked at Bruce.

"Asshole," Davie shouted, looking into the sky. "That's Johnny. Bruce here hired him to be your pilot. Shi-it," Davie said, turning to Mary. "Like a damned kid on a tricycle, him and his rich man's toys. God save us." He spit in the dirt. Elizabeth thought it was rather odd for Davie to be criticizing a daredevil. Wasn't that just what he himself had been just a little while ago? She looked closely at Davie. Was it a class thing? Rich man's toys, he had said. Maybe he'd had a blue-collar background and was envious of someone who could afford an airplane.

"Just a little exuberance," Bruce said, trying to speak calmly. It was the third screw-up this morning: Davie and the elephant, Elizabeth disappearing down the slope, and now daredevil Johnny and his Cessna. He kicked at a rocky outcrop. He was tired of Johnny's tricks, but he envied Johnny's free-living sense of fun, his independence, his life on the edge. The playboy of the wildlife crowd was Johnny's reputation, but good in the field. Bruce had tried to live that life himself years ago when he had started his work in Africa, but he was too introspective and too responsible.

And how would Johnny be on this expedition? In a fight or dangerous situation, he would be out front. When there was no crisis, Johnny could create his own dangers. And he was obsessed with elephants, especially the big bull.

He was willing to do anything to get to know the jumbos as intimately as possible, up close. But they needed his knowledge, skills, and airplane to do reconnaissance f rom the air — his skill as a pilot.

At least this trip wouldn't be dull, like some of the tourist groups he used to guide overweight couples, the men mainly interested in beer and sex, the women taking snapshots of flowers and of each other, but mostly impatient for their guide to produce lions and elephants. W anting it easy. At least most of this group had done fieldwork and, he hoped, would be tough enough. It was one of the things that had persuaded him to take this job and come back to Tsavo.

The sun beat on his head. He took of f his hat, wiped his forehead with a handkerchief, and, looked once again into Tsavo.

The view struck him as it had every time he entered the park, as a view into another world. Something about the limitlessness of Tsavo and the way the light played into the flat lands in the distance made the landscape bluer, turned yellows to orange, oranges to reds. It seemed an ancient Earth, a timeless wilderness, a wounded landscape. It attracted him as some women attracted him. A little mysterious and very dangerous. He wanted to stay and just watch and wait for — what? He was having a difficult time pulling himself away from the view, even though he knew that he needed to get the group started to his first campsite. He felt that the land had called him back, a strange feeling, the worst kind of idea to roam around in a supposed scientist's head.

Elizabeth strode past him, between him and the far off view. With her long black hair and very white skin, he thought, she could be a young witch of children's stories. Like to touch that skin — smooth. Makes things complicated. There is a connection between them, he thought, the bewitching landscape and the all-seeing bewitching woman.

He pulled a strip of jerked meat from his pocket, took a bite, and held it out to her.

"Elephant or gazelle?" she asked.

"Impala, actually. Want to try some?" He handed her the strip, and she took a bite from the same end that he had bitten, her teeth and lips touching what his had just touched.

Damnable woman, he thought.

"Good," she said. "Appetizer or dinner?"

"Dinner's always a surprise. Wait and see."

She smiled at him. He was about to put the strip of jerky back into his pocket, but her look challenged him. He hesitated, then took a bite where she had just bitten, his teeth and lips where hers had just been. For a moment he wondered if she could bewitch him with her lips and teeth. Nice, straight white teeth.

"So you're a geologist," he said.

"*Geomorphologist.*"

"Ah. You study the shape of Mother Nature's skin."

"And how her skin ages."

Tough. But pretty. She did not look like Tsavo, with her black-and-white coloring, but she gave off a feeling — almost a scent — like Tsavo. She stood, chewing, not speaking. She seemed to be waiting him out. "And what will you do here?" he asked.

She swallowed. "Look at the erosion, for one. See if the elephants have been — like cows — a geomorphic force, as one of my colleagues put it."

"Make the world go 'round, do they?" he replied.

"No, down," she answered. "Erosion to sediment."

"Yes, of course." He turned. "Time we got going. Tell me more later."

* * *

Joseph returned to the Manyani Gate just as Johnny's airplane passed low overhead. He immediately grabbed his rifle. He recognized the Cessna from its coloring, the number on its side, and the way Johnny flew it. That tight figure eight done very near the ground identified him for sure. Joseph watched the plane skim the treetops and head toward Lugard Falls. So Johnny was working with Bruce. Joseph turned on his two-way radio and made a call to the nearest people working for him. He told them the location of Bruce's team and said they should get out of that area and leave the scientists alone; they should not be discovered. He directed them north and east into Tsavo, on a route that would take them around and away from Bruce.

CHAPTER 10

Discovering Dead Elephants

Look at the behemoth, which I made along with you and which feeds on grass like an ox.

The Bible, King James Version, Job 40:14-16

Leaving Lugard Falls, Bruce led the team deeper into the park, farther from the Manyani Gate and the paved highway, farther from towns and cities. He had asked Paul to ride up front with him so they could talk about the work to be done. Cecile squeezed himself into the back with Horst and a lot of field gear.

Bruce saw vultures circling ahead, so many that they made a three-dimensional spiral in the sky, black streaks against the blue like somebody's vision gone bad. In his rearview mirror he saw Davie's Land Rover slow almost to a stop. The circling vultures were another distraction, but it might mean dead elephants. Although Bruce was anxious to get the group settled in camp, they had to look, and anyway it was right along their route. This surprised him a little: Why would a big animal die just by chance on the well-worn route to his often-used camp by the river?

Bruce drove slowly toward the circling birds. His view was obscured by tall shrubs, so it was a shock when they entered a clearing to find two dead adult elephants lying on the ground, the larger one with its tusks cut off, the other with one tusk showing a cut from a power saw. Cecile gasped in horror. Bruce cut the engine and, with characteristic caution, first surveyed the scene from within the vehicle.

"Stay still for a while. The poachers may still be around," he said quietly. He reached under the driver's seat, pulled out a pistol, and shoved it into his belt. He picked up a pair of binoculars, also under the front seat, and scanned the area. Then he listened.

"One of them still has its tusks," Horst pointed out.

"They'll probably come back for those tusks. Stay quiet here for a minute while I look around." He took another pistol f rom the glove compartment and handed it to Paul. "Just prudence," he said. "You know how to use this thing?"

Paul nodded.

Bruce opened his door as quietly as he could, but to Paul, in the stillness that surrounded them, it sounded as loud as two crashing vehicles. Bruce went over to the driver's side of Davie's Land Rover and the two talked quietly. Then he went and talked with Michael in the third Land Rover and suggested that he stay to watch out for the others from near his vehicle. Davie got out and walked toward the carcasses with Bruce, then stopped and watched the circling vultures through binoculars. Michael emerged and began to search for signs of the poachers — tire tracks, broken twigs — but stayed near his vehicle.

Left alone with Cecile and Horst, Paul examined the pistol Bruce had handed him. He was used to hunting with rifles and shotguns with his father back home in Oregon, but he hadn't had much experience with pistols. He tried to imagine himself with the rifle his father had given him, hiding in the bush and trying to shoot an elephant where the bullet might kill. A lot more of a challenge than a hundred-pound deer or a thousand-pound elk.

Paul watched Bruce and Davie reach the dead elephants, circle the carcasses slowly, looking for signs of poachers, and then move outward, disappearing into the bush. The soaring vultures rose higher suddenly and broke from their geometric spiral, skywriting that visitors had reached the dead elephants. Paul began to imagine poachers bursting out of the thicket with automatic weapons, and tried to think what he might do if that happened. He fingered the pistol, moving the safety lever on and off. *Click, click, click, click.* The Land Rover would offer little protection.

After what seemed a long time, Bruce and Davie appeared out of the bush, and Bruce motioned for the rest of them to get out. He told them they had seen no one nearby and it was probably safe to walk around, as long as they were quiet. Michael pointed to tire tracks in the soil. Bruce hunkered down to examine them, scratched the side of his face, then rose and walked carefully alongside the tracks toward the dead elephants.

"Very curious," he said quietly to Paul. "New tires. The kind used on new Toyota Land Cruisers — the latest thing in back-country travel here. Not the equipment of the old poachers. This is a well-funded group, I'd say."

Bruce showed Paul that the stomach of one of the elephants seemed to have been blown apart. He shook his head. "Most unusual," he said. "Somebody threw a hand grenade at this elephant. See here — and see bits of metal in that tree. That's what a grenade'll do to a person. Saw it in the Korean War. Never saw it used against elephants. It's hard to kill these jumbos, but this is a cruel way to do it. Used to be the poachers would try to get submachine guns. This is a step up."

"If they're this well armed, maybe whoever's supporting them believes there are plenty of elephants out here. Maybe they're even counting them, like we are," Paul said, a feeling of dread creeping up his spine.

"If I didn't know better, and he wasn't in jail, I would have said it's the work of the Snake," Bruce said. Michael said that the man known as Snake had been out of jail several years now, gently reminding Bruce that he had been away from Kenya quite a while.

"Who's that?" asked Paul.

"A poacher. Snake is a pun on his last name, Kenjoy, which sounds like "'kijoka', the Swahili word for snake," Michael explained. The Snake was famous for the amount of ivory he sold, and was finally caught and put in jail. And he was known for his extreme carefulness, rarely being seen killing an elephant or taking its tusks, and always having his workmen remove all the evidence, all of the elephant's body, and afterwards smoothing the ground to make it look as if nothing had happened.

"Not good news," Bruce admitted. "Snake is always the cleverist of the small-time poachers. It had long been know what he did, but it took years for the rangers to catch him at it and then to corner him and get him to jail."

"Once a pretty good young man, now gone bad," Michael said, "but I don't think this was Joseph's doing. Too messy. Not his kind of poaching."

"Yes, he was always a kind of neatness fanatic at school, wasn't he Michael" Bruce replied. "Then who?"

"Looks more like the kind of job those guys in league with the government have done," Michael answered. "Fast, sloppy, messy, not much hunting experience, heavy weapons. Throw things and run." Michael turned to Bruce. "Too bad about Joseph. Could have been a good ranger instead of a small time poacher."

"You liked him, didn't you?" Bruce said, but Michael was already speaking to Elizabeth, explaining to her what he believed had happened, as Paul and Mary listened.

Horst, binoculars dangling from his neck, looked away to the horizon. Now he had to deal with dead elephants — with their dried blood and guts showing. It didn't seem to bother these researchers, with their curiosity about everything in nature. Their eyes on the ground, they couldn't see or understand the work he was doing, the international political work — saving nature in the large — the bigger picture. And, thankfully, he could do his work without getting his hands dirty.

"Tsavo's so delicate — if you put even one species out of its balance, you can upset the whole apple cart," he said. "Especially the elephants, because they're so dominant. When will we learn? If we aren't spraying DDT to control malaria out here, we're killing elephants because we think it's good for them or us."

Bruce turned to Horst. "Two of these are a year's income for an average chap from Kenya or Somalia. It'd be hard to resist if you were in their place."

Both Cecile and Horst said it could never happen to them.

"Don't say that until a jumbo charges you." Bruce smiled grimly. "Or until you try living out here on two hundred dollars a year, like the poachers, or like 'the Little People,' as they're called, natives of Tsavo, who hunt with poison darts. Talk about brave. Drink the muddy water. Get a stomach full of worms. Lose a few relatives to the crocs. It's easy to condemn them on our fat American and British salaries."

Walking up to the men with Mary, Elizabeth heard a loud rustling and felt the ground shake. Before she could even think about what it might be, a huge bull elephant charged into the clearing. At first she thought he was heading for her and she was going to die, but instead he headed f or the two carcasses and pushed at them, turning now and again to shake his head at the people, making clear that he wanted them out of the way.

Bruce pulled her and Mary back toward the Land Rover, and the rest hurried for cover as best they could. From behind the Land Rover, Elizabeth peered out at the huge animal and saw its broken tusk and torn ear. It was the same bull that Davie had taunted. She hoped it didn't recognize any of them.

After what felt to Elizabeth to be a long time, the elephant stopped trying to get the dead elephants on their feet. He turned toward Elizabeth and Bruce, looked at them in his somewhat nearsighted way, fanned his ears out, trumpeted, made a start toward them, and then turned and dashed away. It was all over in just a few minutes. Mary looked pale and Elizabeth felt a little faint. Davie and Cecile, however, were talking excitedly about how great it had been to be so near the elephant. Elizabeth saw Bruce dash into the bush after the elephant.

Bruce chased the big bull, running as if his legs had taken control of his body and his mind. He felt he was an observer, seeing himself and the elephant crashing through the bush. Something was forcing him to chase this elephant, some need within him, feelings or thoughts that had lain dormant for a decade, buried in Bermuda, or so he had thought. What did he want from that animal? Just to watch him? That hardly made sense. W hy this elephant? The elephant was quickly out of sight. Bruce's legs slowed as he gained control of himself. He turned and walked back to the others, feeling a strange combination of satisfaction, for having gotten near the big bull, relief, at having been able to stop following him, and that constant yearning in the pit of his stomach. As he came into the clearing, he saw Elizabeth looking at him quizzically, and he was embarrassed.

"What do we do now that we know poachers are nearby?" Elizabeth asked, looking from Paul to Michael to Bruce. "Start our work as we planned? Or do we have to stop everything we came out to do go home?"

Bruce replied that they would set up camp first and then talk about possible changes in their plans.

* * *

Joseph had been watching the circling vultures, knowing that they were flying over the two elephants that had been had killed. Would Bruce and his company pass that way? He watched, curious, alert, and uncomfortable. If Bruce and Michael came across the carcasses, they might assume he had killed these elephants, but he hadn't. Damn messy job, and left out in the open so anybody could find them, especially with the vultures circling overhead.

How well did Michael or Bruce remember him from the church school they all attended so long ago? He preferred an element of surprise, if he needed to attack Bruce and his team. The bat-eared fox approached, taking Joseph's eyes off the horizon for a second. He was alarmed, therefore, when he saw the vultures suddenly soar upwards and out of their geometric spiral. Bruce and Michael must have come across the two dead elephants and could see that someone had been using chain saws on their tusks.

Joseph moved silently toward the dead elephants. What the hell, he thought, I'll go and see them all friendly like, act as surprised as them and make sure they know I didn't do it. He hid his rifle, checked that his pistol was hidden under his field jacket, spit on his hands and wiped them across his hair, to neaten it, then brushed the dust off his hand and his field jacket, and as quietly as possible did the same to his trousers. Satisfied with how he would look, he walked toward the opening where the dead elephants lay, making as much noise as he could so they knew he was coming, and not think he was a danger to them, kicking some dead branches on the ground as loudly as he could.

"Well, , look who's back in Tsavo after all these years." He walked over to Bruce, hand out for a shake. "Welcome back old school buddy," he shook Bruce's hand. Bruce accepted it limply, then turned away, frowning. Joseph turned and smiled at Michael.

"And what brings you out here, Michael? Just for old times to see your buddy? And who are these people with you — what are you all up to? Going in for leading tourist groups, looks like."

Seeing that Bruce had walked to the edge of the clearing and was staring out into the distance, his back to Joseph, Michael guided Joseph to Paul.

"This is a scientific research team, studying elephants. From the U.S. Paul, here, is their leader."

Joseph shook Paul's hand. "Honored to meet you. What kind of scientific work will you be doing?"

"All sorts. Mainly counting elephants — trying to find out how many there are. Start monitoring them."

"Not easy, counting these jumbos," Joseph said, looking at Paul's group, with a long look at Mary and Elizabeth.

Elizabeth shivered when Joseph stared at her. She was surprised at the similarity between him and Bruce. Both almost the same height, similar build, lots of muscle. But Joseph was nowhere near as handsome. His face was narrow, his chin pointed, and there was a faint scar coming down his left check from under his hat. Some kind of fight, it must be from, she thought, one of those scary types, easy into violence.

"Doing a lot of it from the air," Paul said to Joseph. "Best way to count them."

"Yes," Joseph said, understanding immediately. Johnny was also back in Tsavo. Aerial counts — great. Just when he thought he had Tsavo to himself, government-hired poachers were creating a mess. And now these Americans, with Johnny up in the air all the time, likely to spot him doing a little poaching. Just exactly what he didn't need. He'd have to be careful with them around. Best to get rid of them one way or another. And he thought he had the perfect setup with Bruce gone and Michael not very active. He'd been able to kill plenty of elephants, poaching them his way, nice and neat — ivory quietly sold off, leather too, to the locals, anything useful moved out and the rest buried or gotten rid of one way or another. Leaving no sign.

"Bloody glad you're here trying to help the jumbos," he said to Paul. "Look, I know Tsavo pretty well — ask Michael and Bruce — maybe not quite as well as them, but if you need help, shout. I've got some new Land Cruisers and lots of field equipment."

Joseph quickly turned away from Paul, before Paul could think to ask any questions about what he was doing with all that new equipment, and looked at Horst, who seemed completely different from the rest of the Americans — older, upper class. He walked over to Horst, Michael staying with him.

"And this is Horst Grobben," Michael said.

"Representing the International Endangered Species Consortium," Horst said, "here to protect the wilderness." A connection with the U.S. Government and a bunch of international conservation groups, Joseph thought — could be either another real hindrance or, come to think of it, it might be something he could use. He shook hands with Horst,

"Very glad to meet you. And my offer to Paul, *to help in any way I can*, stands to you as well," he said. "Sorry mess this is. People killing elephants and not even using the carcasses. Not your way, is it Bruce?" he said, turning to Bruce, who still wasn't acknowledging him.

"Well, I'm glad to have met you all. Michael will know how to contact me if you need any help." He shook Michael's hand, waved at the Americans and quickly walked away, going out the opposite side of the clearing from where he came in, so they wouldn't know where he had left his Land Cruiser. Damn it to hell, he thought as he kicked at some bushes. He'd have to get rid of this group, one way or another. His mind went back to Horst. He could be the key. Clearly there was no love lost between Bruce and Horst. Could be a great opening for him. But he'd have to play it right.

CHAPTER 11

The Old Bull Searches

Bulls, despite their independence, are still sociable and are rarely found more than a mile from another bull or family unit.

Iain Douglas-Hamilton, *Among the Elephants.*

The old bull kept moving, traveling eastward farther and farther into the park. The sun was behind him, westward, when he left the woodlands and came into a vast open area with scattered trees, many standing dead, some still green. Raising his trunk, he picked up scents of men and vehicles and something else unknown to him: the smell of explosives. He followed those scents for a while, which took him along what Bruce would have recognized as tire tracks, and Land Cruiser tracks at that. Ahead, in the shade of a small grove of fever trees, two other bull elephants stood together, pulling leaves off nearby shrubs and chewing on them slowly.

As the old bull approached, the other two turned their heads toward him. He came alongside and stopped, and, putting his trunk over each, one at a time, rubbed their backs. One was a mature bull much younger than himself; the other very young, not long ago pushed out of his herd by the lead females. The three males made low rumbling sounds from what would seem to us to be their stomachs, and the older of the two rubbed against Zamani Baba. They grazed and browsed together, moving slowly in and out of the shade cast by the trees, sometimes breathing some loose sandy soil into their trunks and blowing it over their backs. Doves called incessantly; other animals rustled through the vegetation. A nesting pair of weaverbirds, their basketlike nest shaking from a twig as the elephants pulled leaves from their tree, flew out and over the elephants. A rock hyrax looked up at these giant relatives and scurried away, rustling the grass. A crowned hornbill watched silently from a nearby tree, his red bill bright as a stoplight. All seemed peaceful.

The young bull wandered over to one of the nearby trees and started to push at it with his head until the tree shook, then made a few additional weak charges at the tree and shaking it each time until Zamani Baba raised his ears and trunk, trumpeted briefly, and made a quick, short thrust at the young bull, who immediately backed away, then returned slowly and ate quietly, keeping the other bull between himself and Zamani Baba.

A male lion crept through the tall grass nearby and lay down, looking with sleepy, half-lidded eyes at the three elephants. Definitely no meals there, so he took to washing his head with a paw. Zamani Baba turned and stared at the lion and began to approach him. The lion closed his eyes and pretended to sleep, keeping one eye open just enough to make sure that the elephant did not charge. Zamani Baba continued slowly toward the lion, who rose up and walked slowly and proudly away, as if the decision to move on was completely his own idea.

When the sun was angling downward in the sky, the old bull wandered away from his companions and noticed a slightly different scent of people and their vehicles. He followed it and was soon out of sight of the other two. He followed the scent from grasslands into dense bush, then stopped and lifted his trunk, sensing something nearby. He heard the strange sound of a motor vehicle and saw one come over a low rise and then disappear into the bush. A bat-eared f ox followed the vehicle. The bull turned to the east and moved farther into Tsavo, farther from the road, from the places touched recently by people, and over the next days traveled among his own kind within the wildest regions of Tsavo.

Once he was out of sight, that shiny new vehicle came out of the bush and stopped. Joseph got out and studied the ground, found the tracks of the big bull and studied them for a long time, the bat-eared fox watching and darting along to elephant tracks as if searching for small prey.

CHAPTER 12

Camp

---

*For I do not make so blindly for the end of my journey, as to
neglect anything useful that may turn up by the way.*

Sir Francis Bacon

lizabeth watched from the backseat of Davie's Land Rover as
they came over a rise and down into a grove of palm trees,
which looked refreshing and lovely, especially after their travel
through the harsh Tsavo plains, their meeting with the old bull,
and discovery of the two dead elephants. Water flowed from a well,
clearly an artesian, therefore man-made, Elizabeth realized, making
the settling all the more charming. She checked her watch. Almost
4:00 pm. Getting late to set up a camp.

Bruce and Michael stopped and parked their Land Rovers
and trailers neatly next to each other. Davie parked alongside, and
Elizabeth got out. She pitched in with the others to set up camp.
Soon they had a rectangle of tawny-colored tents in the center of
which was a cooking area and a large tent with walls of mosquito
netting and a waterproof nylon roof, a place to work, meet, eat, and
relax. A bit of geometric order, Elizabeth thought, in the midst of
what so far had been chaos or close to it. Beyond, in a dense patch of
palms, a large metal tank had been tied high on the trunk of one of

the trees, and a spigot extended from it, forming a shower. A shower curtain had even been rigged beneath it, making use of the water from the natural artesian well.

Mary and Elizabeth stood in front of their tent. A small gazelle appeared briefly beyond the palms, jumping, almost bouncing, then dashing away. Mary smiled, delighted, and said that the camp was a small, lovely paradise, adding that she had wanted badly to see Africa and its wildlife, but had dreaded the heat and dryness, and earlier today that seemed to be all Tsavo offered. Heat, drought, weirdness, and death. "But now — " she began to say.

"Camping in style," Elizabeth agreed. She was enjoying the sound of water flowing from the artesian well, like a small brook back home. The setting was delightful compared to her experiences in typical American research camps — rough affairs rigged with what people could backpack into American wilderness areas. Still, something made her uncomfortable; the earlier sight of the dead elephants didn't help, and the possibility that the group was at this very moment surrounded by dangerous animals and even more dangerous people, perhaps like Joseph friendly on the surface but a small time poacher underneath, added to her discomfort. And then there was the obvious tension between Joseph and Bruce.

She saw Bruce walking to the edge of the campsite and staring out into the plains. The one person, she thought, who might be able to allay her unease. She joined him, but he seemed lost in thought. He smiled at her but said nothing, so she strolled out a bit farther, smelling the aromatic plants, the dusty soil, and other earthy scents, venturing as far from Bruce as she felt comfortable. The view of the landscape captured her professional attention, and she began to think about the geological origins of Tsavo. Wandering back, her mind full of earth and rocks, she was startled when Bruce smiled at her and took up the conversation they had begun at Lugard Falls as if it had never stopped.

"Make the Earth go round, do they?" he asked.

She looked at him in surprise, trying to pick up the conversation.

"Cattle and elephants and the like, as you said at the Falls," he continued, "erode the land, change its shape, do they?"

"Some say," she answered, and they talked quietly for a while. When she started back to her tent, he accompanied her. She felt at ease next to this experienced guide and Tsavo expert, and a handsome one at that, tall, dark-haired, elegant, British gentleman loosened up by some experience in the States. When they reached the center of camp, Bruce excused himself to go help Michael. Elizabeth wandered around looking for Mary so she could talk things over with her, but she saw Mary and Paul sitting close together on a log. When had this started? she wondered. Back in the States, Paul had shown no romantic interest in Mary, or herself, for that matter. Maybe she had been missing something. She felt a touch of envy, and thought about Bruce. She saw Michael, busy doing something, tall, elegant, exotic, intriguing. Get off it, she said to herself, you're here as a professional to get a job done.

* * *

Later, a pair of crowned hornbills circled the camp. The male saw Elizabeth walking among the tents. He flew near her and spied a tall acacia tree with a large hole in it, a likely nesting tree, settled on a limb just above the hole, and watched her. His mate landed next to him, and they looked in silence at the people and their strange objects, watching, perhaps wondering, whether this would be a safe place for their eggs and hatchlings.

Only Mary saw the birds circle and land. She had read about hornbills and was fascinated by them, especially by the way that they built their nests in holes in trees. She thought about the female who would soon be encased within that nest, safe, protected by a solid wall of wood and fed and protected by her mate. The thought gave Mary a melancholy, lonely feeling. One of the hornbills swooped down near her, circling and watching her. She felt a connection with it, as if it were trying to say something to her, something important, perhaps a word of friendship and welcome, perhaps some kind of warning.

Horst saw her by herself, looking somewhat forlorn, so he walked over to her and talked with her about the camp, about herself, and how she was feeling. This cheered her up, because Horst was a well known and important scientist in her field. At the same time, he made her uncomfortable. He was standing too close. She was used to men being obvious, making fools of themselves around her. Like all of them, Horst appeared to not have the slightest idea that she, if anything, was feeling a little sorry for him.

Leaving Mary, Horst wandered outside the camp until it was just still visible in the distance. He was surprised to see Joseph, who waved to him from a distance from camp.

"Hello, Horst Grobben, sir," Joseph said. "This is a happy coincidence. I've been wanting to talk with you. You said you represented an international environment organization set on saving the wilderness and these jumbos. It's going be hard to do, as I'm sure you saw yesterday, especially now that there must be some big-time well-funded poachers killing the jumbos like those we saw on the way to this camp of yours." He kicked a rock, watching Horst, who had said nothing.

"Let me tell you, with that kind of operation those fellows must have good connections with the government to start that kind of poaching. None of this traditional one-at-a-time occasional killing of a jumbo by the locals. I know this place well enough and know how to work against those big timers. I could help you and your organization."

"Thanks, I'll keep that in mind," Horst answered. "But you know, we've been thinking Bruce could help."

"Maybe ten, twenty years ago. Not now, not after the mess he got himself into shooting a lot of jumbos and claiming to be doing good," Joseph answered. "Nobody would go near him for that kind of help, who knew what he did. Besides, having him and his science team wandering around, most of them complete novices — no matter how smart they are, they'll just be in the way. Might get hurt, say, during a battle against these poachers. Best if they weren't here, tell the truth."

"Well, I appreciate your kind offer and will definitely keep it in mind," Horst said.

Joseph turned and was gone with a conspiratorial wave.

Horst took a seat on a flat rock. His thoughts raced. Joseph might be the very opportunity he had been looking for — a way to get Bruce and Michael out of the way, to get in charge of the situation. Then he could bring in the large environmental organization he was working with and, with Joseph's knowledge and help, find the big-time poachers and get rid of them. This ponderous science stuff was just interference. The important thing was stopping the poachers. Hmm. that would be working with a petty criminal, but he's just a small time occasional poacher, and clearly as a result Joseph knew a lot about finding elephants and where the other poachers would be going. No, Joseph taking an elephant here and there wasn't a problem in the long run. Yes, this was a very likely way to go. But Horst always moved slowly, always thought about things and let them settle in his mind. Usually, opportunities arose without him having to do anything but watch, and it looked like he would have plenty of time to do just that, given the pace at which Bruce and his science team were going about things.

CHAPTER 13

Musth

---

*The Nantucketers . . . in all seasons and all oceans declared
everlasting war with the mightiest animated mass that has
survived the flood; most monstrous and most mountainous!
That Himmalehan, salt-sea Mastodon, clothed with such
portentousness of unconscious power, that his very panics are
more to be dreaded.*

Herman Melville, Moby Dick

E lizabeth watched as Paul turned the steaks on a grill over the
flame of a green camping stove that hissed bright blue flames
against the darkening land. A night bird called. She thought
she heard hooves of some large animal, then digging and scratching
sounds, but she wasn't sure.

The cooking smells reached all the team and they were soon
standing or sitting near Bruce. He explained what he called the
meal drill, telling the newcomers that their meals were cafeteria style
and everybody helped with cooking and cleaning up, no matter
what they had seen in Hollywood movies about African safaris. He
showed them a stack of plates, cups, and utensils, and told them
that in addition to steaks the menu of the night included salad —
vegetables still fresh from Nairobi markets — and rice and beans

"for our vegetarian friends," he said, looking at Cecile. Better enjoy the fresh vegetables while you can. And dessert was cake fresh from Nairobi.

Bruce pointed to three large buckets, the first held soapy water for the main wash with a sponge, the second bucket had clean water for a first rinse and the third a final rinse. "Anytime you want, come and get your steaks. Beer and other drinks are in that cooler — as long as we have a little ice, that is. Help yourselves."

"Sanitation, order, and symmetry out here in this Tsavo place. Yep, that's what we're doin'," Howie said to Elizabeth, suddenly standing next to her. It was another of Howie's strange comments, she thought.

"Are you saying it's chaotic, disordered, and dirty out there?" Elizabeth bantered back, pointing beyond the camp.

"Not at all. Regulated randomness. Certain uncertainties. Well-regulated irregularities. Chances of your choosing."

"Heck, I don't have a clue what you're talking about, and sometimes I don't think you do either."

Paul broke in, seeming to take Howie's comments seriously and saying that he thought Howie might be describing an American wilderness, but he was expecting Tsavo to be purer, more regular. "Having some of the kind of universal harmony that Einstein believed in," he said.

Howie grinned his wide grin and pushed his glasses against his nose, wacked the dust off his red and white baseball cap, and put it back on his head.

Horst handed Elizabeth a plate and motioned for her to go ahead of him. It was the time of day when he tended to feel down. A lengthening shadow from one of the palm trees fell across his face. Why had he pushed so hard to get himself invited on this safari? He stepped back and let Howie, Mary, and Paul go ahead of him too. How many years had he fought for nature? For places like Tsavo? For himself — his career? He was getting close to fifty, for God's sake. Maybe this was a younger man's job. Just the other day, in Geneva, as he gave a speech about conservation, he felt that he and nature were intertwined, but out here he felt separate and, truth to tell, alone. The energy he had felt after talking with Joseph seemed to drain out of him.

He would rather be in a Geneva rathskeller, hobnobbing with his buddies, the ones who had trod the international conservation circuit with him for decades. They had laughed when he told them he was going to Tsavo, especially when he described the expedition and its purpose. "Really, Horst, you doing fieldwork? You're joking. You'd better stick to your international negotiations, saving the world, not go running around out in the bush dirtying your sports jacket," one of them had said.

Looking around now, Horst had to agree. Aside from everything else, he was put off by the kind of people Bruce had gotten together, claiming to "do ecology." Women. Blacks. Blue-collar types who'd never even gone to college. Earnest types like Paul. Weirdos like Howie. Horst shook his head. And he was tired of dealing with Bruce. The two of them had sparred over the years, each with a very different viewpoint about places like Tsavo.

Horst had been glad when the news came to Geneva that Bruce had left Africa. His main professional enemy had been defeated. He had happily spoken out about Bruce the elephant killer. He had come on this trip to see what might be done to stop Bruce's approach, which seem informal and too small scale to have any effect. Yes, and he had been glad that his colleagues in Geneva had approved of his trip, in fact made sure it was funded. They, like Horst, believed the only solution to the elephant poaching and the overall threat to elephants was through large-scale approaches, and working with the governments, however corrupt they were, to persuade them, God knows how, to stop their poaching.

His unexpected meeting with Joseph upset him especially. On the one hand, perhaps Joseph could really be a key to Horst's goal of stopping Bruce and his team. On the other, for what reason could he trust this fellow, who had recently been in jail for poaching?

Seeing Horst was lost in thought and looking downcast, Elizabeth reached back and handed him a plate, and smiled at him, hoping to cheer him up. Bruce slapped a steak on it. Horst took a tin cup, put some ice in it from the big Styrofoam case, and found a log to sit on. He filled the cup with gin from a flask he kept in his jacket and looked out through the scattering of trees at the plains, which seemed to continue forever. At least he could try to enjoy the simple purity of the plains. He saw Elizabeth watching him and gave her a smile. She sat down nearby, and he offered her some gin from his flask, getting up and finding a glass for her and a little ice. Mary sat down next to Elizabeth and politely accepted a little gin as well. This was more like it, Horst thought, and chatted with them, his eyes on Mary. Paul joined them, sitting between Mary and Horst.

They began to talk again about the big elephant they had seen.

"Zamani Baba," Michael said, joining them with a nod and a smile, "Zamani Baba."

"What are you saying?" Mary asked.

"Swahili. Sort of," Michael said. "It's a rather oblique reference," he explained, "meaning something like Old Father, Old Father Elephant. They all know him. He's ancient. I didn't know he'd survived the die-off. It's good to see him. Even before the drought, he was the biggest. And even the poachers were frightened of him. He killed many."

"We used to call him Old Ragged Ears," Bruce said, sitting next to Elizabeth. "So, he's back, and you saw him. Different from the other elephants, you know. Yes. The eldest. The wisest, some say."

"He reads your mind," Michael said, laughing, "but you can't read his."

"You're joking," Mary said. The darkness and the beer and Horst's gin seemed to be freeing the people up, Elizabeth thought. You couldn't see the expressions on people's faces, so maybe that made it easier to talk.

"Wait till you meet him again," Michael said. "You talk about Mother Nature. Well, Old Ragged Ears is just as unpredictable."

"Is that a belief of your people, Michael?" Mary asked politely, eyes wide.

"No, no, not Maasai. It's my own idea. I got it from those English public schools they sent me to. Ruined me. As I told you before, they tried to turn me into an English gentleman, made me study all those old Greek and Roman legends. Bruce encouraged them, so it was all Bruce's fault."

He moved closer to the lantern. Elizabeth could make out his slightly amused expression.

"Lucretius, I remember him best, and Ovid, all the gods running around dressed up as animals, making love to pretty women." Michael smiled at Elizabeth. "Taught me all that Lucretius stuff about Mother Earth, how she's getting old, wrinkly, you know. So, I thought, she needs some young male to make her young again. And the best one for her is Zamani Baba. Father Elephant, Father Nature."

"Is he always dangerous?" Mary asked.

"Depends," Bruce answered. "He seems to like some people, not like others."

"Oh, he'll like *you* — *ndiyo*, yes. *Kisora mzuri sana. Ndiyo.*" Michael laughed to himself.

"What?" Mary asked. "What?"

"Michael thinks you'll get on fine with that old elephant," Bruce explained gently.

"Oh?"

Bruce smiled at her. "He has an eye for the ladies, Zamani Baba, does, especially during the breeding season. The male gets into quite a state. It's called *musth*. Musth is a liquid that drips from a big gland near his eyes, sort of like tearing."

"Makes him very aggressive," Michael put in.

"Some say it's a kind of euphoria," Bruce said.

Elizabeth laughed. "Come on, a euphoric elephant? You're kidding."

"Not at all."

"Okay, then, what are the signs of euphoria in an elephant?"

"Excitement. Swiftness."

"Fearlessness," Michael added.

"He's already got that, we saw it today."

"Love and passion," Bruce said.

Davie interrupted. "An' an elephant in musth dribbles urine too, all the time."

"Oh, charming!" Elizabeth said, "Now that sounds like an old elephant, all right,"

Cecile spoke up. "I hope they won't shoot that wonderful creature."

"Well, Cecile, we'd better look out for him, try to protect him," Davie answered.

"Protect *him* when he almost stepped on the Land Rover like it was a toy? I'd say we need protection *from* him," Elizabeth said.

An owl-like bird sounded from the darkness beyond the camp. A dry breeze rustled palm leaves above the campground. A Coleman lantern focused blinding white light on the faces so that Elizabeth saw the others only as silhouettes. The rest of Tsavo, bodies and all, seemed shadows.

Elizabeth could not see anything beyond Bruce, whose face was as sharply distinguished by the lantern as a ship's captain on a bridge under a spotlight.

"Just how dangerous was that bull that Davie challenged today?" she asked.

"Dangerous as hell if ya don't understand him," Davie cut in.

Bruce looked at the new Americans. "Davie's just trying to scare you. Sure, if you don't understand them and don't respect them, elephants can be dangerous. But if you respect them, keep your distance, and learn about them, you'll all be all fine."

Toward the end of dinner, the conversation soured as everyone started talking about the dead elephants, poachers, and what the team should do now — if they could still do anything to help the elephants, and, even more broadly, whether they should stay and do their work or just give up immediately and go back home for their own safety. Paul seemed especially quiet and looked uncomfortable. Horst, too, but Elizabeth didn't know him well enough to know what that meant. He puzzled her and disturbed her in ways she did not understand.

Elizabeth was surprised by how many different points of view were expressed, and by some overt hostility among some of the people. Perhaps she had been naive, thinking that everyone on the expedition would agree on the goals. Most disturbing, Bruce seemed to dislike Horst — and Horst, Bruce. She sensed a deep, underlying anger between them that bothered her most. Horst kept talking about the need to preserve the balance of nature and insisting that the only way to do this was to keep people out.

Horst accused Bruce of killing elephants for no good reason, alluding to something that Bruce had done in the past that Elizabeth was not aware of, and Cecile joined in, saying all sorts of sentimental things about individual animals. But what was the difference between Cecile and Bruce? Bruce clearly admired that one big elephant. Wasn't that sympathy for an individual? She glanced around. Davie sat by himself off to one side, frowning and smoking and looking angry at everyone. Where was the sense of loving to be in the wilderness, in the plains and savannas of Africa that attracted so many tourists?

Her idea of a scientific field trip was a bunch of geologists who agreed on just about everything and had a good time searching for answers to questions they all thought important and, more to the point, clear. Not this undercurrent of hostility, and many different agendas. It didn't bode well for their work, or for their survival, for that matter. She was even having doubts about her compatriots, Paul, Mary, and Howie. They weren't saying much and seemed weak. No, that couldn't be right about Howie; he wasn't weak, just weird.

Just how dangerous were the poachers? Horst kept saying it would be wiser for them all to leave immediately.

"Damn well better watch yourself, buddies," Davie said. "I've seen death everywhere out here — vultures at too many carcasses of all kinds. If it ain't one thing, it's another in Tsavo. Once, just a few miles from here, I came 'cross one of them poison-arrow fellows, one of those little people, dyin' of thirst, vultures circlin'. I tried to help him, but I was too late. You'd think he'd a known if anybody woulda where to find water and how to survive. But he got caught somehow."

"Not common, though," Bruce said.

"How 'bout your ancestors goin' after them man-eatin' lions? How many railroad laborers did they eat before your grandfather or whoever killed them? Lotsa them from India, didn't know nothin' neither. Didn't know anything except to shake in their tents all night and scream when they saw the lion comin'."

"Now, Davie, let's not be so melodramatic," Bruce said. "That was another time."

"Tell that to the vultures. They're lookin' for them times to come back, man, and lookin' for you tryin' to walk outta here searchin' for water."

Paul, ever quiet, spoke softly to say that he thought they were able to deal properly with the animals, respecting their needs and rights, especially with Bruce, Michael, and Davie himself bringing so much experience to the group. But his attempt at smoothing the conversation did not work.

"You'll kill them all, you will," Cecile said bitterly, hauling himself up. He put his Panama fedora hat on his head, and in the darkness, with a black shirt over a very white neck, looked like a mad preacher making a prophecy. "You'll kill them all before you're through," he said again, shaking a finger at Davie. Cecile talked about the sad plight of the elephants, and his commitment to do God's work to help save His creatures. Bruce stood up and went over to Cecile, putting his arm around the portly man's slumping shoulders. "Come on, we're all here to work together, aren't we?"

"I'll stay at all costs, poachers or no poachers — all the m ore so now that I've seen the murdered elephants," Cecile said.

Michael talked about the history of the poachers. Both he and Paul said that this one incident was not enough to decide to leave. Only Horst had argued in favor of leaving, and Elizabeth wondered what this might mean about him, but she could not fathom his motives. In fact, Horst continued to be of two minds. One was just to get clear of this place, away from this mostly amateur group.

But the opportunity with Joseph seemed too good. In the end, he thought, he probably should take a chance on Joseph. Otherwise, fleeing back to Geneva, he would look a fool for having gone to Tsavo, giving his professional buddies another chance to laugh at him. He hated to be laughed at. That more than anything edged him to stay and see what he could work out with Joseph. In the end, they all decided they would stay unless things got worse.

The camp suddenly became quiet, the only noise the now-loud hiss of the gas lantern, spewing white light into the night, darkening it by contrast like rain wasted on a hot pavement. Davie lit another cigarette, threw down his match and ground it into the soil. "Shit," he said. "Time for bed," and walked away toward his tent. One by one the others left the circle of light for their shelters.

* * *

Joseph camped south of the Galana River and west of Bruce's group. He spent his evening talking with a small group of men he had hired to help him poach some ivory, some very experienced whom he had known for years, and some new recruits. First he told them about what appeared to be the arrival of a big time poaching operation, describing the sloppy methods and advanced weapons evident at the site of the two dead elephants. Then he warned the people who worked for him about Bruce's team of scientists, and asked two of the most experienced to keep track of Bruce's people, to know always where they were. He told the rest to keep away from them, to be invisible. But he also knew that he at least some of the time he had to follow Bruce, because Bruce was the best at knowing where the elephants would be. Joseph had gotten pretty good at getting to the elephants, but he knew down deep that nobody understood the jumbos better the Bruce.

Joseph's men understood this put them in a squeeze, between keeping their small time and careful harvesting of elephants continuing, but keeping that unknown to Bruce and team, at least as much as possible, and avoiding contact with the new heavily-weaponed foreign poachers. Joseph went on to explain that they were doing pretty well, but he was being offered more and more money for ivory and was under pressure from those who had hired him to get much more, faster. He was trying to get an idea of where the elephants might be concentrated, and if there really were as many as those who funded him speculated.

CHAPTER 14

Cecile

The recent past is invariably the most treacherous because, lacking perspective, we understand it the least.

Landscape architect Grady Gammage, Jr.

I n the brightening light that quickened after dawn, Bruce drove a Land Rover to the edge of the old landing strip where Johnny was going to set his plane down. He had asked Elizabeth if she would like to go with him, knowing that he really should have brought Paul, who was at least formally in charge of the American contingent, but Bruce let his curiosity about Elizabeth and his attraction to her overrule. Michael went too, as planned. At the last minute Cecile had jumped into the Land Rover, saying he wanted every opportunity to scout wildlife. Bruce was annoyed but hadn't wanted to turn around and kick Cecile out.

Driving up and down the grass runway, Bruce stopped occasionally so he and Michael could pick up a branch or any other debris and throw it or drag it as far away from the landing strip as they could. Then they parked off to the side and got out. Bruce motioned to Elizabeth to join him and strolled away from the airstrip to the edge of the grassy clearing. Michael and Cecile left them and continued to walk along the airstrip, keeping an eye out for wildlife that might stray onto the landing strip and looking out for poachers as well. At first, Cecile watched how Michael worked, and helped, but then he began to look around, hoping to find something more interesting than dead branches. After all, it was his first chance to be out in this true wilderness and he couldn't wait to look for wildlife. Michael was busy and Bruce was talking with Elizabeth a good distance away. He decided they weren't paying him any attention and wouldn't care if he looked around a little.

Indeed, Bruce was paying no attention to Cecile, assuming he was busy with Michael. Too full of memories of this place, at first Bruce was silent, stopping now and again to toss a branch into a grove of trees. But slowly he began to talk to Elizabeth. "I used to land here all the time," he told her. "That was in the good old days, when this place was loaded with elephants, and the tourists were starting to come. But then the elephant population went up and up. That was when I got myself into a lot of trouble. I took on the job of reducing the elephant population." He stopped to pull m ore dead branches off the landing strip.

"Once we shot a whole herd of elephants here. Come along, I think I can find where it happened." He walked westward, looking at the ground, then stopped and bent down. He picked up a large elephant tooth, about ten inches long, yellowed with age. It looked like a fossil but was large as a chunk of firewood. He told Elizabeth that the killing of the elephants had happened right there. Her eyebrows raised, she asked what he had done. He explained that the whole thing had started when he and others involved with elephant conservation saw the great destruction that the elephants were doing to Tsavo — creating the much more barren place that still remained and that Elizabeth was seeing. "There were so many jumbos they were running out of food, and tearing down trees and shrubs and eating the bark. They changed Tsavo from the dense forest my father had seen — what Howie rightly called a park for elephants where you couldn't see any. Sheldrick, the first head of the park, had gotten the poachers under control — he had mounted a kind of anti-guerrilla warfare against them. And the ironic result was that there were way too many elephants."

"Why didn't the elephants just leave the park?" Elizabeth asked.

Bruce paused and looked into the distance. Elizabeth saw sadness in his face. "Well, this is a huge park, as Howie pointed out. And the jumbos just would not go outside the park boundaries, they just wouldn't cross the railroad, the paved road, and the dirt track, the three forming the boundary," Bruce replied.

Bruce was silent again, and Elizabeth took a moment to look around at the landing strip and its surroundings. She saw in the distance that Michael, now quite a ways down the landing strip from Bruce and herself, seemed to be keeping an eye on Cecile. But Michael had found some new tire tracks and was bent down studying them, his mind for the moment preoccupied with whom might have recently been nearby. He assumed Cecil was still just behind him, following.

Bruce, still looking into the distance, not directly at Elizabeth, continued to talk. "I decided to make a profession out of elephant control — formed a company to reduce the overabundance of the elephants, and we tried to do everything in the most humane way, including the way we killed the jumbos, and we tried to make sure that almost every part of an elephant got used for a good purpose, especially as much as possible to help the local people," Bruce said, looking into the distance.

"Some said that if we were going to shoot any to reduce the population we should have culled an animal here and there from each of the herds. But the elephants are such social animals that shooting one elephant in a herd would be terribly hard on the other animals. They remember each other. They care for each other. You see, my idea was to minimize the suffering of all the elephants — not just physical suffering but their emotional suffering too, thought I was doing a good deed, and saving the elephants from themselves — population control was the goal."

The lines on Bruce's 's face deepened as he told Elizabeth his story. It had been more than ten years ago, in a Land Rover bristling with submachine guns. They had driven up to a herd of about forty elephants, a herd they had picked out the day before from the air.

There was another Land Rover with them, with more armed men. They braced the guns on the hoods of the vehicles and, staying as quiet as they could, waited for the herd to approach. W hen it was close enough, they opened fire with all of their guns, killing the entire herd in a few minutes. The noise left him deafened. The sight of the dead and dying elephants had hurt him deeply.

Bruce fell silent.

Meanwhile, Cecile, far down the landing strip from Bruce, had wandered quietly away from Michael and gone into some thick brush. He had heard something make a small noise and once inside the vegetation saw a small lion cub, or maybe there were two. Yes, two. They were so cute that he couldn't resist moving toward them, not thinking about where the mother might be.

Elizabeth waited patiently for Bruce to continue with his story, imagining the scene of massive killing of elephants. Then she said, "So you believe elephants have emotions and can feel sadness and loss of others?"

He looked at her, but did not give her a direct answer. "We decided that the most humane thing would be to kill an entire herd. I didn't like doing it, but I thought it was necessary. And we made sure that the hides got used, and we gave the meat to villagers. We gave the ivory to the villagers as well, and they could sell it. After we shot the herd, we studied every animal — aged them from their teeth. This tooth must not have made it back to archive." He held the great tooth upright, big as a human skull, looking at it. "Guess I didn't get to know that elephant very well," he said, turning the tooth over in his hands.

He explained that they measured everything they could think of about the elephants — never let a scientific opportunity pass, was his goal. Science information that would tell them how badly the herd had been doing, so they could manage the park for them better in the future. For one, they measured fat on the kidneys, which he explained was a good index of their health. "Yes, we did it to help the elephant population, to help the species, and we tried to do it as humanely as possible and as fast as possible. I suppose it's on my mind all the more because of the poaching we just saw."

He fell silent. The wind blew through the tall African grasses. A secretary bird scurried busily away from them.

Cecile meanwhile was trying to move slowly closer to the lion cubs. He bent down and quietly called to them. But getting their attention seemed to take forever. He knew he needed to be careful, but the lion cubs were so appealing, and it would be his first direct contact with these creatures.

"And then what happened?" Elizabeth asked softly.

"Everybody hated me. They called me a Nazi, said I was seeking the 'ultimate solution to the elephant problem.' People threw things at my home in Nairobi, even threatened to bomb the house. Once somebody shot at my airplane when I was flying over here. Put a hole through the wing of my Piper Cub. I tried to do good, and everybody hated me for it. Then came the drought, and the elephants died, just as the better scientists said they would. More died than we ever would have shot. We estimated that six thousand died in the drought. In the process they destroyed all the trees and shrubs as far as you could see from the Galana River — the river was their last stand. We would have shot about half that many if we'd had the support of the people and the government. But no, they're all just mushy inside about elephants, like Cecile. Do everything to build up the herd, but then leave it alone, nature would know best — like bloody old Horst."

"What did you do afterward?"

"Hung around for a few years. Then left. Went to Bermuda. I thought perhaps I would find peace there."

Now Elizabeth knew that this was the terrible event that ate away at Bruce.

I'll never forget seeing the lead female of that herd drop and fall onto her side, giving her calf a few seconds to see that she was down before he was shot as well. It was all over in a few minutes. Then silence. Silence and death. T he smell of elephant blood everywhere. Tons and tons of carnage. No sport in it, nothing but death."

"What's good for the population isn't always so good for the individual, and vice versa," he added.

Elizabeth reached out and touched him, taking his hand. He didn't seem to notice.

"They're a lot like us, you know," Bruce continued. "Elephants live about sixty years, reach puberty at about fourteen. They live a kind of nomadic life — like our early ancestors, except, of course, that elephants are strictly vegetarian. Teenagers are a problem. Mothers kick the teenage males out of the herd when they reach fourteen. Too much trouble." He was quiet for a few minutes, then began again.

"Elephants are like life itself. The essence of life. Big and smart. Thoughtful animals. I'm not a religious person---not in any ordinary way so to speak---but there's something almost spiritual about these jumbos. I don't know. Not like the other herbivores you see out here. The small tommys—Thomson's gazelles — rush and panic, not much up here" — he pointed at his temples. "Good eating, but not much sense. And the rhinos — there's nothing as dumb as a black rhino. But the elephants — there's something special about them."

"Think they have regrets?" she asked.

He gave her a strange expression, almost a smile, but a sad one. "Don't know. Maybe."

Elizabeth listened. Clearly, he needed to talk and not be talked to. Perhaps it was easier to open up to an American woman who was still a stranger, whom he might never see after this trip.

Michael was not in view.

At this moment they seemed alone in the unbounded Tsavo plains, in the silent grasslands and savannas, perhaps the fatherland of the most ancient human beings, separated from the rest of civilization. Elizabeth heard the buzzing of insects, saw a small bird fly past, heard once again the incessant calling of doves. High above, vultures soared in the distant updrafts.

Elizabeth heard the drone of an airplane that appeared low on the horizon. The plane flew to the west, turned straight in, and descended in a gentle glide until the wheels softly touched the ground; Elizabeth could not even hear or feel their impact. Johnny spun the plane around with a flair and taxied over to where they stood, the plane blowing sandy soil in Elizabeth's face.

Cecile heard the sound of the airplane and realized he had to leave the lion cubs, but he wanted to make one more try at direct contact with them.

Johnny cut the engine and jumped out, grinning. "How's my boys and girls?" he called to the two of them and to Michael, who waved, but continued on his course, then looked around for Cecile.

Elizabeth was impressed. Johnny, with his long blond hair whipping in the wind, white shirt open at the collar, and khaki trousers, had the debonair look of a professional pilot just off a commercial flight and the adventurous look of a hippie setting off on some new conquest. A shotgun was slung over his shoulder. He walked to Bruce with an easy, long-legged gait and gave him a pat on the back, then turned to Elizabeth, stood back to admire her, and graciously stepped forward to shake her hand as Bruce introduced them.

"Our geologist," plus her name, was about all the introduction she got.

Johnny smiled at her. "Bloody empty, Tsavo," he said, his pale blue eyes looking first into Elizabeth's and then beyond "I didn't see more than twenty animals all the way through the park. Not like it used to be. Except a herd of about sixty animals as I was making my approach here, not more than a mile north.

Elizabeth smiled at Johnny and looked past him to see a man on horseback a distance away riding toward the landing strip.

"Who's that?" she asked, pulling up her binoculars. "He looks like an old man right out of the nineteenth century. Is that a sword slung down on one side of his saddle and a long rifle down the other side?"

Johnny looked and then shook his head. "I'll be damned. He's famous out here. Been riding around Tsavo like that for years. Some say he's always looking to help people in trouble. Some say the opposite. Lots of superstition about him."

"What do you mean?" Elizabeth asked.

"Another one of Tsavo's peculiarities," Bruce said, seemingly trying to make little of the man. He turned around, looking for Cecil and Michael so he could get everyone together and they could be on their way.

"Peculiar, alright," Elizabeth said. She pulled up her binoculars and looked toward where the man had been. There was no sign of him, only a small trail of dust.

* * *

Cecile, still focused on the lions, picked up a small stick and waved it at the cubs, hoping it would make them curious and bring them closer. It did. So focused on the cubs, he did not see the mother watching from the thicket. She crouched down and began to move, ever so slowly, toward her cubs.

Cecile's heart raced with excitement. Here in this desolate land he might achieve a moment he had long dreamed about — direct and wonderful contact with a wild creature, and two absolute charming ones at that. He began to move closer. That was too much for the female lion, who charged him, knocking him down and biting his neck. He screamed. Bruce, Johnny, and Elizabeth heard the scream. They began to run toward Cecile, but they were twenty yards or more from him. They saw that Michael was already moving into the brush where Cecil had been.

From the thicket of shrubs and small trees near Cecile, Joseph appeared, rushing out, with a rifle. He tried to get the lioness off of Cecile. Firing his rifle just over the lioness's head, he got her to turn away, but Cecile was badly bitten and bleeding. Michael arrived with his sword out. Joseph picked a knife out of his field jacket and the two chased the lioness, who at first stood and roared at them, but then quickly moved to save her cubs, disappearing into the brush.

Michael and Joseph were bending over Cecile when the rest of the group arrived. Johnny was completely perplexed, not knowing who Cecile was or what he was doing lying on the ground, and couldn't believe that he was seeing Joseph. But always a person of action, he immediately joined Bruce and Michael. No one was able to stop Cecile's bleeding, and he lost consciousness. They were so focused on Cecile that they failed to notice Joseph leaving them, quietly moving away toward where he had seen the lioness take her cubs.

CHAPTER 15

A Flight to Voi

Don't you know that love and death go very close together?

Joseph Conrad

Bruce called everyone together as soon as the group returned to camp with Cecile's body and told the others what had happened. This was not the first time that he, Johnny, and Michael had dealt with death of a companion in the Tsavo plains and they handled the situation much as they had done in the past, first, telling the those who had not been at the airstrip what had happened. Then, not knowing the religious convictions of everyone, Bruce held a brief interdenominational ceremony. A prayer to God on behalf of Cecile's soul, appreciative words about him.

He explained that Johnny would fly Cecile's body to Voi and arrange for appropriate handling of the body and shipping by air to his family. Johnny would also contact the family, by phone if possible. Michael would go along to help, even though that meant bringing Johnny's Cessna 182 close to its maximum carrying weight. Bruce knew he had to remain to help the rest of the team, one by one, deal with Cecile's death.

Moving quickly, Johnny and Michael wrapped Cecile's body in a large plastic bag that had been brought along to collect vegetation samples and then drove Cecile's body back to the airstrip in the Land Rover they had used that morning. Bruce went into the meeting tent and sat down on one of the folding chairs, inviting each of the team who had not been at the airstrip to talk with him, one at a time. Davie and Howie followed him and said, each in his own way, briefly, that they would do whatever Bruce wanted them doing to help. Davie was well acquainted with death through his research of vultures, and he, of all the team was least disturbed by Cecile's death. He watched Howie, wondering what was going on with that strange dude, but could not tell a thing. Then he realized that Howie was calm, surprisingly practical, and spoke to Bruce about what they might do to keep the group going, if that made sense at all. The three of them were soon deep into a discussion of their options and what actions needed to be taken right away.

Elizabeth went off with Mary and in private told her what she had experienced. Elizabeth, disturbed by it all, but under control, knew that Mary would be very upset, and she was, not only by Cecile's death itself — she of all the group liked Cecile best — but by the reality of death in the tall grass and bush, killing by the very wild animals she both feared and sought to fathom. It was, Elizabeth knew, for Mary, the realization of her worst fears

Elizabeth, doing her best to deal with her own feelings, felt that the adrenaline that had gotten her this far seemed to be fading. She was having enough trouble controlling her own emotions, but knew that Mary needed her help. She was relieved when Paul found the two of them and, with a simple look at Elizabeth, made clear that he was there to help Mary, and Elizabeth as well. Although as new to Tsavo as the others, he was more experienced in wilderness and had dealt with death of a companion in some of the big woods of Montana, killed by a grizzly. Paul sat on the ground near the two women without saying anything. He offered the some tea and a few cookies and waited for either of them to speak.

"Paul, I've been wondering about something," Elizabeth said. "How come that guy, Joseph, was right there when the lion attacked Cecile? I mean, it was awfully nice of him, brave of him, to jump right in and scare the lion off. And then to help us try to keep Cecile alive. But it seems strange that he was right there."

Paul was quiet for a few moments. "Yes. Hard to imagine he just happened to be wandering by, good luck so to speak, now that you mention it." He looked away into the distance. Elizabeth knew Paul was thinking, and in his usual way, took his time, wasn't one for small talk. So she said nothing, just waited, not especially easy for her.

After what Elizabeth thought was a long time, Paul turned back to her. "It can't have been just a coincidence. But you know what that means." Again Paul was silent for a few moments. "He was following us, or at least on his way to seek us out, one or the other. But why? And isn't he the guy that was in jail for poaching and just got out? What's going on here?" Another pause. "I'll go find Bruce and Michael and ask what they think," he said.

* * *

Horst was absolutely furious with Bruce and could barely control himself. He wanted to have it out with him. But he saw Howie and Davie, talking with him. He waited until they left and he and Bruce were well out of hearing.

"What the hell were you doing out there on the airstrip?" Horst said, almost spitting the words out. "How could you have let Cecil get killed? How could you let him even go near two lion cubs. You, who's in charge? What kind of screw up is this?"

Bruce interrupted. "I beg your pardon, Horst. Don't talk to me that way. Yes, I accept full responsibility for what happened. I'm afraid I failed to understand how inexperienced Cecile's was. I thought he had had more time in the wild. Apparently not. You should know as well as I that this is a tough place to work, with plenty of dangers."

"But you brought them here. It was your idea."

"Again, I have to beg your pardon. I was asked to lead this group. This expedition wasn't my idea at all. I didn't pick Cecile and I didn't pick you. However, I *agreed* to lead a group with Cecile and you."

"But you know damn well you loved being asked to come back to Tsavo. We all know how guilty you must feel given how you screwed things up here before, long ago. And now you're well on your way to screwing things up again —"

Bruce interrupted again. "Horst, nobody invited you on this trip. You volunteered. You knew I was going to be in charge. If you don't like what I'm doing, leave. Johnny will get you out of here as fast as you'd like, tomorrow, or the next day."

"Not on your life. Damn it, Bruce. Somebody's got to make sure things don't get even worse, and that the international conservationists aren't made to look bad."

"And you're the one to set things right. Is that it? You, who've had so little experience in the wild. You think you could do better? Shit." Bruce turned away and looked into the distance. "Horst, I know that I cannot force you to leave. Your people would not let that happen. But if you stay, I'm bloody well in charge, and you will go along with how I do things. Clearly, we have very different ideas about people and places like Tsavo. You want all people out. I want people involved, in touch with this incredible wild place — in touch with their deepest, oldest feelings. You and I both want to "save nature" as you would put it, but very differently. I want it to be helped and kept a place that people can come to. You want it left alone. And I even want members of my team to be able to do a little exploring on their own. Well, you've got the big time contacts, I know that. I'm just a guy on my own. But somebody did ask me to lead this project and I'm doing it. Hell, I know I'm not perfect, but neither are you."

"It's not perfect I asking for," Horst said. "Christ, a lot less than perfect would be good enough. Just don't make us conservationists look bad by getting everybody you've brought here killed. And doing science out here when there's big time poaching. That's not perfect. Not by a long shot. But I'm not leaving. *You* shouldn't even be here. I'll do whatever I damn please, thank you very much."

Horst strode to the edge of the camp, doing his best to calm himself down. Now what to do, he wondered. I've got to get that Joseph person involved, he realized. Joseph was the only person he had met so far who was completely independent of Bruce and had about as much knowledge of Tsavo — maybe right up there with Bruce and Michael — and seemed not to like either especially. He could be key to getting rid of Bruce and taking over the expedition himself, maybe with Joseph filling in the role of guide and armed guard. Yes, but how to find that fellow?

Toward evening, the group quieted, each with their own thoughts. Bruce dug out a bottle of Scotch he had brought and passed it around with cups. He lit a small fire, and slowly, one by one, all but Horst came and sat near the fire and to Bruce. Thus the evening passed.

CHAPTER 16

Among the Elephants

---

*It is in the compelling zest of high adventure and of victory,
and in creative action, that man finds his supreme joys.*

Antoine de Saint-Exupery

Several days passed before Johnny and Michael returned from Voi, as the team adjusted to Cecile's loss and gradually got back into their work. Bruce was not sleeping well at night. Today Johnny and Michael were to be back, and Bruce realized that the best thing he could do for the group was to get them out of the camp and in close to the elephants, to renew their fascination with nature and the wilderness. He explained his plan for the day to them over breakfast, adding that they could do it in honor of Cecile, for what more would Cecile want of them, if he knew how badly they all felt over his loss, than for the team to continue what they had been sent to do, so they could help save these beautiful creatures, as Cecile had put it.

And so the day's trip began. Davie said he would prefer to search out some sites for him to do his vulture studies, and asked Howie if he would like to go with him. He was getting to like Howie, even though he didn't understand him — or a lot of what Howie said for that matter. In fact, that was what he found so appealing about

Howie, a true character who didn't seem to care about status, money, or success in an ordinary way. Howie agreed to go with him.

Horst asked Davie if he could join them. He had been watching Davie the past few days, and a new thought had occurred to him. Before Cecile's death, he had thought that the only way to get Bruce out of Tsavo and away from this project was getting rid of the entire science team. But now he realized there was another alternative — get rid of Bruce and Michael, and then, as a representative of his international organization, he could take over the team.

Joseph could become his Michael, and Davie, along with Joseph, could help find the elephants and the poachers because Davie was so familiar with Tsavo and knew how to deal with dangerous situations. He might even be better than Bruce, given how Bruce had screwed up with Cecile. Yes, he could not only lead a team that would get rid of the government-involved poachers, and he could show that he was leading an important scientific survey, a new approach. Yes, this had an appeal. But he had to get to know Davie better. Clearly, Davie had his own strangeness and limitations. Paul, Elizabeth, Mary, and Howie could stay and do their science stuff. But what about Johnny? Maybe he would leave if Bruce were forced out. More complications. He'd better get to know Johnny better. After all, the two had, at least in some ways, similar backgrounds --- upper class, educated, moved around in rather elite circles. Yes. Perhaps he could take over the day-to-day stuff that Bruce had to do, with me as the leader.

Davie accepted Horst's request that he accompany Davie the next day. Bruce was glad that everybody was going to get out of camp and that he wouldn't have to deal with Horst during the day. His spirits lifted as he thought of watching elephants with Michael and Johnny. He could continue to educate Paul as a kind of future leader in the way he had been, and he would have the company of Mary and Elizabeth. Sounded very pleasant.

A little later, Bruce heard the sound of Johnny's plane. He told the others to get their gear ready for their field trips for the day and drove alone out to the airstrip to pick up Johnny and Michael After the three of them had tied the plane down, Bruce gave them some coffee out of a thermos and suggested that sit down and talk a while before going back to camp. He asked how things went in Voi.

"Everything went okay — the usual," Johnny said. "Got everything flown out. Called the relatives and talked with them. Took a good bit of explaining, as you can imagine."

"We saw something on the way back that won't make you happy," Michael broke in.

"We decided it would be a good idea to take a look around while we were in the air, see if much else was going on," Johnny began. "Climbed up to 6,000 feet and got a good look. Saw one clearing that looked messed up — maybe carcasses, maybe trees knocked down. So I made several low passes and yes, there were a lot of dead elephants, ivory cut off, not much else taken. Just left to rot, easy to spot."

"Couldn't have been Joseph's work," Michael said. "You remember — the neatness freak. And he was always very careful when he killed the jumbos. Left as little evidence as he could. Didn't destroy trees, didn't mess up the soil, got rid of as much as he could cart way. Probably sold the hides and meat to the locals."

Bruce nodded yes. "Those guys are in league with the government."

"Looks like it," Johnny answered. "They'll likely be trouble for us. Certainly won't want us interfering. And whether we do or not, they likely will think we are. Might put a cramp in our science."

Bruce said nothing, just looked down the airstrip, thinking, and was quiet for a while. Johnny got up and did a walk around his airplane, checking everything, knowing that when Bruce wanted to think, he did and was never hurried. Michael stood up and looked into the vegetation nearby, walking a short distance, never out of easy talking with Bruce.

"We've have to tell the rest of the team," Bruce finally said. "But not until this evening. Got to raise their spirits. We're going elephant watching today."

Johnny smiled broadly at this. "Good plan. 'Bout time."

"I'll talk to them at dinner. I need to mull over how to do this some more anyway. So let's get the team out doing more sightseeing," he got up and walked over to the Land Rover.

The three of them drove back to camp and helped the rest of the team prepare for their outings. After Davie left in one vehicle with Howie and Horst, Bruce, Michael, and Johnny, gathered Elizabeth, Mary, and Paul and drove to where Johnny and Michael had seen elephants earlier from the air. The Land Rover bounced over rough terrain and then, to Elizabeth's surprise, slowed, crawled. The three men went on a silent alert. The machine stopped in an open grassy field with a few acacia trees here and there looking dead, half-dead, or dying, and the men were out of the Land Rover before Elizabeth knew what was happening. They were looking westward toward a large number of elephants, maybe the length of two city blocks away.

She pulled herself out of the Land Rover. The sun beat down from a cloudless sky. In the blinding light and dry heat, the scenery was as difficult to see as if it had been twilight or a night lit by moonlight. Heat waves made the elephants seem to float up and down and change shape, like ship mirages on a waveless sea.

Bruce had not been able to talk about what had happened the past few days. Elizabeth decided it best to not mention any of it. It would take some time for everybody to come to terms what had happened. Finally noticing her, Bruce came over and handed her a pair of binoculars, then quietly climbed up on the hood of the Land Rover. Wasn't he going to explain the whole damn thing to her? What the hell were they doing? Just sightseeing, or was there some purpose to all of this?

She took up the field glasses and looked through them from left to right. The word "herd" didn't exactly seem to apply to what she saw — individual elephants, each seeming to do its own thing. Far to the left was a mother and calf, the calf nursing, the mother chewing on something Elizabeth could not identify. To the right of those were three or four large animals pulling at sparse grasses. A lone elephant seemed to be digging into the ground. Two young bulls pushed at a small tree, one at a time as if it were a game. The one consistency was that everywhere she looked she saw peaceful activities. Still, it wasn't like watching a herd of domestic cattle on a ranch, all doing pretty much the same thing at the same time — grazing at the same time, chewing their cud at the same time, walking back to the night's enclosure at the same time.

Bruce motioned to the others and they all got back into the Land Rover. He drove slowly but steadily toward the elephants. The vehicle moved even slower as they continued their approach.

At fifty yards Bruce stopped, and everyone peered out. The elephants paid them little attention. A very large elephant stopped grazing, turned, and looked at the Land Rover, staring, like the big bull she had seen with Davie that first day, as if it were slightly nearsighted, head slightly back, peering through bifocals. Its trunk went up in the air perhaps trying to catch their scent, but its ears stayed back, and finally it returned to grazing.

Johnny opened the front passenger door quietly and stepped out, then walked a short way toward the big elephant. Elizabeth saw that Michael was shaking his head "no." Apparently he didn't approve of Johnny's approach on foot. Aha! Perhaps there was some kind of competition among these male elephant experts about who was going to be the most macho and who was going to learn the most. When did men *ever* learn? Still, nobody said a thing.

Elizabeth heard a commotion to her right, the noises of large animals moving. Johnny was suddenly back in the vehicle, and Bruce turned the Land Rover around and moved back from the herd. Elizabeth saw a group of Cape buffalo moving toward the elephants, perhaps five or ten, she hadn't counted. Although these were very large animals, they were dwarfed by the elephants. The buffalo must have wanted to move into the grassy area where the elephants were grazing.

Several of the larger elephants were standing still, staring at the buffalo. Then the largest of them started to do just what Elizabeth had seen the big bull do during her drive with Davie on their first day in Tsavo. The elephant started to pace at right angles to the line between herself and the buffalo, moving her head up and down, with ears and trunk out. Ah, that's got to be the matriarch, the lead female, and she's warning the buffalo that she expects them to leave, Elizabeth realized. Those motions were not just for people, but for any animal.

They seemed to have a selection of messages that they communicated by body language, but when the message did not get through, they seemed genuinely puzzled and thoughtful. If there was ever a sign of intelligence in an animal, it was, ironically enough, this inability to decide what to do. It made the elephants incredibly appealing to her.

Suddenly the lead female made a short and surprisingly fast dash, perhaps two or three paces, stopped abruptly, and sniffed the air. She fanned her ears out, raised her trunk, trumpeted, and charged. The buffalo put their heads down for a moment, then turned and fled. Joined by several others, the big female chased the small herd some twenty or thirty yards, then stopped and watched to see what they would do. The buffalo ran for a ways, then slowed and walked away. One stopped and turned, and the matriarch made another quick dash at it, and it turned and ran. In a few moments the buffalo were no more than dust rising from the dry ground on their way south.

The lead female rejoined her herd and began to graze. After about ten minutes, Bruce quietly opened the driver's door and got out. Johnny was immediately out of the front passenger's side, and the two started off toward the big female. Elizabeth wasn't sure what to do. She didn't relish the idea of approaching the huge animals on foot, but she did climb out. Michael did too, and bent down and talked with her quietly, telling her that he and she should stay back; that Bruce and Johnny were extremely experienced around elephants and could make a close approach. He did not tell her that he thought they always went in too close — too close for the sake of the elephants, who from his point of view deserved their own space, and too close for Bruce's and Johnny's safety. No, that he would not tell her.

For what seemed a very long time, Bruce and Johnny moved slowly toward the great animals, stopping frequently. What in the world were they trying to prove? Elizabeth wondered again. How could they do this after what had happened to Cecile? Did Tsavo make everyone crazy? And what the hell kind of science was this, a kind of testing, perhaps taunting, of the elephants? She decided it was something else; that the two men were drawn to the elephants for reasons they might never be able to explain to her.

She thought about the consciousness and purposefulness of the elephants — the smell of the soil, the feel of the sun and the dry air, the sounds of Tsavo. She tried to figure out the meaning of the many feelings stirring within her. Was she just feeling a kind of empathy for the elephants' well-being, like Cecile had felt? She didn't think so. Her feelings certainly weren't the desire for a hunt and kill. So what were they?

She looked up to Michael, as if his very demeanor might carry the answer. He stood tall and straight, watchful but calm, his rifle pointed downward in his left hand and his spear, as long as himself, in his right hand. Johnny was now so close to the big female that he had attracted her attention and she had turned to f ace him just as she had faced the buffalo. Bruce remained farther away, writing in his notebook.

The big female took a few slow paces toward Johnny. At first Johnny stood still, but then he backed away slowly. Thank God the guy had at least an ounce of sense, she thought. When he reached Bruce, the two of them backed away until they reached the Land Rover. Before climbing in, they turned and watched the elephants again, seemingly transfixed. To Elizabeth, they acted as if they were drugged on elephants, addicted to them, and had to have their fix. But she was beginning to feel that pull herself, that fascination with another form of life that might be, in its own way, intelligent.

The sound of the engine caught her attention. She saw that Michael had put away his weapons and gotten into the driver's seat and started the engine.

They arrived back at camp to find everyone busy getting settled. Paul and Mary were talking together with maps spread out on the ground and notebooks open. Horst and Davie were arguing about something. Horst was smoking a pipe — she could see a red glow rising from its bowl — and Davie was smoking a cigarette and waving his hands and shouting. She looked over toward Mary and Paul wondering whether she would be an unwelcome interruption if she joined them. Something was definitely brewing between those two. They turned from the maps and sat in camp chairs. Paul put his arm around Mary as if to shelter her from the world. Mary leaned into him, a tear streaking her cheek. She was processing Cecile's death. Elizabeth knew it would take a while, likely until she was back in her tiny island of civilization and human society.

CHAPTER 17

Air Attack

With exaltation at the beauty of nature comes wonderment as well, and the belief that man comes closer to the heartbeats of the creation when he is alone in primordial harmonies.

Clarence Glacken, historian and geographer
of the idea of nature

J ust before dawn, Bruce dressed, pulled himself from his tent and took a deep breath. Tsavo at first light — his favorite time of day. Nobody else was stirring, so, even better, he had Tsavo to himself. The visit to the airstrip with Elizabeth had disturbed him more than he ever could have expected. Too many bad memories; perhaps he should not have come back. Now Cecile was gone. He had failed already.

His mind was churning. Not just reliving those terrible memories. Other things were eating at him. He was supposed to be leading this group with great efficiency to succeed in a difficult, short-lived task, and little that he had done so far had gone well. Truth to tell, he wasn't sure how they could accomplish what they were asked to do in so short a time with so few resources. They were supposed to report back in a month about the status of the elephants and an estimate of how many there were. That was hard enough to do under the best conditions in a place like Tsavo.

But now there was Joseph not long out of jail and doing who knew what? Trying to appear as a reformed, good guy. But Bruce knew he could never trust the Snake. And worse, now there were big-time poachers with contacts with the government, going to go after big kills in a short time, not caring if there were any elephants left when they were done. The worst of the worst. At the moment he had no idea how he was going to deal with them. Avoid them the entire time? Seemed impossible. Fight them? On our own? Not a chance in hell. Best avoid them now if they could. Maybe they could get enough work done to have some impact. These type of poachers even made Joseph look good. Maybe Joseph really was reformed. He had been a pretty good kid in school, some of the time. Bruce wasn't sure at the moment about anything ...

Why had he agreed to lead this group? Why had he accepted the terms offered with an almost impossible schedule and poor resources? Could he find a way out of this mess? Who among this group could get the job done?

As he walked away from the tents, a European bee-eater, one of his favorite birds, perched on a nearby tree and displayed its beautiful chestnut-colored crown and sang its clear, liquid-flowing notes, then flew up and circled high overhead and sped away. It must have just arrived from Europe for the winter. Higher up, two eagles soared in the early-morning updrafts. He squinted to see them; black on the front of the male's wings, white to the rear, hawk eagles they were, soaring as a pair as they always did. For a moment Bruce wished for a mate. Nature, in the warming light, seemed peaceful and perfect, and he wished he felt the same, but he did not.

A crowned hornbill flew by, a flash of a large red bill in the morning light. It landed on a nearby acacia tree and emitted its mournful cry, as if expressing something deep within itself in empathy with Bruce's turmoil.

Why did this group he was leading disturb him so much? Why did that off-the-wall Davie bother him? What about Howie in his multicolored crazy-quilt clothes? Was he going to be just in the way or helpful in his odd way of thinking? And then there was Horst. An image of him stuffed up in his corduroy sports jacket flashed through his mind. His professional enemy for such a long time---- Horst was usually able to outwit him in any political arena. Maybe it was too many different opinions in a small group — a group that would have to become tightly knit in a short time. He was tired of the public arguments over what was right for the animals and what was right for people. Years ago he had thought he had solved those problems for himself. Then, realizing that he had not solved them and having left Africa, he had thought he had left those problems behind. But there they were, encompassing him, and he didn't like them rising to the surface again, like the eyes of a crocodile rising to the watery surface of the Galana River.

A secretary bird scurried past, busy as usual, like some damned store clerk or accountant or government bureaucrat, troubled by nothing and seemingly with no imagination. Damned smugness of the avian world. A vervet monkey chattered at him from an acacia tree, busy, busy, busy, without a care in the world.

And then there were the two women. Mary was pleasant enough — beautiful, decorative, helpful, trying to please, not too demanding, but not that interesting either. She seemed to have a fixation on measuring everything, but somehow that interest did not seem to go deeper — science seemed to stop with her at the surface, like the beauty of her face.

Elizabeth. Now there was an intriguing woman, but why did she disturb him? She made him feel that she could see inside him, know his thoughts, invade his privacy. And he had revealed himself to her, perhaps too much. And Paul, the best of that American crowd. At least some wilderness experience and a little hunting. Been in tough situations — obviously, somehow he got that limp, haven't found at how. Had a lot to learn, but could be relied on in a showdown. He showed that with Cecile's death.

Not able to cry out like the crowned hornbill, Bruce strolled into the plains, into its privacy. He began to feel alert, energized, perhaps even a little happy. Things to discover everywhere. He tried to empty his mind of all but Tsavo. Deep breaths, scents of pungent plants. See, smell, hear, abandon all but his senses, leave behind his cares. He saw a good-sized boulder surrounded by tiny flowering plants. Something so simple and beautiful in the morning light. This was truly being alive, a feeling he always sought but could find only when he was in an unbounded wilderness alone or with someone like Johnny or Michael, who could feel the same things and did not require a lot of talk and explanations.

He didn't even see the twin Beechcraft until it was a few yards above him, then the arm reaching out with some kind of gun, looked like an automatic weapon. Why the hell was the big aircraft here in Tsavo? Took some talent and experience to fly that machine and land and take off in Tsavo. Could be done, but took some flying skill. And who could afford the damn thing? Christ, don't get distracted, they're aiming at me, he realized. He dropped to the ground as bullets whizzed by his cheek. The plane circled back. He threw himself next to a large rock and angled his body for cover. Michael appeared to his right and fired at the twin Beech, hitting a wing, but not the fuel tank as he intended. It was enough to throw the plane into a downward spiral but the pilot pulled the plane up at the last minute. Then it was gone.

Bruce couldn't breathe. Michael ran to him and pulled him up. Bruce stood shakily, then squatted to get back a regular breath. Michael scanned the horizon.

"Who the hell was that?" Bruce asked.

"My guess is government-connected poachers, but it could be government men themselves."

"Jesus. That twin can outfly Johnny's Cessna 182s — more than 200, maybe 250 mph."

"We should find out if they've got more than one — what other equipment they have," Michael said. Bruce started back to camp, then turned to see Michael watching him with concern.

"We're not going to discuss this at camp. We'll make a plan once I get my head back on straight."

"Right," nodded Michael.

CHAPTER 18

Science and Baboons

Somebody better help me, 'cause I can't help myself.
Somebody better help me, 'cause I can't help myself.
I ain't doin' too badly. I'm a bran' new man.

Junior Wells, *Hoodoo Man Blues*

Bruce and Michael were up soon after dawn the next morning,, talking about being shot at from an airplane, and a twin Beech at that — unusual and expensive. "Not your typical bush plane," Bruce said quietly. They agreed they were going to have to investigate what was going on. They could not do the simple thing of going to police or some other government office in Voi. There had been too much corruption and involvement by the government, to the very top, in the ivory trade. They were on their own. Ironically, Horst's contacts with the international nongovernmental conservation groups seemed to be their best bet, which meant they would have to bring Horst into this discussion and trust him, which neither of them wanted to do.

"You know, that shooting from the twin Beech," Michael said. "That might have just been a warning to keep away."

"If we just go about our business, making clear to them that we are ignoring them and doing our science, they might leave us alone, is that what you mean?" Bruce said.

Michael nodded, yes

"Getting this month's worth of information about the Tsavo elephants is all the more important to the conservation groups and to the elephants themselves, matter of fact," Bruce said.

Michael nodded again.

"Then we'd better just get on with it, take it as far as we can. Then get out, get back. I've set up a meeting of the team this morning to go over our research plans," Bruce said. "Then we can do a little sight-seeing with Johnny's Cessna, to see how bad the situation is."

"Best be careful where you fly, who might see you," Michael said.

After breakfast, Bruce called the group together inside the tent set up to serve as an office and meeting room. It had a folding table and chairs and mosquito-netting walls. They all crowded around, sitting as best they could. Bruce asked Paul to lead the discussion since he was the head of the American scientists and was abreast of the latest techniques and methods. It also would give him time to pull his thoughts together. Was it even safe to go on? Could any work get done under the circumstances they found themselves in?

Paul took several folders from a backpack and was preparing to speak when he noticed a troop of baboons edging into the camp behind the tent. Bruce saw them and glanced back at Paul to make sure he saw them too. Some of the baboons came over to the mosquito netting at the rear, looking in and seeming to listen.

Sitting on camp chairs or stretched out on the ground, the rest of the people were unaware of the visitors, except Michael who stood with arms folded as he watched the baboons and looked the people over. Davie sat on the ground and cleaned the bottom of his cowboy boots with a pocketknife. Johnny sat on a poncho on the ground. Horst sitting in the only desk-type chair, pulled out his tobacco pouch, filled his pipe, and began to smoke. The baboons looking on found this especially interesting. Howie sat in a lotus position on the ground, palming his yo-yo. A young baboon watched the yo-yo intently.

Bruce toyed with the idea of stopping the meeting and dealing with the baboons, but he decided to let things go on, in part because he hoped the baboons would go away on their own, but also because he thought it necessary to test how well the four Americans could deal with their work amid Tsavo's typical distractions. Now was the time to see if he would be able to mold this group into a functioning unit.

Paul cleared his throat and began. He lamented that they had had little time to prepare before the trip began, and he reviewed their goals: that they had been asked to report back about the status of the elephants — whether their numbers had increased or decreased since the big drought and die-off, and what kind of shape they were in — and to do so in a month, because international meetings to decide the fate of Tsavo's elephants were going to take place in November. "And we were also told to look out for any poaching and report back about that. Try to get an estimate of the amount of poaching," he said, frowning.

"Sure. We can stop by an' ask them how many they hope to kill," Davie said. "They'll like the company."

"I knew it, I knew it," Howie said, smiling. "'Paul told me this was just going to be a great vacation, a trip into a lovely wilderness — failing to mention anything about this people wild-side." He laughed. Bruce was impressed and pleased with both of their reactions. Howie seemed surprisingly calm and unphased. Good. But Bruce thought Paul, although calm, seemed uncomfortable, hesitating as he spoke.

"We have to get some kind of useful knowledge in a limited time," Paul said. "We're going to use a series of camps and make a series of measurements at each and also along the way between camps — vegetation, soils, geology."

"And we'll count elephants from the airplane," Johnny interjected, "That's something we do know how to do, done it for years."

Mary spoke up. "You can tell a lot about the animals, even about how many there are, by looking at plants. It's hard to count wildlife directly, one by one, even from the air — either you can't find them or see them — and you only get a rough count. But you can easily see the effects of herbivores on vegetation. If the plants look like they're being destroyed and not recovering, that's pretty good evidence that there are too many animals feeding on them." She clearly enjoyed talking about her specialty.

"We've gotten much better at that with the aerial counts," Johnny said. "It even surprises me. You'll see."

One of the baboons began scratching in the soil just by the tent, shaking the tent and distracting Paul, but he tried to concentrate.

"Mary is saying that if we can't count the jumbos accurately, we can estimate their number by looking at the trees, shrubs, and grasses," Paul explained. "We can come up with a relative abundance, so to speak — too few, too many, just right. The Goldilocks approach, I call it."

"But how do you know if anything you find out is really true?" Horst asked.

"You never do, if you put it that way," Howie cut in. "This isn't about truth. It's about science and life. Try thinking 'statistics.'"

"Good research design," Paul spoke over him.

Bruce, listening, wasn't sure that this group was up to making the fast survey that was required, at least one that would hold up in the scientific circles that would criticize what they did. Howie was more on the mark. How would they really know anything for sure? It was never easy.

Paul took out maps that showed Tsavo's topography, explaining that the maps were crude, twenty years old, never updated, but all they had to work with. "The folks who asked us to come here didn't even check to see if such basic information as maps were available." He shook his head in disbelief.

Horst interrupted, apologizing for doing so, and saying that he sympathized with Paul's desire to do a detailed study, but there just wasn't time for it. "Why not just do one big flyover and see what's there? We know the answer already. I've seen just one live elephant! We can write the report right now. 'Tsavo elephants in trouble. Active poaching. Need help. Send money. Make Tsavo an international preserve.' What else'll we need? I can make a few phone calls and get the money. That's part of the reason I was asked to come here. Contacts. It's all politics, you know."

Horst and Bruce argued for a few minutes about the necessity of doing more than that, Bruce on the side that only good science could provide the answers.

"In this country?" Horst asked. "They'll just as likely ignore science, period. You know the talk, don't you?"

"What talk?" Mary asked.

"There's talk that some high government people here are involved in the illegal ivory trade — maybe even supporting the poachers. Possibly some outsiders as well — white guys from Europe joining the poachers. If that's the case, what's the good of all this science?"

"If it's all politics, why did you bother to come all this way to be part of this scientific group?" Bruce asked.

Elizabeth frowned. They hadn't even started work and already they were arguing among themselves. Why couldn't they just get on with the work they had agreed to do? And there was an underlying fear among some of them. She smiled to herself, thinking that Cecile's death had become the elephant in the room. She was distracted by a noise outside and turned in her seat to see a baboon digging in the soil, which was more interesting to her at the moment than the conversation.

The others, still unaware, continued their discussion. "I thought there were international agreements about ivory," Mary said.

Bruce, hoping the baboons would not become a problem, watched them but also nodded and replied. "Yes, there is an international convention. Countries that signed it agreed not to trade in any endangered species or any product of one, like ivory."

A big male baboon jumped on top of their tent and bounced up and down, shaking the entire structure. Everyone sprung from their seats. It was like being on a boat rolling in a stormy sea, and for a moment Elizabeth thought she was going to lose her balance. She almost felt seasick. What next? The baboon whooped, then jumped down and found a banana that somebody had left out. Another big male came over, and the two started fighting over it, screeching angrily and rolling around in the sandy soil.

Bruce started toward the zippered doorway to deal with the baboons, but before he could reach it, Howie saw a young baboon enter his own tent and rushed to rescue his things. Several baboons jumped onto a table outside the tents and started turning over everything that was loose. One pulled a 35mm film canister out of Howie's backpack and tried to chew on it, then tried opening it as if it were a nut, but it kept slipping out of his mouth. A female baboon snuck up behind him, grabbed it away, and jumped down. He chased her, but she was up a tree, hooting at him, before he could do anything. He spied a jerry can of gasoline and forgot about the female. He went over to the can, smelled it, and tried to turn it over. He bit at the cap.

Up in the tree, the female tried to open the film canister just as the male had done. She bit it and pulled at it without success. Losing interest in it, she reached out and plucked a fruit from the tree and let the film drop. It fell on the ground near a baby baboon, who grabbed it, jumped up on the table, bit it once, and dropped it almost exactly where it had been originally. Howie rescued it and put it back in his pack.

Elizabeth grabbed a folding chair and dashed out, swinging it at the big male baboon. "Get out of here, you bastard!" she shouted. The baboon bared his teeth and hissed. Horst got between her and the baboon. "Take it easy, Liz! We're in his territory!"

"The hell we are," she said.

When Howie approached to lend a hand, his red and white hat fell to the ground and was grabbed by a baboon. Elizabeth picked up her chair and swung it at the baboon, catching the animal just behind the ear. It dropped the hat. She swung again, hard enough to let the animal know she meant business, but not hard enough to hurt it. The baboon ran off, stopped, turned back, and hissed. She ran at him, and he scrambled away into the bush. "Got the sonofabitch," she said, and waded into a group of baboons, swinging the chair like a scythe. The animals retreated.

Bruce watched Elizabeth with great amusement.

Now everybody was out of the tent chasing after the baboons and trying to lclean up after them. One young male got into Horst's tent. Mary rushed over and tried to get it to come out, but Michael, who had gone around to the back, motioned to her to move. Of course, she realized, as long as she was in front of the tent, the baboon would be afraid to come out. She felt stupid. She joined Michael at the back of the tent. Howie was already there. "Now this is what I call an in-tents experience." Michael and Mary paid him no attention.

Mary beat on one side of the tent, Michael on the back, and Howie on the side opposite Mary. The youngster shot out of the doorway and scrambled off, following its troop. Bruce joined Michael and Davie, who were now helping Elizabeth scatter the rest of the baboons. Michael went after them with his spear, swinging it to scare them away. Bruce pulled his pistol out of his belt and shot into the air. The entire troop, whooping and bellowing, rushed away, scampering over anything in their way, scattering papers, ripping bags, knocking tent poles down. One grabbed a wrench as it took off; another a screwdriver that had been lying on the hood of one of the Land Rovers; another had somebody's hairbrush.

Inside the meeting tent one of those odd winds of sunbaked country whirled through and blew Paul's papers off the table, scattering them all over the tent. Paul sighed and began gathering them up. Howie helped him. They were keeping themselves under control, Bruce was pleased to see. He left the tent and went over to Elizabeth, a big smile on his face. "I want you to know you've got a new fan," he said. "You've got a lot of guts."

She laughed. "Better watch out, you might be next," she said. "Actually, I'm a black belt in two of the martial arts — started learning about them from a boyfriend in high school." She gave him her nicest smile. "Hey, how come you took so long to do anything? You're supposed to be our trusty wilderness guide."

"It was too much fun watching you," Bruce said.

* * *

Joseph had been using his two-way radio for several hours, contacting or trying to contact all the men working for him in Tsavo. He sat in the shade of an acacia tree marking a crude map, labeling it with circles where his men told him there were elephants, and putting inside the circle symbols for few and many. He wished again that he had Bruce and Johnny working for him, and Johnny's airplane out searching for elephants. How much easier that would make his work, as long as nobody who could create problems for him knew what he was doing.

He was going to have to look into the airplane idea. An airplane would make it easier for him to know where Bruce was. But meanwhile, hunting for elephants was as risky as playing poker, a game he loved. He enjoyed a game of chance, but with all the money involved, he would like to reduce his risks. Unfortunately, the big-time strangers doing massive poaching were likely to ruin his game. What could be done about them? Horst came to mind again as perhaps the only avenue. Not Bruce. He was too independent to have those kind of political contacts. And he made the politicos angry, telling them the truth all the time. One thing Bruce never had learned to do: lie a little.

CHAPTER 19

Bruce takes Elizabeth for a Flight

The machine does not isolate man from the great problems of nature but plunges him more deeply into them.

Antoine de Saint-Exupery

Once the baboons were gone and things had settled down, the group prepared dinner. Johnny, Michael, and Bruce discussed the need to find out more about the new, big poaching that seemed to be going on. A flyover was clearly the best way to check this out, and Bruce explained that he had offered to take Elizabeth on a flight so she could get a better sense of the geological structure and formations of Tsavo. He thought this was important so their geologist could give them insights and guidance.

"Uh-huh," Johnny smiled. "Structure and formations, eh? Of Tsavo or Elizabeth?"

Bruce smiled and turned away. Familiar with Johnny's love to tease, he did not respond. So the plan was made, a flight to introduce Elizabeth to Tsavo's geology combined with a hunt for these new poachers.

The next morning they were moving down the airstrip with the noise of the wind and the engine in her ears, and then they were in the air, turning and climbing. She had had an uncomfortable night, thinking about Bruce, who at first had seemed the perfect man — wise, knowledgeable about all things natural — but then he had revealed a more complicated, more troubled, and perhaps darker side. And there was the new concern about massive poaching and danger from the poachers to the team.

Elizabeth's thoughts were swept away by the wind in the airplane's wings and the rumblings of the airframe. During their ascent, Bruce pointed out their camp. She peered down, seeing it as a little island of civilization in the vast Tsavo plains. She could see her friends, Paul, Mary, and Howie, putting their gear into one of the Land Rovers, getting ready for their first day of field work. The camp seemed lonely and sad, not the great center of African adventure she had imagined herself going to before she had left the States. Part of it was Cecile's death, but there was more. Each of her friends was troubled in some way, and her heart went out to them now as she saw them as tiny beings, alone, isolated in some way even from one another. Nearby a small group of gazelles grazed peacefully. How she wished her friends were as settled within their surroundings and as peaceful as the beautiful animals.

Bruce flew north over the Yatta Plateau, keeping low to look for signs of people, he explained to Elizabeth, shouting above the engine's roar, and also looking for signs of the old bull elephant and trying to make sure she could see more of the terrain. He was happy to be with her; Johnny was right in what he had said the night before. She intrigued him more and more.

Jesus, it was noisy inside these little airplanes, Elizabeth thought. She could barely make out what Bruce was saying even though their bodies were almost touching, *were* touching when the plane banked or he moved to adjust something or other among the many controls.

After fifteen or twenty minutes, by her watch, she began to relax a little, and her thoughts turned again to Bruce. In the airplane he seemed a different person than he was among the elephants yesterday — in control, calm, professional, courteous, a gentleman.

The underlying waves of uncertainty and disturbance that emanated from him yesterday at the landing strip and on the first night at dinner seemed not to exist; he was a calm lake.

They continued to fly low to the ground, not much above the treetops, and Elizabeth felt she was seeing the countryside from a fast-moving walkway, stretching before her, seemingly forever, reddish soil, gray-green shrubs and occasional trees, dying and half dead, more or less evenly spaced, to the horizon and into the hills beyond to the north, a red-running landscape, gray-green woodlands, brick-colored earth tones, onward and onward.

Then they approached Lugard Falls. "You're looking at one of the largest lava flows in the world," she shouted to Bruce.

"Different from book knowledge, isn't it?" he shouted back.

Bruce asked if she had ever seen anything like it.

"You can go to the Columbia River Valley in Oregon, where Paul's from, and see another huge lava flow — or the tops of part of it, in the river," she said, "but that's about it, from my experience."

She was fascinated to see Lugard Falls from the air, where the Galana River cascaded over the edge of the lava plateau, passing through a small fissure. She saw white water and thought it would be quite a challenge — probably impossible — to float those falls in any kind of watercraft. Too steep. The water rippled and churned, as if it were alive, like a Loch Ness monster or a plaything of Poseidon.

From the air, the falls looked narrow enough to jump across. The puzzle of the landscape began to come together in her mind: lava flowing over cold rock; water cutting through one layer, then through another. This was the kind of understanding she had always sought, to see and to know the land as a single piece, now made possible by the view from the air, from within this cramped, noisy machine, gears and wheels and pistons and valves.

She fell into a reverie, watching the cascading falls as if they were full of river nymphs, half-expecting to see their white shapes ripple below. She could see several crocodiles sunning themselves along the banks of the river where it leveled out below the falls. One slipped into the water and began swimming, half-submerged, just below the falls, approaching a small gazelle drinking by the shore, its feet in the river. She pointed out the crocodile swimming toward the gazelle, and Bruce immediately put the plane into a steep dive, banking sharply so that they circled the crocodile. Fun, she began to think, yes, very much like a motorcycle ride on her own or with one of her boyfriends when she was in high school. Bruce circled so that her side of the plane looked downward, and Elizabeth watched the crocodile approach the gazelle.

"It's a Tommy — a Thomson's gazelle," he shouted. She nodded but the information meant little to her.

He brought the plane to treetop level, making sure he cleared the top of the falls with his turns, and leveled off, continuing the turn. The crocodile was just visible under the water as it reached the gazelle, grabbed it, and pulled it underwater. At that moment, Elizabeth felt herself part of life and death within Tsavo. Along the edge of the river, also watching the crocodile, was a man on horseback. He seemed to be wearing leather, surprising in this warm climate, and she swore he had a sword and a rifle. An odd old man on horseback watching a death scene. It seemed to be the old man she'd seen at the landing strip. Strange, she thought. It made her shiver.

"They call it the Athi River above the falls, the Galana below it. Shows how different the river is when it runs on the plateau and of f the plateau," Bruce said.

They left the falls and flew on to drier country eastward, beyond where they had traveled by Land Rover. They crossed a nameless dry streambed, at this time of year a slightly meandering series of sandbars, the river's path marked by the line of yellow-barked trees — fever trees Bruce shouted to her — and fan-leafed palms along what she believed would be the stream's shore during the rainy season. She saw an elephant pawing into one of the sandbars. Bruce again put the plane into a steep circle and the elephant looked up, put out its ears and raised its trunk. He or she was obviously trumpeting at them, standing his or her ground against the strange beast in the air.

Bruce loved seeing the jumbo trumpeting and standing his ground — it was a bull — this greatest of all land mammals unafraid of an airplane, threatening it. He would have circled the bull several times but was concerned about making Elizabeth airsick, so he leveled off, climbed and flew on. "That jumbo's digging for water," he said. "They know where to look, too, like your water witches in America. Where they dig, they almost always find water. I suppose you do that, too, you geologists." He smiled at her.

"Sure, all us geomorphologists can water-witch," she quipped.

Bruce turned the plane west. After a while he told her that they had crossed the park boundary — marked clearly from the air by a dirt road, a railway line, and a paved highway. Elizabeth thought that as soon as they were outside the park the light seemed to change, to soften, become gentler, as if they had passed from one world to another. She looked behind and could see the amazingly sharp effect the starving and dying elephants had had on Tsavo ten years before, the land inside the park a dull yellowish-brown, while the land outside, beyond the reach of the elephants, a deep green from the thick cover of trees and shrubs.

Bruce put the plane into a turn and crossed back into the park. The volcanic plateau stretched north to the hills that led to Nairobi — to the horizon, more or less. Bruce stole a careful look at Elizabeth while she was watching the scenery below. She looked very pretty, he thought. Mary was prettier, but Elizabeth intrigued him. He hungered for a woman, for sex and for comforting companionship, and he preferred the tougher, more mysterious Elizabeth to Mary. Attracting women had been easy for him, and he was usually quite confident about his chances of success, but Elizabeth kept him off balance. He couldn't read her; strange, he thought, because he could read most wildlife well. One of his favorite sayings about women came to his mind. Oscar Wilde wrote it. *Women are to be loved, not understood.* That seemed to typify Elizabeth. He didn't think he could ever understand her completely. Yet there was much he could learn from her professionally and much they could share as professional colleagues, if that could happen.

Bruce saw another plane, seeming to be flying in the direction of the camp. "There's a plane, about six o-clock, going the other way, toward our camp," he said. Fortunately he was still east of the other plane, so the sun could have blinded the other pilot and he might not have seen their plane. Bruce banked and climbed, seeking to put the plane at an altitude that would force the other pilot to look directly into the sun to see them.

"Think it's poachers?"

"Could be. It's that fancy, expensive plane Michael and I saw the day before yesterday — Twin Beech — a two-engine Beechcraft. Pricey. Tail-dragger — small turning wheel at the back, not in front. Easier to land on grass and dirt. One of the few twins you can use out here. Don't see many. Whoever owns that has some money or a rich uncle, so to speak. I can't think of anyone who would be flying out here today." His heart rate rose.

"I wish we could ignore them for now," Elizabeth said. "Everything is so amazing from up here. But we can't, can we?"

"I'm going to stay between him and the sun for a while and see where he goes. Then we'll decide," he replied. His thoughts raced: *pretty fancy plane, that. Not the best to bang around on rough ground, though. Could be some Hollywood tourist, or the like. A little tony for poachers, but they're surprising us, aren't they?* But he was careful to show a confident attitude to Elizabeth.

Elizabeth was comfortable letting Bruce take care of the situation. There wasn't much she could do, and, at least in these situations, she was growing to trust Bruce as her Tsavo guide and leader. Without noticing it, she was leaning against him.

"Excuse me, but you've got to move your arm," he said. She blushed and sat upright.

"Sorry."

"No problem," he answered, his eyes on the other plane. It seemed to be traveling aimlessly, making turns almost at random as if in response to a passenger's wishes. The Beechcraft eventually turned and began to fly north toward Nairobi. Bruce slowed their airplane and let the other one fade into the distance.

Then something big on the ground caught his eye and he banked the plane so as to keep the sight from Elizabeth. He saw a small camp with several vehicles and tents, and next to it what looked like a massive killing of elephants, lots of their huge carcasses. He banked the plane away from the tents and climbed sharply, trying to minimize any chance someone on the ground could identify Johnny's plane.

Once high enough, he circled and looked down at the tents, again banking to keep the view from Elizabeth, who inadvertently took his arm to brace herself. Bruce saw three vehicles and they looked new, as did the tents and other equipment. It added up to a camp of poachers. He flew low over the elephant carcasses. Just as he expected, only the ivory tusks cut off, everything else left to rot and no attempt to hide anything. Had to be government protected and involved in a massive, quick kill, an in-and-out operation. Their worst fears realized.

"Sorry," he said. "I thought I remembered a natural spring near here, but I guess I was wrong." He flew away from the camp, descended sharply, leveling off just above the ground. He wasn't about to add to Elizabeth's worry at this point, although he didn't mind the fact that she was still holding his arm. He flew low over the ground to suggest he was still looking for the spring.

Elizabeth thought their wheels must be almost touching the ground, but they were actually about 50 to 100 feet above the sparse grassland. Everything was rushing by Elizabeth. She felt a combination of thrill and fear. Bruce was silent, searching for any sign of people, looking for equipment — guns, vehicles, whatever. He flew a somewhat wandering path to make it appear they were just tourists searching for any wildlife.

He noted the camp's position, making a mark on the flight map tucked beside his seat.

"Maybe I'll come back later and have a look again," he said. His thoughts were much more complicated. He would talk this over with Michael and Johnny. The only good news was this camp was far from their camp and far from where the team planned to start their scientific measurements. Maybe, just maybe, they could get their work done and get out safe and sound. Risky, no doubt about it. He would have to explain the risks honestly to the team and let each decide whether to stay and see the job through. Okay, fine, we're done here, he thought. He put the plane into a climb.

"If you've seen enough of the plateau, let's follow the Galana River for a while, then go northeast to the really arid country," he suggested. He banked to the right and climbed, and the ground fell away. Bruce put what he had seen about the poachers in a compartment in his mind, and focused on what Elizabeth needed to see. He had learned over the years that the only way to get through and survive out in this wild country was to compartmentalize.

"Now that we're off the lava flow, we're over metamorphic and igneous rocks," Elizabeth told him.

"In English and louder," Bruce requested. "Remember, I'm just an ignorant old wildlife guy."

"Yeah, sure," she laughed. "It's ancient bedrock. Granite and its relatives — rocks that make up the very bones of the continents. We're looking at the skeleton of ancient Earth in a way our ancestors who roamed this country for hundreds of thousands of years could never have seen it. And we understand its chemistry and mineralogy. It's a whole different way to see the land. For thousands of years people have dreamed of seeing the world like a bird does, and here we are, doing it." She paused, admiring the view. "Farther south, way over there," she pointed, "the rocks are much younger. Permian and Tertiary, so I've read."

"What's that tell you?" Bruce asked. The terms were not unfamiliar to him but he could never remember what times they actually referred to — and he was having the usual trouble hearing another person in the noisy cockpit.

"Dinosaur stuff. Way before people," she shouted. "Permian's just before the dinosaurs. Tertiary is the age of mammals. Dinosaurs are in between. Look off to the south," she said. Bruce banked the plane so that it headed west and Elizabeth could get a good view. Then he did a one-eighty so that he could see it too, turning in a half-circle to the south.

"You're seeing land formed, oh, hundreds of millions of years ago," Elizabeth said. "Just think, from this small plane we can see more than two hundred million years of Earth's history, at least the

top of it. It's a view few have seen before and fewer have understood."
They flew a while longer until Elizabeth said she had seen what she
needed to see.

After he parked and shut down the engine, he looked at
Elizabeth. She hesitated a moment, then leaned over and kissed
him lightly on the cheek. For a moment their eyes locked. Bruce
was about to set aside his better judgment and pull her toward him
when she took his hand and squeezed it. "Thank you," she said, and
opening her door, she climbed out, feeling very confused.

As they drove back toward camp, Elizabeth wished that Bruce
would take her hand or say something affectionate, but he seemed
distracted. She asked what was on his mind, and he talked to her
about what had to get done that day. He told her he wanted to
spend some more time with Howie to decide how they could most
efficiently get a quick count of the elephants, and he told her he
had promised Davie that there would be some time during the trip
for him to continue his studies of vultures. Bruce pointed to the
sky in the distance and Elizabeth could see many vultures circling.
She took a deep breath and focused on her professional role in the
expedition.

They had not quite reached camp when she saw Davie jogging
toward them.

* * *

Joseph had seen Johnny's plane take off and had watched it and
then the other aircraft, the bigger twin that Bruce was following.
Why was Bruce following that other plane? Did he have more people
working for him in it? He did not recognize the newer airplane, but
he was concerned that some of his men might be visible to whoever
was in it, or to Bruce. Perhaps they were looking for poachers — and
now Bruce had an extra airplane just for that purpose. He turned
on his walkie-talkie and radioed some of his men in the plane's path
telling them to take cover until the sound of the aircrafts faded away.

How he wished he had a pilot's license and his own airplane. But
he could never afford it. It was Bruce and Johnny, born into families

with money, who could have those things. Rich man's toys. Even their research and their constant talking about saving the world, rich man's hobbies. They didn't have to *make* a living, they could just *enjoy* their toys and their life. Even though he and Bruce went to school together, were school chums, there was always this difference, himself, the poor unimportant white boy — more of them than those British colonialists, for God's sake, more of them than their Michaels — their Maasai — those people who so fascinated the Bruces and the Johnnies, the exotics. Rich man's toys, they were, so their Michaels got better schooling, better jobs. The three schoolmates were friends as kids, but now look at them. Michael part of those elite. Himself always scraping by. And what kind of living? Doing what he knew best and was best at, hunting, out in the wild, as good or better maybe than Bruce. And what was the difference between him and Bruce? Bruce who "culled" elephants — killed them — in the name of population control, goody-goody. Himself, killing fewer as a way to make a living, and considered a criminal.

The bat-eared fox suddenly appeared, rushing at him, being chased by a cheetah. He quickly stepped aside and held his rifle pointed at the cheetah, just in case. Brought him back to the real world, not that world of persons and personalities. He slapped his head with his hand. My God, that other plane, the big twin. Fancy equipment. Lack of care about anything except making money fast. No doubt a well-funded, large operation that could bring in the big international conservation organizations and force the government to stop all poaching. Dammit, they could put him out of business, too. Better get back to Horst and get him on his side, help him stop those poachers so he could continue to make a living, for God's sake. As these contradictory thoughts tore through his mind, he wandered back to his pickup, trying to think what to do next.

He drove as close to Bruce's camp as he thought was safe, so nobody would hear the motor noise, and then walked silently to the camp's edge, keeping behind the vegetation so nobody could see him until he saw Horst. He caught Horst's eye and pointed to a path leading away from the camp. Horst looked around and then walked as casually as he could to that path and way from the camp. Joseph handed him a walkie-talkie, showed him how to use it and what frequency to contact him on, and told him, speaking quietly, to call as soon as he could get away for a hour or two so they could talk and make some plans. Before Horst could ask any questions, Joseph was gone, seeming to Horst to have vanished as quickly as an impala could dash away into the bush.

CHAPTER 20

Vultures

Every day I went back to the scene to watch the slow disintegration of this huge elephant corpse, black with flies, and crawling with worms. The stench was appalling. . . I watched the first vultures arrive and settle on a nearby tree, necks outstretched and bent, looking like old men in winter coats sitting on benches at a murder case."

Iain Douglas-Hamilton, *Among the Elephants.*

D avie talked rapidly, pointing to the vultures circling in the sky beyond their camp. He reminded Bruce of his promise to let him spend some time studying vultures in exchange for being one of the drivers on the expedition, and said that the circling vultures meant there was some carcass out there. Usually, Davie shot an impala or a Thomson's gazelle, or some other animal and used it as bait, but here was a perfect situation, he explained. Tsavo had provided the bait, or a lion or leopard had.

Elizabeth sensed again a violent intensity in Davie and thought about the pistol he'd had stuck in the back of his pants at their first camp dinner and had pulled out when he was talking with Cecile. Just how violent was Davie, and how insistent on his own way? And how would Bruce handle him? There was an air of male violence between the two men, and she wondered again how much of Davie was inside Bruce, only better hidden beneath a more polished exterior and demeanor. Bruce gave Davie a questioning look and glanced over knowingly at Elizabeth, as if to say, "I knew it."

"Hey, man, I can take these newcomers with me, teach 'em more about Tsavo," Davie argued, pointing at Elizabeth. "You can tell a lot about what's goin' on in the whole park by lookin' at vultures. Double-E," he said, turning to her. "You know, they're at the top of the food chain, and if they're doin' well, then the whole system's okay."

Bruce reminded Davie that poachers might be nearby but he reluctantly agreed, as long as Davie took along one of the two-way radios. Davie jumped into the backseat and rode to camp with them. He told Elizabeth that Paul and Mary had already agreed to go with him and he hoped she would too. She looked at Bruce for a clue to what she should do, but, damn him, he drove along expressionless, as if he were still piloting his plane and out of contact with his passengers. She nudged him, and he looked at her, a little surprised. "You could learn a lot from Davie, Elizabeth," was all he said.

"Whatever," Elizabeth replied, annoyed, and decided to go.

Davie gathered Paul, Mary, and Elizabeth around his Land Rover and showed them his equipment as he loaded it in. He pointed at some boxes in the back of one of the Land Rovers and laughed. "That's an explosive net I brought along to capture vultures — just a little dynamite blows the net over them faster than they can fly away. See 'em fart when that happens. And worse! You folks come with me. I'll show you what's what. No academic theory crap — real science."

They drove the Land Rover where the vultures were circling and found a dead animal, just as Davie had said. It turned out to be a Cape buffalo. Davie stopped the Land Rover about fifty yards from the carcass and began to unpack gear. He took out a roll of fine black nylon netting and a plastic toolbox, then walked over to the carcass. Elizabeth asked what had killed it, but Davie did not answer; he seemed preoccupied with his preparations. Seeing the people approach, the vultures soared higher, but continued to circle.

From the toolbox Davie took a small hatchet and wooden stakes. He unrolled one of the nets and stretched it over the dead buffalo. He drove stakes through round metal rings into the ground at two corners of the net, so that one side of the net was fixed in place. Then he took what seemed to Elizabeth to be small sticks of dynamite, unraveled the other end of the netting, pulled that end away from the carcass, and fastened the charges to the rings at the outer edges of the netting. He attached electrical wires to the charges and pulled the wires back about fifty feet, then connected the charges to a small detonator box. After that, he put up a small tent, with the entryway facing the carcass. The tent was large enough for the four people to sit comfortably on the ground inside and watch. He took several more cases out of the Land Rover, stacked them in the tent, then tied back the mosquito netting and sat down inside, toward the front, motioning for the others to join him.

The four sat together just inside, not visible to the vultures, and watched. Davie looked now and again through binoculars at vultures flying overhead, his long neck stretching. "Gotta be real quiet and stay inside so they'll come down," he said in a low voice.

They waited. Elizabeth watched the sun climb overhead. Heat waves wrinkled the landscape. She sat in silence, barely daring to shift her feet. Paul and Mary were also silent. Paul rubbed his bad leg. Mary took a peak through her binoculars at the soaring birds. She whispered to Davie about which species they were seeing, and he told her, pointing to some of the black shapes in the sky. She took out a bird guide and wrote notes in it; neat, circular script and lots of numbers, Elizabeth noticed. Slowly, some smaller vultures descended, soaring low and looking carefully around.

"The smallest ones always do that," Davie said softly. "They ain't big enough to fight off the big boys, so the smallest ones gotta take the biggest chances and go in first. Kinda like a baseball lineup — have a small, fast guy first up to get on base and the power hitter up fourth."

"Doesn't seem fair, does it?" Elizabeth said.

"Nope, nothin's laid out fair on the Tsavo plains, 'cept maybe death." Davie picked at his teeth with a small twig, momentarily lost in thought. If he were to tell his deepest thoughts and feelings, it was the confrontation with death in nature that gave meaning to his life. It was at these times, when his mind was focused and intent, studying the details of vultures, that he felt most alive. But why vultures? Other people asked, and he often wondered himself. Something about growing up poor in Brooklyn, always being the underdog, living in a family of grave diggers. He was too smart for that job, but his family was too poor to send him to anything but a nearby community college. And even there he had to pay his way by working in the family business, digging graves. At first the cadavers and the coffins had frightened him, but he grew used to it, and discovered it was a great attention-grabber.

"And how are you working your way through school?" other students would ask. "Helpin' out in my daddy's business," he would say.

"Oh, how nice. And what's that?"

He would look them straight in the eye. "Grave diggin'."

It always got a reaction. He was the kind of person who did not stand out, whom people ignored or forgot they had met. But his job shocked them — they remembered *that*, all right. He imagined that some of the girls found him a little fascinating, too.

He heard a rustling and turned to look. It was just a Thomson's gazelle passing by in the bush off to his left.

He'd had a sympathetic ecology teacher, someone who at one time had worked with Horst. That teacher took an interest in him and told him to find a specialty in which he could excel. Memories of his ecology course field trips flashed through his mind as he sat in the tent with the three visitors — trips to Long Island's sand dunes, finding washed-up dead crabs, finfish, an occasional gull, once even a dead pilot whale. The college was so poor that the only animals he could dissect and study were those he could find himself. He had watched turkey vultures converge on carcasses and became interested in their behavior.

Even though the stench was overpowering and clung to his clothes, he had dissected the pilot whale, trying to find out why it died. When he finished work for the day, he would swim in the surf with his jeans shorts and T-shirt on to rid himself of the smell. From that, the path had led to becoming the world's expert on vultures. It was clear and simple.

Hell, let 'em think I'm weird, all them highfalutin, mostly rich enough not to have to work too hard if at all do-gooders who "study" nature as a hobby. None of that airy-fairy sittin'-in-a-clean-office-writing-equations-on-a- blackboard stuff for me. Anger welled up, and involuntarily he clenched his hand into a fist and jerked it in a punching motion, barely missing Elizabeth, seated immediately to his right.

She jerked back, startled. "Are you all right?" she whispered.

He nodded. "Yeah, sure, I'm okay." She really wasn't so bad, he thought. And just sitting near Mary was a thrill. He decided he was in love with her. Even Paul was a decent sort, he had to admit. They were just an inexperienced academic bunch. He ought to relax.

They sat mostly in silence for an hour, according to Elizabeth's watch, while the vultures circled and circled. Elizabeth was thirsty, but Davie offered nothing, and nobody dared move. The smell of decay filled the air. Then out of the corner of her eye Elizabeth saw something moving through the thornbushes. Davie put a finger to his lips. A leopard came out of the bush and began to circle the bloody carcass, pacing a long circle that brought it behind the tent and then around again. It made the circuit three times. Elizabeth glanced at the others — Mary was pale; Paul looked grim and determined.

"She knows somethin's funny about this setup. That's why she's circlin' and not just feedin'," Davie whispered. "It ain't easy to fool a leopard."

The leopard came in closer, moving stealthily from their left side so that it was soon between their tent and the dead buffalo. Elizabeth thought she could almost reach out and touch the big cat.

Paul moved his bad leg as carefully as he could, but the leopard heard it and, turning toward the tent, looked directly into Elizabeth's eyes. The leopard's eyes were steely blue. She thought they were the most threatening thing she had ever seen — sheer violence, the complete predator. The leopard stared at her for what seemed many minutes. It crouched lower, its eyes fixed on her. Then it glanced at Davie, who continued to sit absolutely still. Nobody moved.

Paul, more experienced with wildlife and hunting than Elizabeth, realized that none of them had a gun. He had a knife. He tried to think what the others could use as weapons. Finally, the leopard turned away and walked toward the carcass. It reached the body and sniffed at it. Paul was certain the leopard would begin to feed, but it backed away and turned toward the tent again.

The leopard's coat glistened over a seemingly well-fed belly, or perhaps it was pregnant. It moved slowly toward the tent, crouched low, back bent, like a cat stalking a bird. It was so close Paul could smell its fur and hear its breathing. Everything else was silent, as if they were watching an old silent movie. But this was real. Too real. Paul very slowly unsheathed a knife he had in his belt, but thought it would be of little use if the leopard charged. Mary edged closer to Paul, her eyes on the leopard. At least one of their group might be dead in a few moments, but there seemed little they could do.

Elizabeth looked from Paul to Mary to Davie and back to the leopard. She was frightened but fascinated. Who had talked the other day about raw nature? Life from death; death from life; vultures at the top and bottom of the food chain, whatever. What would she do if the leopard attacked? Use some of her martial art skills, kick the leopard in the teeth, maybe.

Suddenly, Davie sprang up, grabbed two of their metal canteens, and rushed out of the tent banging the canteens together and yelling at the top of his lungs. The leopard stopped. Paul grabbed his own canteen and banged it with his knife to make as much noise as he could. He stepped out, yelling loudly too. Elizabeth followed, shouting, but Mary hung back. The three people were completely exposed, making as much of a racket as they possibly could. The big cat rose from its stalking crouch and stood facing them uncertainly.

Then Mary grabbed her metal clipboard and pen and, standing in the tent doorway, began banging them together.

Davie moved forward, shouting and banging the canteens, his unkempt hair flailing, his scraggly beard moving up and down as he shouted. He had no weapon, but he advanced. There was an ominousness in his movements, and for a moment Elizabeth wasn't certain who was more frightening, the steely-eyed leopard or Davie. But then the big cat turned him and growled. Paul banged his knife on his canteen. The leopard growled again, but backed away, turned, and moved off into the thornbushes. It turned toward them again, almost hidden, and they advanced, making even more noise. Davie moved to the carcass and beyond, Paul and Elizabeth following. The leopard wheeled and walked away. It looked back one last time and fixed its cold eyes on Paul's and then on Elizabeth's, as if telling them that next time it would get them. Then it moved off slowly. They watched it slip into the distant bush and disappear.

Elizabeth and Paul returned to the tent and sank down, drained. Mary was already there. But not Davie — he still banged the two canteens together, hair flying, eyes wild, spittle at the corners of his mouth. He walked toward the bush where the leopard had vanished and was perhaps lying in wait. He held his arms lifted far from his body, like a vulture's wings, and his back was hunched over. He went over to the carcass, looked about some more, then returned to the tent. The strong smell of human sweat filled the tent. Davie put down the canteens, opened one and took a long drink, then sat down.

"Good work, guys. This happened to me once before when I was alone. But that time the leopard circled an impala carcass for three hours."

"Thank *you* for saving us," Elizabeth said. "That was a brave thing you did." Mary and Paul agreed.

Davie glanced at her, at Elizabeth, then at Paul. "Pretty gutsy of you two as well," he said to Paul and Elizabeth. "Not many people woulda gone out there with me, especially ones like yourselves who haven't spent much time in the bush."

Elizabeth wondered why Davie had not used the pistol that she'd seen him pull out of his pants pocket the night before.

"Better to do something than just sit and watch," Paul said. Mary looked up at Paul and then at Elizabeth, but said nothing. "Too bad we didn't have a rifle," Paul added.

"Yeah, you'd need something big, not a handgun," Davie said. "But we try not to kill the animals here, y'know. We're supposed to be studying them and protecting them, and we're in their territory." He was silent for a moment. "Funny how bangin' metal gets 'em to move off. Wood or rocks, they don't move. Somethin' man-made, that gets 'em."

The vultures had retreated and were again circling high in the blue-white sky. Elizabeth felt her heart settle down.

"Old leopard scared 'em off," Davie said, "but not for long. They'll be back. Time for some lunch first, though." He opened a pack and took out some beef jerky, crackers, cheese, and cans of soda, which he passed around. Elizabeth smelled sweat and decay on his hands as he passed her the food.

"This is the way I really like it," Davie said while they ate. "The wild without people. You guys prob'ly think I'm just a heartless bugger. Brooklyn grave digger. But I have deep feelings. I love this wild place. Empty. No stinkin' crowds, like at Coney Island or even Prospect Park." He snorted

"Y'know, it's a sad fate. We're so smart, we can think about Tsavo and know about it, and yet be so dumb we can't connect to it. W e gotta struggle to fit into nature. You think Tsavo's hard, don'tcha? W ell, when you spend as much time as I do out here, and in other wild places — not just Africa but wherever they call me 'cause they need help with vultures, condors, whatever — I see through it. Everybody's strugglin' to try to fit into nature. Our nature's inside us" — he pounded his breast. "Shove us out of that nature into civilization — Nairobi, New York City, whatever — " he pointed vaguely toward the horizon — "and we, dumb asses, we gotta find our way back, fit ourselves in. It's the pain of bein' human."

"Hey, you just said something that hits right to the center of what I've been trying to figure out," Elizabeth said, "and maybe you're the one who can answer it."

Davie turned to her. "Me?"

"Yes. You and the others — Bruce especially — are so hung up on elephants. And I'm going along, not being a biologist, trying to figure out what's so important about them. What *is* it?"

Davie was silent for a while, looking out over the plains. "Y'know, Liz, I wondered about that too. Still don't quite get it. But now that you mention it, maybe it's about what I was just sayin'."

"The pain of being human?"

Davie looked at the buffalo carcass, then off into the bush where the leopard had vanished, then back at Elizabeth. "That big tusker I showed you guys? Old Ragged Ears? Whatever the hell he is, he sure don't have to wonder whether he fits in, or how. Y'see, Bruce's whole life is Tsavo and its animals. I think that elephant kind of represents all of nature to him, and he's tryin' to figure out what that means to him. He'd never say it to you though, no, not the great white hunter admittin' he was confused about anythin'. Maybe Bruce and all the rest of 'em think if they understand Old Ragged Ears, they'll find a way back in. They're all outside, ya see." He waved his hands around in a big arc, and as he did so, the smell of excrement wafted over to Elizabeth, Paul, and Mary. Mary's hand strayed to her necklace. She twisted it back and forth and then held on to the pendant.

"Well, Davie, you've sure succeeded in immersing yourself in something that smells pretty damn strong, whatever you want to call it," Elizabeth said. "You're right, we seem to have alienated ourselves from nature, with our Dove soap and face creams and deodorants and sun block and alcohol and antibiotics."

"Yeah, I use all that crap too when I need it. What the hell. We ain't gonna turn our backs on penicillin. But that stuff came from some old guy lookin' at a bread mold and then makin' a commercial product out of it. And think about this — what was the first main use of penicillin? Savin' soldiers in World War Two so we could send 'em back into battle. That's your humanitarians."

"But, Davie, these vultures don't seem much more humanitarian, or moral, to me. Or that leopard," Elizabeth said.

"Yeah, but they're natural, don'tcha see? They don't rationalize. They don't talk do-goodin'. Look at Horst — you think there's a vulture here as connivin' as him? They're too stupid to be mean on purpose. They just act mean out of naturalness."

Elizabeth talked with Davie about the old bull elephant.

"He knows me, Zamani Baba. Him and me, we been around each other. He knows," Davie said.

"I guess he wouldn't have trouble catching *your* scent," Elizabeth joked.

"Go ahead, laugh if ya want. He knows about nature. About people. He's the spirit of nature himself, whatever you think. So I stink. I know it. That's my job, my chosen profession. To stink. You can think and stink, y'know."

"No doubt, but it's pleasanter, at least f or old civilized me, to think and not stink," she said.

Davie had a wild look in his eyes. Paul tried to signal Liz to lay off. It was one thing to philosophize, it was another to tread on the edge with somebody as unpredictable as Davie. But Paul couldn't catch her eye. She was watching Davie with a half-amused expression on her face.

"Take care now, Liz. That big daddy tembo will getcha one day if ya don't watch out. Or somethin' else will." Davie gave her a sinister look.

Paul wondered if Davie might have a limit, a threshold that he would reach suddenly and then become violent. Seeking to derail him from that path, Paul dug in his pack and brought out a small sack of fruit-flavored hard candies and passed them around. They had the desired effect — the four of them sucked contentedly in silence.

Davie was suddenly all business again. "Okay, now we gotta quiet down and wait out them birds again."

And so the four of them sat in silence once more, each lost in private thoughts. Even inside the tent, Tsavo's heat beat on them, blinded their eyes, blew dust in their noses and ears. Tsavo was not listening, not caring.

Above, the vultures soared slowly in lazy circles. Time seemed to stop. Elizabeth stared at them. Some of the vultures circled low, some a little higher, and another group circled almost beyond eyesight. The circling vultures were hypnotic. They made the sky look three-dimensional, giving it a depth that she had never seen before. For a while she watched dreamily. But time dragged. It was so much a part of this work, she thought, hours of waiting, moments of action. The nature programs on television never showed the long, boring hours, never communicated the thirst, the heat, the fatigue.

"That big tembo, as you call him, that elephant, he's a puzzle," Mary said quietly. "He seems so intelligent, as if he understands us. At first I thought he would kill us, but now I think maybe he's on our side."

"Our side of what?" Elizabeth asked.

"I don't know exactly how to put it. One moment I think about him as if he were a pet dog or something, and the next I think of him as the wildest of things. It's a puzzle."

"I told ya you'd thank me for gettin' us near him," Davie said. "Just like I said, they're fascinatin' animals. You'll tell your grandkids about him — if you live to have any."

"And what would the world be like without them?" Mary said, half to herself.

"Something magical would go out of it," Paul said. "No doubt about it. Ever watch an elk? A big bull elk? They're fascinating too. I learned that hunting them with my dad in Oregon, tracking them. We think they're dumb, but they're smarter than you'd think. Compare them with a cow or a chicken. That bull elk can fend off a pack of wolves — if he's healthy, that is. I've seen them do it. And an elk is nothing compared with that big old elephant."

"Who's the more rational, an elephant or a dog?" Elizabeth asked.

"Elephant, hands down," Davie said.

"Elephant or cat?"

"All a cat's got is independence. No comparison."

"Okay, a whale then."

"Don't see how you can compare 'em, scientifically I mean. You can have your opinion if you want, but they're too diff'rent to really compare."

"What's the closest?"

"What's this rationality thing, anyway?" Davie asked, looking at Elizabeth.

"Oh, just a hobby of mine," she said. "Come on, Davie, we're talking here the basis of Western civilization."

"And I thought we was out to catch vultures. Well, whaddya know. You want to talk Descartes, do you? Fine with me — I've read his stuff. But not now, Liz. We're out here. Let's just enjoy Tsavo. Look 'round you. Chance of a lifetime."

"He's right, Double E," Paul said.

"Descartes an' elephants in the middle of Tsavo. Now I've heard everythin'." Davie shook his head and spit at an ant that w as wending its way toward the tent. "How 'bout an ant or a termite? Wanna talk Descartes an' them?" He spit at the ant again, nearly drowning it.

Around midafternoon, some of the smaller vultures circled just above the treetops. And eventually one landed on the dead buffalo. Davie held his finger to his lips. The vulture tore at the flesh in the gaping hole, sticking its head up to its neck into the rotting meat, eating rapidly. Seeing that the first small vulture had landed safely, the others began to drop out of the sky. They descended onto the dead buffalo faster than Elizabeth would have believed possible. Soon the carcass was crawling with the big birds, like ants on dropped food at a picnic. They stirred up the stench of the rotting flesh, and the smell flooded the tent.

Now the scene looked primeval to Elizabeth, as if she had been cast into another time, before human beings, a reptilian time. The vultures ate and fought among each other for space to reach inside the body. Their heads became covered with bits of meat and dried blood. The largest vultures came in last, but once on the carcass they shoved the smaller ones aside. The struggle for existence took place right in front of her. Before many of the smaller ones were pushed off the carcass, Davie pressed the lever on the dynamite box and the charges exploded, blowing the net over the dead buffalo and trapping all but one of the birds. That one vomited, defecated, and flew off. The rest of the birds struggled to get through the net and began to vomit and defecate.

Mary fanned her face with a rolled-up piece of paper, trying to fend off the stench. Davie laughed. "They do that to lighten their loads, so if they get free they can take off easier."

"Weight and balance," Paul added. "I learned that in my flying lessons."

Davie laughed again. "Yeah, like Johnny tossin' out a few pieces a baggage when he's got a fat passenger."

No one took their eyes off the birds. The stench grew stronger, rolling in waves like surf against a shore. Mary put a handkerchief over her nose. Elizabeth pulled a red bandanna from her pocket and put it around her f ace. Meanwhile, Davie began his work. He walked out to the net-covered carcass that crawled with trapped vultures. He carried heavy gloves, a large, dirty scale, canvas bags, and a carpenter's tape measure. "Yo! How 'bout givin' me a hand?" he shouted to Paul.

Paul understood it to be as much a challenge as a request. He came over right away. "Just tell me what to do." He was used to dealing with dead game, but not usually this rotten.

Davie put on heavy gloves, the kind falconers wear, and loosened an end of the net just enough to reach in and grab the nearest vulture. The bird bit and struggled until Davie stuffed it into a canvas bag. Vomit and excrement leaked through the rough cloth.

"Grab my notebook," Davie said over his shoulder to Paul. "Write down what I say." Mary stood up and came over to Paul and Davie; her interest in measurements overcame her reaction to the terrible smells, and she offered to help too. She took the notebook from Paul and wrote down the numbers as Davie called them out. Davie put a hood over another vulture's head, quieting the bird, and then forced it onto the scale, holding the bird tightly without putting any downward pressure on the scale. Paul helped him. Davie called out the weight, and Mary recorded it. Davie then stretched the bird out and measured it from head to tail, then from a wing tip to the center of the breastbone, and called out both numbers to Mary. Then he removed the hood from the bird and let it go. It vomited and defecated again, staining Davie, the scale, and the ground around it, and flew off, squawking loudly. Paul managed to move out of the way and was unscathed.

Davie measured each of the vultures the same way. There were twenty-two of them, and the entire process took more than an hour. By the end, he was covered with vulture vomit and excrement. He began to roll up the net, now also filthy, and put away all his gear, placing a lot of it in the very rear of the Land Rover, just behind the second seat. He packed up the tent with the help of the others and put it into the Land Rover too. Then he took the notebook f rom Mary and, with stinking fingers, pointed at the numbers.

"You see, there's a lot a variation in size in some species, less in others. We had four kinds of birds on this buffalo. In general, these birds were heavy, in good shape. They must be feedin' well — either there's a lotta elephants and few other big plant eaters, or they're bein' shot at a high rate and there's a lotta carcasses. That's one use of my data, as an index of the size of prey populations. I'd say there's both a lotta elephants and a lotta of poaching."

Mary offered to help Davie analyze the data. Davie was so pleased by the offer that he was speechless, and Mary didn't know whether he accepted or not. He put the notebook away, then took a canteen and rinsed his hands, but Paul saw that the rest of his clothes and his arms, neck, and beard were crusted with gunk.

Davie went over to the Land Rover. "Time to go. We done what we could here. Hop in. Don't let the smell getcha. That's just nature, ya know." He stared at the two women, challenging them to say something. They said nothing. Mary merely crawled into the middle seat, keeping as far away as she could from the putrid net and other gear. Elizabeth stared defiantly at Davie, but said nothing and seated herself in the back near all the stinking equipment.

Paul sat in front next to Davie.

As soon as they got back to camp, they washed as thoroughly as they could with water from the artesian well. Davie washed the worst of the gunk from his nets and sacks. He was especially careful with the net, spending the best part of an hour pumping water from the well into a bucket and repeatedly rinsing the net to make it as clean and odorless as possible. He soaked the canvas sacks and hoods in the bucket and washed them, too. Mary couldn't get near the stuff without retching, but Paul and Elizabeth helped with the cleaning. They'd passed Davie's first two tests — the leopard and the vultures — and they weren't going to let him win this last one.

"I've got detergent — want to use some?" Elizabeth asked as she stuck an especially foul-smelling sack into the bucket.

"Is it scented?" Davie asked.

"Yes."

"That's the worst. Perfume puts 'em off more than their own puke and shit — they prefer what's natural, I s'pose. They've evolved over a long a time — they play it safe by avoidin' the new an' novel."

"Makes sense," Elizabeth said.

Howie, who had wandered over and was chatting with Paul, said, "Unlike whales or dolphins, a puking vulture's just not a great bumper sticker. Picture a bumper sticker with a puking vulture on it and the message 'Save biodiversity, Save the world!'"

"Who knows what's more important, whales or vultures?" Davie said. "A condor's just a big American vulture, and look how much money folks have spent savin' them. For me, it's realism instead of idealism. Shit's real."

* * *

While Davie was keeping Paul, Elizabeth, and Mary busy catching vultures, Horst decided it was a good time for him to meet with Joseph. Bruce was occupied with Michael and Johnny, and that made things easy. He passed the three of the by, saying he would be spending the day writing up reports and walking near the camp, to familiarize himself better with Tsavo. He walked about a half mile from camp, down the path where he had met Joseph and called him on the two-way radio Joseph had given him. Horst sat on a log, thinking. It wasn't long before Joseph arrived and they discussed how they might cooperate to stop the big-time commercial poachers. Horst explained his connection to the international environmental organization. Then he asked Joseph to tell him more about himself and how it was that he knew Tsavo so well.

Joseph realized he had no choice but to tell the truth, so he told Horst about his going to school with Bruce and Michael, but never having their money and contacts, had had to find his own way. He admitted that he "occasionally" killed an elephant and sold its ivory and anything else that people living near Tsavo would buy. He did his best to make it sound like he was just an honest guy who loved the wildlife, but had no other way to make a living.

Both men were on edge, neither trusting the other but believing that had no choice but to work together. Horst ended the conversation by saying as soon as he could get to Voi he would call back to Geneva and get funds, people, and equipment, and would pay Joseph for his time for helping them find the poachers. The people he would bring would attack them and try to drive them out of business and away. They shook hands on the arrangement, each walking away wishing the other could be trusted, but not quite believing it. And so passed much of Horst's mid-day, after which he returned to camp, got out his notebook and did begin to write a log of what had been happening, as a beginning to his report back to the international organization.

CHAPTER 21

Rocks and Personalities

Barring love and war, few enterprises are undertaken with such abandon, or by such diverse individuals, or with so paradoxical a mixture of appetite and altruism, as that group of avocations known as outdoor recreation.

Aldo Leopold, *A Sand County Almanac*

Bruce walked over and watched Elizabeth, Mary, and Paul help Davie clean the Land Rover from the vulture trip. At first he stood to one side, listening to their conversation, but then he came over to Elizabeth and asked her how things went. She answered briefly, smiling. She looked from Bruce to Paul and found herself comparing the two. Bruce had that rugged look of experienced outdoorsmen — little weathered wrinkles in his face, as if his skin had been eroded and shaped by wind and water, as if he had become part of the outdoors. Paul, in contrast, was smooth-skinned, handsome in a quiet way. There was something much more complex about Bruce and, to Elizabeth, much more intriguing.

By the time they finished cleaning up, it was dinner time, which went by quickly as Davie talked with Howie, and Bruce sat with Paul, Mary, and Elizabeth and talked quietly about their day with

Davie. Bruce listened to each, but seemed focused on Elizabeth, not on Paul or Mary. Elizabeth felt flattered.

Horst, preoccupied with his afternoon meeting with Joseph, talked a little with Bruce but then lit up his pipe, got himself a glass of gin, and got out his notebook, continuing to write.

After dinner, Paul and Mary went for a walk, while Elizabeth and Bruce continued to talk. She felt some of the intimacy return that she had experienced on their airplane trip. They strolled beyond the edge of the camp, and once out of sight of the tents, Bruce put his arm around her waist, gave her a little hug, and then took her hand to help her over some rough ground — hillocks of bunch grasses, dead trees half hidden among tall grasses. Elizabeth attracted him, no doubt about it. He wanted to be with her and he didn't. She would be an interference in his reasons for coming back to Tsavo. The key to it all seemed more and more Zamani Baba, the biggest of the big, the oldest of the old. It was becoming a fixation with him; at times he could step back from himself a little and realize that it was irrational, but mostly it seemed simply a logical conclusion from everything else he thought about. He had been thinking more and more about that big elephant in the past few days, and now was hoping to get this team working well enough together and situated safely enough for him to take a few days to go off alone in pursuit of the old bull.

If he got involved with Elizabeth, he would be reluctant to take that trip, or at least would be preoccupied with her. He hadn't found any woman he felt close to in Bermuda; no one *simpatico*. Lots of pretty women there, and he'd had several affairs, but most of the women he had met there were involved with international financial businesses, something that was taking hold on that island, and they were too materialistic for him. He had searched for his Miranda within that tempest, but hadn't found her, was the way that he thought about it.

Truth to tell, he had been very lonely in Bermuda, divorced from his British-born wife, who had left him when he became impossible to live with after the terrible events in Tsavo, the killing of the elephants. He had managed to shut out those feelings for a while in Bermuda. But then they had come back to the surface. As sure as water rose in Tsavo's dry streambeds during Kenya's long rains, feelings had flooded up within him, and finally he'd decided that he couldn't live in Bermuda any longer. This opportunity to return to Tsavo had seemed to come at just the right time. Now that he was back, though, too many things were disturbing him, and he wasn't so sure he should have returned.

And here was Elizabeth, who appeared to have everything he'd always wanted in a woman, and something more — a mysteriousness that he could only think of as bewitching. Her black hair and very white skin, her uncanny ability to read him, her forthrightness and her questions that probed deep — uncomfortable questions. He wondered if it would be safe to tell her about the poachers — or whoever had tried to kill him.

Maybe he was better off to shut a woman like Elizabeth away from himself forever, to live more simply, to pick up where he had left off ten years ago, become once again just that professional nature guide, work with Michael, in many ways his closest and best friend; seek adventures, live on the edge with Johnny. Get himself an airplane. A sleek Mooney, the sports car of single-engine planes. No one else he knew had one in Kenya, and he could soar over Tsavo in it faster than Johnny's Cessna. His mind flew far away along these flights of fancy until Elizabeth's voice called him back. She asked him if he was daydreaming, and he excused himself, saying there was a lot on his mind, and focused on Elizabeth, the here of the here-and-now.

Letting go of her hand, he bent down and picked a pebble from the ground and handed it to her. "What's this smooth rounded whitish stone doing here if our camp's downstream from a huge lava flow?" he asked. Why weren't the rocks all lava, black and brittle?

Before she could answer, he began to ask her questions about the geology of Tsavo — intense, specific questions. What was that rock over there? What was the latest theory about the origins of kopjes, those strange rock outcrops, famous in the Serengeti but occurring here and there in Tsavo. She told him that technically those lumps of rock sticking out of the plains were called inselbergs, and explained that they were the remains of hard granite and other ancient rocks that once were mountains towering over the plains, and that the higher land had eroded and its sediments had filled in the lower areas, making the landscape more or less flat, but some pieces of the hardest rocks remained, and those were the kopjes.

She wished the conversation had not turned so professional; romance was more in her mind. She looked at him and wondered whether a kopje, a hard, solid rock and isolated hill, was the right metaphor for Bruce, or, instead, whether there were some serious cracks in his inner depths, so that he would, so to speak, break up and erode away. She herself felt immutable and tough. Those outcrops, she decided, were a pretty good way of thinking about herself.

She took a hand lens from the small field pack that served also as a purse, and looked at the stone Bruce had handed her, then passed the stone and the glass to Bruce, explaining the stone's geological history as he examined it. It was a water-washed thing. Born in a break-off from some wall of stone, probably during some rainy-season flood, it had traveled a long distance and a long time down the meandering streams of Tsavo, having a kind of life of its own, being bounced and pushed and tossed and tumbled by water for years, probably centuries, rubbing and scraping other stones, the process smoothing them all.

"Don't you ever feel that you're like one of these little water-washed stones — we call them fluvial, for river, pebbles — tossed and turned by the other people-pebbles so some sharp edges get ground away and you become more settled, rounded, contented?" she asked.

"'Flowery way of describing my life," Bruce answered. Night had fallen and in the darkness he pulled her to him and kissed her.

CHAPTER 22

Random Numbers and Tourists

Give me knowledge, so I have kindness for all.

A saying of the Plains Indians of North America

The next morning the scientists in the crew took time to set out plans for their work. The lunch hour came quickly. Horst, cutting a sandwich carefully with his knife and fork, glanced down and saw that Howie appeared to be reading a book that seemed only to contain column after column of numbers. He asked Howie about the book, while Bruce and others listened in. They, too, had been wondering what Howie was up to.

Howie replied that it was a book of random numbers. Bruce walked over to have a look. "You're kidding — good reading?"

Howie smiled. "Sure is, if you're after the truth. It's for sampling. You pick a point at random and you start there. That way there's no bias. Mother Nature tells it like it is. She tells you what she's really like, not what you want to believe she's like."

"Nonsense," Horst said. "We in ecology always sample in a regular way. Pick a line, stop every ten meters, whatever, and measure things. That's the way nature is, orderly, perfect, beautiful."

He smoothed his hair back and looked at Mary, who had also joined them and was carefully peeling an orange while she listened.

"This is a regular way," Howie said. "It's used all the time. A path to knowledge. Yessir. Sample at random, learn the truth."

"Best seller, eh?" Bruce said.

"So to speak. Selling better than the book I wrote, anyway."

"That's a good one. A bestseller on dirt," Horst chided

"Well, it's the real dirt about everything," Howie answered. Elizabeth groaned.

"But pretty soon you won't need this book," Howie continued, "because one of those new little calculators will do this for you. Push a button and get all the random numbers you need."

"A calculator that gives you random numbers?" Horst was getting annoyed. "I thought calculators calculated — did arithmetic and mathematics and all that."

"Yeah, but this is a kind of mathematics, Horst." Howie pulled at the brim of his red-and-white baseball cap, lowering it somewhat over his eyes like a card shark playing poker, then stared directly at Horst. "Since this bothers you, to tell the truth, they aren't really random numbers, they're pseudo-random numbers."

"Random numbers that are not random?" Horst shook his head

"It works out naturally from the mathematics."

Paul wandered over, a cheese sandwich in one hand and a cup of coffee in the other.

"Here's how it works, Horst," Howie continued. "If you have a method to produce numbers, that means they are actually not random. You can reproduce the method, so the method is methodical, not truly random. They're just numbers generated in a way that you can't tell from random." He took off his baseball cap and scratched his head.

"Can't tell from random? Chance that isn't chance?" Horst asked. "What the hell's that supposed to mean?"

"It's random like that big old elephant we saw the first day. Random but not random. Predictable but not totally predictable. And like the baboons yesterday, although they were less predictable and more random, I have to admit."

"Nothing random about that elephant," Horst replied.

"Well, I didn't think he was all that predictable," Howie said.

"And that lion that got Cecile, it wasn't so random," Horst said.

Bruce was interested. Maybe Howie was the one who understood how they could get their job done in the time they had available.

Horst pushed his finger onto the open page of the book.

"Hey, careful, Horst, don't get dirt in my book. This'll be a collector's item someday."

Horst pulled his finger back quickly. Howie grinned. "Nobody's ever printed a book of random or almost random numbers before our time, and when they have calculators to do it, nobody will publish these anymore. It's like a rare and fragile species that appears on Earth for a short time and goes extinct. You're looking at a soon-to-be extinct species of book."

"Books that go extinct that have random numbers that aren't random?" Horst said, wiping his hands and face carefully with a piece of paper towel.

"Especially first editions. This here's a second edition."

"Improved the plot, did they?" Bruce joked. He was feeling better about this group, or about Howie at least.

The others wandered away, back to the table inside the tent to get more food, but Bruce sat down on the ground next to Howie and Paul.

"Seriously, Howie, you know we have a big problem here, trying to count all the elephants in Tsavo in a month." Bruce explained to Howie that Johnny and a few others had worked out a way to count elephants from the air. They would sample a part of a park and then extrapolate to the rest of the area. But Bruce wasn't convinced that they were using the best methods to search out elephants or that

143

they could get a good sample of all of a park from such a small part of it.

The key to it all, Howie told him, was how to pick a point to start counting and then what kind of pattern to search through Tsavo to understand it best and to find elephants.

Howie explained that this mathematics had its roots in practical problems. "All this random-number stuff got started during World War Two," he said, "when some mathematicians were asked to figure out the most efficient way to hunt submarines when you couldn't see them and didn't know where they were going. They invented game theory, and discovered that the most efficient way to search for something you knew nothing about was at random. If you don't know anything, the path to knowledge is a random search. Pretty ironic, isn't it?"

"But we do know a great deal about elephants — what kinds of habitat types they prefer and where we found them most in the past," Bruce answered.

"Okay! Then we can design our sampling to make best use of that. Yep, old jumbo sure ain't a submarine. Let's do it!" Howie answered, turning to a new leaf in his notebook.

Horst had had enough. This weird and useless joking by Howie was the last straw. He went over to Bruce and said that he needed to say some things to the entire group, and whether or not Bruce was de facto in charge, he himself was representing a major environmental organization and it was important that he explain some things to the group. Bruce agreed. Purely objectively, Horst had a right to talk to the entire group and present his point of view, whatever the relationships had been between the two. So Bruce brought everybody together once again and explained that Horst wanted to tell the group about his work and his role.

Once again the group gathered in their meeting tent, this time without baboons and with Howie and Davie sitting quietly and listening.

"Look, I have nothing against your all being out here to do your scientific survey," Horst said, "but it's becoming clear that there is some major poaching of the elephants going on. They poachers are dangerous to each of us, let alone to the elephants. One reason I've been sent here was to look into that poaching. If the elephants are being killed big time, then what use will your science survey be? Those guys might be bringing the elephant population down faster than you can count them.

"So it seems to me that we better have a two-pronged approach. You go ahead with your science. Meanwhile, I'll try to bring in some help against the poachers."

Elizabeth turned to Bruce, who she was sitting next to and said quietly to him that Horst, however difficult and scary a person he was, had a point.

Bruce stood up and said, "Okay, Horst. You're the one with the big international connections. And the organization that sent you over has done good things and I respect them. So go ahead. But we have our obligations too — to the people funding us — so do what you want, as long as you don't interfere with what we have been sent out to do."

"Good enough," Horst said, although he didn't mean it.

* * *

Joseph realized he had to get some ivory. His cash was running low, and he wasn't sure he could pay the men working for him. So he picked his three best and drove them out to a heavily wooded area with lots of cover to hide his Land Cruiser. It was just off a well-worn track, probably started as an animal track and used often by those familiar with Tsavo as a road. Although he was concerned about being spotted from the air, he did not think there was much chance the foreign poachers would know this track. They wouldn't know much at all about Tsavo, he was sure.

He told his men they had two new groups to watch out for. They had to poach elephants as quietly and as hidden from the air as possible. "One's a science team, run by three guys who know Tsavo as good as me, maybe better. They can't find out we're getting ivory. Too much contact with that 'save the elephant crowd,'" he explained. The others are our worst fears, a large operation of foreigners, don't know anything about Tsavo, probably involved with the government — don't care who sees what, shoot everythin' in sight, get in, get out fast. They'll leave such a mess, could bring those international environmental groups here big time. And those groups will try to put us all out of business, even us small-timers, who like keeping jumbos around like they do."

They hunted quietly, silently, staying under cover as much as they could. They shot a few elephants with big tusks so their carcasses fell in the bush that would be hard to see from the air. Then they heard a motor vehicle coming down the track.

"Hide, hide," Joseph said, as he jumped in the Land Cruiser and drove off to intercept whoever was coming. He had not gone far when he was surprised to see a large American station wagon, and even more surprised when it stopped and a white man and woman, dressed like tourists, got out and walked toward him. The woman walked gingerly and somewhat awkwardly on open-toed high-heels, stepping carefully around shrubs and bunch grasses. Joseph saw that she was wearing a sleeveless tank top and pedal pushers and had a tan leather purse hanging on a long strap from her shoulder. She seemed to be limping a little.

The driver was a middle-aged man, hatless and wearing a brightly colored floral short-sleeved shirt like Joseph had seen in travel ads for Hawaii. The shirt hung out over Bermuda shorts. On his feet were sneakers with no socks.

"We're lost and need help," the man said even before they got near Joseph, who had immediately hopped out of his Land Cruiser, trying to look as friendly and helpful as possible.

"Are you park staff?" the man asked. "We've just been attacked by some guys with guns. I thought we were goners."

Joseph did his best to hide his shock. 'Sure, I can help you. Goodness. Where did you meet up with those guys?'

"I don't know. We just drove away fast as we could. We just wanted to get away from them. Got completely lost."

"About how long ago — how long have you been driving since you left them?"

The man looked at his watch. "I don't really know. Maybe forty-five minutes? What do you think, honey?" He turned and looked at the woman. Dazed, she shrugged her shoulders to mean she didn't know and looked off into the distance.

"How many guys did you see?" Joseph asked. "Did they have big trucks or lots of pickups? Any other equipment — chain saws, maybe?"

"Yeah. Big time. Hey, you think they were out killing elephants, getting their ivory?" It seemed a new thought to him. "Jesus. We heard about that kind of stuff, but it wasn't in any of the tourist brochures."

"There's talk of a large operation — maybe foreign guys — working for an international corporation or something, doing just that," Joseph answered. He couldn't believe his good luck in having these lost tourists turn up and tell him that the poachers were out hunting. Knowing Tsavo very well and calculating the couple's drive time, he was able to guess where they were likely to be. Now he wouldn't have to send a scouting team out to locate them.

"Sit down for a few minutes and take it easy," Joseph said. "Don't worry. We will take care of you." He got a thermos out of his vehicle and offered to them. The man took it, passed it to the woman, and they both drank quickly from it. From years of contact with these kind of naive tourists, Joseph knew how to play up to them. He sat them down near their car and waited for them to speak, his goal to make sure they had no idea what he was doing or that he had his team of ivory hunters with him just a short way back. Then a great idea came into his mind.

"Tell you what. If I had time, I would drive out with you and guide you out of the park. But I've got a team working just a little way from here — cleaning out brush and so forth, for the park." The lie came easily to him. "Can't leave them. But not far from here is a team of scientists just starting some kind of studies. Four are Americans, make you feel right at home. There's a local and two Brits with them, know Tsavo as well as me, maybe better — school friends of mine. I'll take you to them and they'll help you get out safely.

"Whew! That would be great! I'm telling you, I've been through a lot of tough times, Korean War and more, but these guys, they scared the hell out of me," the man said.

"Thank you so much," the woman added, tears welling up in her eyes.

* * *

That morning, Elizabeth found herself working with Bruce, Paul, Mary, and Howie in the midst of a large open area, a flat, treeless plain of grasses and desert shrubs. They had begun their fieldwork and had agreed that Howie would choose the location — and all future ones — at random, using his little book of random numbers.

She wished she could talk quietly with Bruce or, short of that, at least get some kind of communication from him. She had expected he would be at least friendly, perhaps even joking with her, or offering some pleasantries after their time together last night. But he was only the professional guide again. Good thing she hadn't actually slept with him. She felt a little hurt, so she retreated to what she usually did: reviewed the facts of her situation.

She had come along on this trip to be a geological adviser to a bunch of biologists. She had expected to see the famous wildlife of East Africa on what would be a kind of paid vacation, since the task of this group wasn't in her primary field. She'd no romantic expectations at all, just a month of travel. On the first day in Tsavo, she had met this handsome wildlife guide and scientist. He had told her a little about him self, which made her sympathetic to him. He had taken her on an exotic, adventurous, and, she had to admit, romantic, airplane ride. And in two days, she was feeling ready to have an affair.

It was as if she had entered into a B-movie plot, one of those African adventure movies of her parents' generation. And this morning she expected something more from Bruce — perhaps the next scene in the B-Hollywood movie plot. What was she? A chump? A pushover?

Elizabeth put those feelings aside and focused on her role as the professional geologist. Mary, however, glanced at her and smiled, so Elizabeth knew that she was not doing especially well at hiding her feelings.

Under Paul's and Bruce's directions, they began by measuring out a circle ten meters in radius, using a flexible, canvas-like surveyor's tape. Mary held a compass and the large reel that contained the tape, and directed Paul, w ho pulled the end of the surveyor's tape. Elizabeth followed, laying another of these tapes along the circle, so that the area was marked clearly.

Mary picked up her field data book. It was an aluminum case combining a clipboard and three-ring notebook, its aluminum cover hinged on the left and closed snugly into a waterproof rim. She was proud of this record book. She had ordered it from a major forestry supplier. Funny how something like that would matter to Mary, Elizabeth thought. Mary flipped open the cover, cleverly made so that it swung completely under the back and formed an easy base to hold. She began neatly filling out a printed form for the plot with basic information: date, location, position, item.

Any stranger watching them would think this group of people were completely crazy, Elizabeth mused, walking in a circle in this barren spot in the bright sun, as if they were carrying out some kind of cult spiritual ceremony. She had an image in her mind of a Disney-like group of little animals, maybe some of those rock hyraxes and some of the gazelles that she and Mary had seen at camp, watching them and chatting among themselves about the odd things these humans did.

Bruce walked the circular plot, beginning at the outer limits and spiraling in. He was looking for animal signs on the ground — hoofprints, droppings. Mary followed, walking the circular path a second time. Elizabeth knew that Mary was looking for signs of animal feeding on leaves and twigs. If Bruce or Mary found anything, each would take measurements, and then Bruce would put samples in plastic bags. Some of the samples were animal droppings; others were twigs.

Elizabeth thought about trying to bring these plastic bags through customs on their way out of Nairobi and entering the United States. "Do you have anything to declare?" the customs official would say. "Just some animal droppings and leaves and twigs," she would answer. She giggled to herself. She didn't know why the whole thing was seeming so absurd to her this hot morning.

She had to get ahold of herself; she knew that they were doing the right things and that the measurements were legitimate science, which they had to do to find out the state of the elephants' habitat, quantitatively. There was just something going on about Tsavo that was giving her this odd way of looking at things, as if she were Alice and this were Wonderland. She half expected to see the white rabbit hurry by, looking at its stopwatch, or at least some Tsavo equivalent, perhaps a white rock hyrax, who would scream at her that he was late. Her companions were taking measurements carefully, and the records would be useful. It was just something about herself that was changing.

When the first round of observations were finished, Howie walked the same area, spiraling in, examining the soil, while Bruce, Paul, and Mary made additional measurements elsewhere. Although the plan was straightforward, the work went slowly, in part because they were still getting used to working with each other, in part because so much was new to them and Bruce was giving them a short course in Tsavo natural history. But mainly because it was so hot in sunlit Tsavo.

"Howie, why couldn't your book have landed us in a little shade?" Elizabeth teased. She had noticed that, as usual, the men couldn't take their eyes off Mary — the perfect beauty interested only in the numbers she was writing in her little book, unaware of, or at least avoiding, the male attention around her. What was Bruce going to do, seduce Mary next? Was that how he amused himself on a safari? She was angry with herself for allowing such thoughts to rise to the surface, and pushed them away.

Meanwhile, Joseph had ushered the American tourists back to their station wagon and helped the woman get in the passenger seat. He told them to follow him. Back in his Land Cruiser, he was thankful that he had had his most trusted guy tracking Bruce and crowd. Using his two-way radio he found out where the science team was working. It wasn't too far away and soon he and the two tourists were within distance of Bruce and his group. Joseph stopped a safe distance away and got out slowly and carefully.

* * *

In midafternoon Bruce told everybody to take a break, and while the others were finishing their lunch, Bruce took Paul and Elizabeth with him to have a look around. They had not gone far when they saw two vehicles approaching.

Looking through his binoculars, Bruce saw a Land Cruiser and what appeared to be a station wagon, an unlikely vehicle for Tsavo.

"Trouble?" Elizabeth asked.

"I doubt it. But no harm in being prepared."

Elizabeth watched him open his backpack and take out a pistol that he stuck in his belt under his shirt. Maybe he and Davie weren't so different after all; she didn't like being around so many guns, and so many loose cannons holding them. Michael had seen the vehicle and joined them.

Through his binoculars, Bruce recognized Joseph getting out of the Land Cruiser, slowly and carefully, clearly trying not to look hostile. "What the hell, it's Joseph," Bruce said quietly. The station wagon, which by this time Elizabeth could see was two-tone black and white and looked new. It continued toward them, slowly and not very carefully.

Paul motioned to Bruce that he wanted to approach and Bruce nodded 'okay.' He motioned to the others to stay back and followed after Paul. A young woman stepped out of the front passenger seat.

The driver's door opened and a hatless middle-aged man stepped out. Joseph, following a fair distance behind them, was walking slowly toward Paul and Bruce, his hands clearly without weapons, smiling.

"Hello Bruce and — Paul is it? — brought you some friends, some Americans even," he said. "Found them not far from here. Got lost trying to tour the park."

The American man and woman hurried over and began talking excitedly at the same time.

"We ran into some guys with guns," the man said.

"We're just on a vacation, read about all the elephants here and drove down from Nairobi to see them," the woman said, nearly breathless.

"We think those guys were out there shooting elephants, stealing ivory. I thought we were goners."

"Lots of them," the woman said. "And big guns."

"Managed to get away and drove like crazy, got lost," the man said, interrupting the woman.

"Then we saw this guy, friend of yours, he said. "He saved us."

"Thank goodness we met up with him!" the woman added.

Joseph just smiled at Bruce. Turning to Paul, he said, "I thought the best way I could help was to bring them to their fellow Americans. Luckily, we found you without too much searching. Thought they'd feel safest and most at home with you and Bruce." He looked at Michael and smiled, silently hoping Michael's appearance would scare the Americans.

"I was hoping you'd be good fellows and let them stay with you while you're doing your science stuff, and you could help them get to Voi," Joseph said.

The man, yet without a name to Bruce, asked Bruce if he worked for the park. Bruce explained that they were not working for the park in any official capacity, but would try to help. Paul asked if either were hurt.

The woman said "They shoved a gun in Bob's face and hit him. See? He's black-and-blue. And they threatened to rape me, grinning at me and shoving me with their guns." She started to cry.

"They made us stand in the sun while they talked about what to do with us — whether to shoot us and leave us there, or let us go," the man said.

"They argued for a long time," she whimpered. "It was so hot. Stifling. I couldn't breathe."

"Where did this happen?"

"We came across this dead elephant somewhere back there" — the man waved his arm vaguely. "Stopped to have a look. It must have died recently, because it didn't smell. And Deborah noticed it had no tusks. W e thought that was a little odd, to tell the truth. Just as we got out of the car, these armed guys appeared out of nowhere. They held us at gunpoint for a long time and asked us all kinds of questions. They took my wallet and all of Deborah's money. At least they left her some identification. Scared the shit out of us."

Howie, Mary, and Elizabeth had come forward and were listening sympathetically. Joseph knew it was time for him to get going before anybody asked him what he was doing.

"Okay," he interrupted. "Got to be on my way. Just trying to be helpful. Bloody big-time foreign poachers. Hope you can do something about that, you Americans and Brits, with your contacts all over the world."

Bob rushed over to him. "Can't thank you enough. Here, let me do something for you, pay for your time." He pulled a wallet out of his back pocket.

"On no," Joseph said, hands in the air. "Just trying to be helpful. Wouldn't think of taking your money, given the trouble you've had. Hope all goes well." He turned quickly and walked to his Land Cruiser, and before the others could say anything had jumped in, started the engine, and was on his way. Looking in his rearview mirror he saw Horst waving him down. The others, preoccupied with the American tourists and their minds also on their field research, didn't notice Horst moving off. Joseph got into this Land Cruiser and drove just a short way out of sight of Bruce and his team, turned off the motor and waited. Horst watched to make sure nobody was paying him any attention, and quietly walked toward where he saw Joseph driving.

Horst was glad to see Joseph, and began talking to him immediately. He told Joseph that Bruce and Michael have been known to get into dangerous situations — and come out with little or nothing to show for it.

"Yes, Bruce's group is in danger, given what you've just told me," Joseph responded. "Especially with what that tourist couple went through and told us. Bad stuff is moving fast." He went on to tell Horst what he knew about the big-time poachers, repeating that they had to have government funding and support, and that these guys, with their big guns, didn't care who they killed.

"Whatever this science stuff they're doing is — whatever its value somehow and somewhere — no scientific report is worth the death of even one member of their team," Joseph added. It surprised Horst that Joseph actually cared about Bruce and his team, given what Joseph had told him about their early life together and about how he was the poor man left out.

Horst explained in more detail to Joseph that he had clout with major international environmental groups that could put a stop to the poaching as well as get the team out of Tsavo. Joseph was intrigued. He had just been trying to get rid of Bruce's team. If Horst could stop the other poachers, all the better. The only problem was with the international wildlife consortium Horst was involved with. He'd need to think this one out before taking any action.

"Get me to Voi and I'll address the situation," Horst said.

"Okay . . . but first I need to tend to some of my own business. I"ll be back soon enough," Joseph replied.

* * *

Bruce watched Joseph drive off, looked at Michael and then at Paul, confusion on his face, and shook his head negatively. Then he turned to the tourist couple. "Bob and Deborah, is it? Don't worry. We will take care of you. Elizabeth and Mary, could you make them feel a little a home? I'll be with you shortly." He ushered the American couple to the two women and then turned and motioned to Michael and Paul and the three of them walked away. Michael was the first to speak, quietly so the others wouldn't hear. He was carrying his spear and rifle as if he wanted to point the rifle toward where Joseph had gone.

"Everywhere we turn, Joseph turns up," Michael said. "No accidents."

"You know as well as I, Michael, he's just as likely out here doing a little poaching on the side, and that's why he's here. Why else?" Bruce responded.

* * *

Elizabeth, in her khaki field trousers, long-sleeved khaki shirt, hiking boots, and floppy broad-rimmed hat, felt dowdy next to this woman, who looked as if she had just stepped out of her Manhattan apartment to go shopping. Elizabeth and Mary got a blanket out of the back of the Land Rover, spread it out on the ground in the shade the Land Rover cast, and invited Deborah to sit down. They gave her water and offered her a sandwich, which she took and ate hungrily.

"We were just about out of water. And food, too, come to think of it," she said.

"What were you doing here?" Paul asked.

"Just came to see wildlife. We heard this was the largest wildlife park in the world, so since we were in Kenya and we had the day off — Bob's out here on business — we thought we'd come check it out."

"No guide or anything?"

"We didn't know we needed one. You don't at parks back home. Just drive in, drive around, drive out. We thought it must be the same here. We thought they'd have a lodge or something, and places to buy snacks. Boy, we were sure wrong about that!"

"Got your sleeping gear in your car?"

"No way. We just drove down from Nairobi and thought we'd take a spin and go back to our hotel there. Damn, I don't know what you call this, but it sure isn't the kind of park we're used to. What the hell is this anyway? All this empty land, and guys with guns!"

"It's a wilderness preserve. The United Nations has listed this as one of the 'Man and the Biosphere' nature reserves."

"I could do without this much wilderness or nature or whatever," Deborah said. "It was supposed to be some kind of romantic place for our tenth anniversary trip. If I get out of here alive, I'm going to Aruba and sit on the beach and drink margaritas." She brushed off her pants, took a small mirror out of her handbag, and carefully checked her makeup. Then she looked Elizabeth up and down. "You do this for a living? Or worse, you do this for fun?"

Elizabeth laughed while Mary watched shyly, standing behind Elizabeth. "A little of both, actually. It probably does seem strange, though."

"Oh, but it can be very beautiful, too," Mary put in.

"And even peaceful and relaxing," Howie added. "But not when you meet up with poachers, of course."

"Boy, you guys are something else. Do you have to wear those safari outfits, too?"

"They're field clothes, very practical out here," Mary said.

Deborah tilted her head and looked Mary up and down. "Come to think of it, that outfit doesn't look so bad on you girls. Maybe there's a trend here. I'm in fashion design, you know. Oh, of course, you wouldn't know. Hmmm . . . a safari look . . ."

* * *

Michael offered to use one of the Land Rovers to lead the couple to a location where they would be safe and where the road out was good and clearly marked. Since the trip would take a day or more, Bruce told the couple that they should join the group for dinner and stay overnight. Back at camp, Horst gave them each a healthy gin and tonic and talked cheerfully with them about what they were doing in Kenya and where they lived in the United States. Elizabeth lent Deborah a pair of pajamas, and Bruce gave them his tent and helped them get settled in it, saying that he would happily sleep outside under the stars.

The bustle around the two strangers to the camp aroused the pair of crowned hornbills who, by this time, had almost completed their nest within the hole in the acacia tree. Soon the female would be caged inside it, walled in by a cement the birds made of dung, bark, soil, and their own saliva. The male, who was busy stuffing some bark into the cement like material, flew up and circled as the Land Rover and the station wagon arrived, and then circled the two newcomers from high above, watching them and then, slowly spiraling downward, he returned to his tree and continued his work, uttering no cry.

When Bob and Deborah had gone to bed, and the others had drifted off to their own tents, Bruce came over and sat down next to Elizabeth. Impressed with her grit in deciding to stay and sensing that she had felt snubbed during the day, he apologized, explaining that as the leader of this group, he had to maintain a professional and externally neutral role with all the members of the team. She knew he was right, and it made her feel better. They talked quietly as he arranged his sleeping bag on top of a poncho near the campfire. Then they sat down together, and Bruce immediately pulled her to him. She was beginning to feel like a high-school teenager with a crush on an upper classman, and she was happy to lie next to Bruce and watch the campfire burn low to red coals. As the fire faded and she grew sleepy, she kissed him goodnight and went to the tent she was sharing with Mary.

* * *

The next day, as promised, Michael led Bob and Deborah out. W hen he returned he took Bruce aside and told him he had seen a huge herd of elephants not far from their camp.

CHAPTER 23

Elephant Encounter

Elephants are among the world's most intelligent, sensitive
animals and possess both empathy and self-awareness.

Ian Douglas-Hamilton
Wildlife Conservation Network Website

I n the far northeast of Tsavo, Zamani Baba once again joined
two other males who were searching the barren countryside for
something to eat. They greeted each other, communicating with
low stomach rumblings, and Zamani Baba rubbed the backs of the
other two elephants with his trunk. They found little to eat — some
dried, dwarfed shrubs, leaves from a few broken acacia trees. They
traveled a long distance, following a search pattern known only
to themselves, which might or might not have been deciphered
by Bruce or Howie or Michael if they watched the elephants long
enough. Whatever it was, it was not very successful, and now the
three elephants were pawing at sand along a dry streambed, digging
for water.

A small elephant herd did the same downstream, but the three
bulls did not join them. Instead, they moved leisurely, rubbing
against each other now and then when they paused briefly from
digging into the sandy soil. One filled its trunk with sand and blew

it over his back. Another wandered off to chew at a dried shrub, but the three bulls always came back together, greeting each other again. After a while, one of the bulls lifted his trunk and moved toward the herd, catching the scents of the females and young. But then he seemed to think better of this, stopped, and returned to the other two.

Then Zamani Baba heard the sounds of the machines that carried people. He moved in front of the two other bulls toward the sounds and stood still, watching, listening, then moved slowly toward the sounds, raised his trunk to pick up scents. Which kind of people would these be — the ones that simply stood in the way and angered him, or the ones that killed?

Two Land Cruisers came into view, not so clearly through the old bull's eyesight, but with distinctive smells, some of which alarmed him, and which Bruce and Michael would have identified as those of gunpowder and other explosives. Zamani Baba moved aggressively toward the two vehicles. They turned away from him and drove toward the herd. The old bull followed, first moving as quickly as the vehicles, then faster, gaining on them. The lead vehicle pulled away from the other, which slowed, then stopped. A man came out and aimed a rifle at Zamani Baba, while the first vehicle sped to the herd. The old bull, ears out, trunk up, trumpeted loudly and rushed at the man. Before he could shoot, the bull hit him with his tusks and spun him around, then stomped on him until he was still.

The lead vehicle had reached the herd. Zamani Baba chased them and sent one man flying, flinging him with his trunk and tusks high into the air, head over heels, cartwheeling and hitting the ground. He did not move.

The other man ran back to the Land Cruiser, jumped in, and started the engine. The old bull wheeled, trumpeted, and charged after it for fifty yards or so, then stopped and turned as the vehicle moved away, out of his sight beneath a cloud of sand and dust. The bull ran back and stomped again on the two bodies. When he was done, he raised his head, put his trunk up high, and trumpeted to the sky.

CHAPTER 24

Old Friends

I am a weary and a lonesome traveler,
I've been a travelin' on.

American Folksong

After dinner Tuesday evening, Johnny took Michael, Paul, and Bruce aside, settled down with them by the campfire, and offered each a lukewarm beer — their ice had run out and there was no way to cool anything. He looked over his shoulder at the others. They were busy with various things, some cleaning up, some talking. Turning back to the three men, he told them that he wanted to start aerial counts of the elephants right away, poachers or no poachers, but knew that some of the others would think that was unwise, and he wanted to get these three on his side.

Johnny felt more comfortable discussing his plans with these men. He wasn't ready to talk with the women about something risky like this, and he didn't like Horst, had little respect for Davie, and hadn't figured Howie out. With these three he enjoyed a feeling of camaraderie. The four of them settled back; it was peaceful — justthree old friends talking together, with a younger man, Paul, to listen and learn. They even chatted briefly about the two women, what might happen on the rest of the trip. Johnny ribbed Paul about

Mary — said it was clear something was going on between them. The others smiled. Johnny then asked Bruce about Elizabeth, at the same time looking at Michael to see if his interest picked up, but Bruce brought the conversation back to their work.

Michael told them about poachers he had dealt with recently when he was working for the Kenyan National Park Service in Amboseli and in the Serengeti National Park in Tanzania.

"Most were cowards," he said with a small smile. "They quickly dropped their weapons when they saw me and my uniform. But the Snake was an exception."

"That's Joseph Kenjoy, the man who keeps popping up," Bruce reminded them. "As we told you, he's nicknamed the Snake because his last name is similar to the Swahili word for that animal."

"One of the most dangerous — and intelligent — of the poachers." Michael added. "He was a schoolmate of ours at the English church school that Bruce and I attended. The school had students from each of the three cultures of Kenya — the British colonialists (here he smiled at Bruce), Maasai (he tapped his spear on the ground as if to say 'here, here') and a Kikuyu. The Kikuyu were dominant in Kenya at the time — both in numbers and in politics. They have controlled the Kenyan government for the most part since independence."

"And Joseph?" Paul asked.

"Oh yeah," Johnny replied, "I forgot our fourth cultural group — poorer white Englishmen. Not very many and most, like Joseph, feel left out and are unhappy about it."

"We were friends — the three of us — in the way that boys who feel like outsiders come together," Bruce added. "I even hired Joseph — along with Michael — to work with me when I started a company to try to control the elephant population. So we go back a ways."

Paul was listening intently. The plot was thickening — or it had been thick and he hadn't noticed. What did the Snake mean to the group? Why was Bruce usually so rude to him if they'd been friends? Or maybe that wasn't really rude, just some kind of old-friends kind of talk. But if he was a poacher, why were they even dealing with him?

"Actually, Bruce taught Joseph pretty much everything he knows about elephants – scientifically, at least," Michael said, sensing Paul's growing concern.

"So, how did he go bad?" Paul asked. "Sure seems like he wants to renew your friendship. He keeps popping up — like a bad penny."

"I understand your concern," Johnny said. We don't know just yet. And you're right that he may not be worthy of trust. He twisted the science that Bruce introduced him to — the need for control of elephant populations — using it as an excuse to increase his illegal harvesting of ivory."

Bruce had been listening thoughtfully, "Yeah, he's got a history, but the Snake's hardly the major problem now," he said. "We should be all right for the time being but we better get the data we were sent here to get as soon as possible. We can use Johnny's plane to keep track of the poachers while we're counting elephants.

The plane is one big advantage we have over the Snake," Johnny offered.

Michael added that Joseph would be especially interested in Zamani Baba, because of the value of his tusks, and that all the poachers loved to brag to each other about the biggest elephants they had killed. Then he told them about the attempt on Bruce's life.

There was a hushed silence. Everything had been rather abstract until now, even Cecile's death. But an airplane flying over Bruce and men shooting from the windows? It was news to Johnny and Paul. Johnny just stared at Bruce for a second and then looked upward, as if for some guidance. He'd had close calls, but he'd never been shot at from an airplane.

"When did this happen?" he asked.

"A day or so ago," came Michael's reply. Bruce clearly was leaving the talking to him.

"Was the Snake involved?" Johnny asked.

"That's hard to know. But it's not his style. Never has been. He sneaks in quietly, kills a few jumbos, leaves no trace. Pretty good business, what they call 'sustainable" these days."

"Should we consider aborting this mission?" Paul asked.

After a long silence, Bruce finally said, "It's very complicated. We don't know who took a shot at me. It could have been poachers, government people, spies, who knows? Yesterday I saw a Beechcraft flying over elephant herds. I agree with Michael — the Snake's probably not involved — he couldn't afford a Beechcraft and, as Michael said, not likely his style. But as far as I'm concerned, it's not time to quit yet. We have to find out more about these new poachers, and meanwhile we can try to get at least the elephant counting done, if not Mary's vegetation studies and Elizabeth's geology, then there's Howie's soil … whatever."

"Won't the final decision have to be made by the entire group?" Paul asked. "I'm afraid I've put us in that situation, because to get Mary and Elizabeth to come along, I had to promise them they would be involved in any major decisions."

Johnny playfully punched Paul's upper arm, "You Americans. Think everything's got to be done by a vote. What do you think, you're on holiday?" He winked at Michael and Bruce.

"It's okay, Paul," Bruce put in. "You're the scientific leader of this team. We'll follow along, but with a lot of advice."

The four men separated, and Bruce asked the entire group to meet briefly in the big tent. When they had gathered, he talked about the tasks that they had taken on, explained what had happened to him, and asked them what they thought should be done.

Mary went pale when she heard the news. Why couldn't they just do the work they came here to do? Elizabeth focused on the fact that Bruce could have been shot, killed. And why hadn't he told her? She was tiring of Bruce's stoic behavior, especially when it came to life and death. But she knew she needed to keep a level head.

"What chance is there it will happen again?" she asked.

"That is hard to say," replied Michael. "We need to be vigilant. And that can be done."

"Vigilance, hell, and who said they were going to be vigilant for Cecile? Us taking them on by just being vigilant?" Horst snorted.

"It seems all of us could be at risk," Howie offered.

DANIEL B. BOTKIN

"I've got to add that my long experience worldwide tells me that the science stuff has to take second place," Horst said, clearing his throat to make his next point. "It's just plain obvious that these elephants are in trouble one way or another and the poachers have to be stopped. If you want to keep the science going, you're going to need more help."

"And just who would that be?" Elizabeth asked. "Where's the help?"

But Johnny interrupted. "We can do a quick elephant count — shorten the research, but get the most important things done. It will take me just a day or two to make some flyovers, covering as much of the park as possible."

Taking a heavy pull on his pipe for effect, Horst said "Take me along when you count the elephants and we can make a quick stop at Voi so I can call and report to those funding this operation. Then we should leave. All of us."

"We've got to count the elephants now, while we can. The trip to Voi can wait," Bruce said. "We have enough gas for several flyovers, and after we've done those and need more fuel, then we'll take you to Voi,"

"Oh for Christ sake, Bruce," Horst replied. "Won't you ever get it? It's the big picture, not your little field work that's at stake here. We got to get help first so you *can* do your bloody elephant viewing."

Bruce looked off in the distance and walked a few steps away from the rest.

"To hell with it," Johnny said. "Bruce, I'll do the counts and on the final pass we will be close enough to Voi to fuel up and get enough extra for more flights."

Bruce simply nodded okay. "Paul will sit behind me on the copilot's side so I can teach him how to do the counting," he said. "Horst can sit behind you, Johnny."

"Put on much weight lately, Horst?" Johnny, smiling, asked him. Only Michael joined Johnny in smiling. Horst focused on his pipe, tapping down the tobacco and breathing in deeply so the pipe glowed brightly and hot smoke flew straight upward. A

164

pair of crowned hornbill flew overhead, once again emitting their mournful call.

"But when we leave depends on what we find out about these new poachers and what kinds of danger they pose for us," Bruce said.

"I agree," said Paul. "As head of the science team, I say we should take some risks — not too great — but not just run away either at the first sign of danger."

Mary, looking up and seeing the crowned hornbills flying just overhead, asked some specific questions about safety.

"Hell with it," said Davie. "I ain't got no fear of them poachers. I worked Tsavo years longer than they an' I know how to find them, avoid them, give 'em a ton of trouble." He thought for a while, watching two hooded vultures circling high above. "Ya know, maybe the Snake could actually turn outta be a help. Think about it."

This unexpected suggestion immediately put Horst off, to think that Davie would be suggesting just what he had decided. But then, on the other hand, that might be a sign from Davie that the three of theme, the Snake, Davie, and himself, could take over and do both the science and politics. Maybe keep Mary with us as well. What the hell, he thought, looking again at her.

When all had had a chance to speak, Bruce asked for a vote, and Paul, Johnny, Michael, and Davie raised their hands immediately in favor of continuing the work. Mary then raised her hand, as did Elizabeth — tentatively. Horst voted against it and made a point of his disgust as he walked back to his tent. Howie abstained, taking out his yoyo for a meditative walk on the edges of the camp.

CHAPTER 25

A Sable for Dinner

It should be a sweet thing to have what is best and richest, if it's for a short space only.

Jonathan Synge, *Deirdre of the Sorrows*

The next afternoon Johnny and Michael went exploring and came across of pride of lions about to kill a sable, a large antelope. They quickly decided that their own dinner would be a better end for the exquisite animal, so they drove off the lions and shot the sable. Back at camp, Michael built a fire and was now cooking one of animal's haunches — the first fresh meat they had eaten for days.

As the scent of roasting meat spread throughout the camp, one by one the members of the group gathered around the fire. Paul sat on a log, watching Michael cook. The haunch was suspended over the fire by two saplings cut and notched so that each of their tops formed a V. The smell of the cooking meat was more than delicious, Paul thought; it perfumed the air with scents of aromatic plants, as if giving back to the air the aromas of each grass, shrub, and tree that the antelope had being eating. Michael showed Paul that he had cleaned and carefully skinned the antelope, so that the skin would be useful to someone, and he had stretched the skin out over a rough wood frame he had fashioned quickly. Paul admired the sable's fur; it was beautiful, like a work of art, with the most unusual markings: a very dark, glossy black fur on its back and sides, and a white underbelly like a dress shirt that contrasted strikingly with the black back. Paul rubbed its fur, thinking that the skin looked like something the animal could have worn to a formal dance.

Watching Paul, Michael mentioned as he cooked that the sable w as a woodland creature, unusual in Tsavo, but not unknown. Paul stroked the pelt some more, somewhat sadly. Mary seemed to share his feelings. Johnny, however, had delighted in the chase, which he described in detail as he brought out a bottle of Scotch and passed around tin cups of it.

"Now you're talking," Horst said as Johnny poured a small amount into a cup from a shot glass. "What's with the shot glass? Just pour it in," he said.

Johnny looked up for a second and then filled the cup to the brim and handed it to Horst with a polite bow.

"That's more like it, my friend," Horst said, taking a swig. "Nothing like it after a hard day's work. Yes, I remember the time we were in Manaus, Brazil, in the Amazon rain forest. Talk about hot! We were out looking at places to do experiments. Those huge trees — Mary, you'd like it there. Been there?"

She shook her head. "We have to get you there sometime, my girl," he said, holding out his empty cup to Johnny. "Those trees along the Amazon, just beautiful. Pictures do not do them justice. And the town — picturesque, to say the least. There was an opera there, you know. The opera house is still there — quite a monument to the past, when that place was the center of the rubber industry. Yes, had some steamy nights there. A little rum made a difference."

After dinner, Paul and Mary left the others and went for a stroll beyond the campground. Concerned for their safety, Elizabeth followed them in the darkness, staying a good distance behind, a flashlight in her pants pocket, no weapon, but alert to anything dangerous. She was convinced that neither of them would notice a lion's nose between them at this moment. They needed protection, and she would be their guard. The male hornbill flew above her, seeming to follow her, as if he too were going to watch over Mary. Elizabeth looked at the bird, puzzling over why it seemed to be following her.

Like Elizabeth, Bruce decided that Paul and Mary were so besotted with each other that they wouldn't notice danger. Putting his pistol in his belt, he made a loop around them to the east and got ahead of them without their noticing. In taking this eastward path, he missed Elizabeth, who had stayed west.

Michael had kept an eye on Paul and Mary even as he and Bruce went about their work preparing dinner. Now, as he did every night, he was going to walk the periphery of the camp to check for any dangerous animals, including poachers. Taking his spear and his rifle, he kept Paul and Mary in view. Michael was so tall that he had to stay considerably back from them, but his eyesight was keen. He had tracked many a human being, and this was a simple situation. He remained far behind, much farther than Elizabeth, and stayed to the north.

Meanwhile, unaware that others were following them, Paul and Mary strolled along until they came to a large tree. Mary sat down, resting her back against the trunk. The twilight would soon give way to the deep darkness of Tsavo's night. Paul settled down next to her, and decided it was now or never. He moved closer to her and let his shoulder touch hers. Then — it was barely an act of will, more a movement over which he had no control — he reached over and took her hand. She did not withdraw it. He enjoyed the touch of her hand. It seemed to radiate light, to blind him to anything beyond their bodies. His arm went up and around her shoulders and held her against him. His arm had suddenly become an independent creature. He was becoming helpless, an odd collection of parts that would not remain under the control of his brain.

Mary turned to him, brushed his hair with her free hand, and held his head. He pulled her toward him and kissed her. He felt that there was no lovelier place in all the world than this patch of half-dead trees in the dry dust of Tsavo. They lost themselves in each other, unaware that any others could be near. She lay back on the sand and welcomed him. In the moonlight her golden hair was the color of Tsavo's sand. Her legs too were golden. She looked up at him and saw the violet-blue of his eyes against the deep blue of the night sky.

They were soon immersed in the golden sand, the three — male, female, and earth — intermingling. Paul felt he and Mary were melting into the very soil on which they lay. Their movements covered them with sand, turning skin a soft golden. Dust within dust. They gave life to the deserted landscape. Mary felt, finally, a part of that landscape, a part of nature, completion of a seeking that had occupied her entire young life.

Michael, catching sight of them, and having checked all around the far periphery, moved back so as not to see them or hear anything they said, but stayed near enough to watch out for them. Bruce did the same. Elizabeth now saw him and watched with great amusement as he moved stealthily toward her, looking this way and that but still unaware of her presence. She decided not to get out of his way. Still, she was surprised that when he did bump into her, moving very slowly, he almost knocked her over. He was a large and powerful man, she reminded herself.

"What the hell?" Bruce said.

"*Shh!*" Elizabeth put her fingers to her lips. "You voyeur," she whispered. "You're so interested in what they're doing that you weren't even looking where you were going. If I were a lion, you'd be dead meat."

"*Shh* yourself," he whispered back. "Why do you think my clients always get home safely? Because I let them screw each other out in the wild by themselves in the middle of the night? God, the scents they'd give off would attract just about every predator in Africa."

"I didn't know it was your job to follow people around even when they're just sneaking off for a quickie," she hissed.

"It's hardly your job, either," he retorted. He put his hands around her waist, pulled her to him, and kissed her, ignoring her halfhearted attempts to push him away.

"Thank God you don't have the hang-ups your Yank colleagues have," he whispered. "You're you, and you know who you are."

"Now we can guard them together," she said. She saw the hornbill fly up and go past her, back toward their camp, back to his nest.

"Actually, Michael's looking out for them on the other side, and I saw Horst go off in their direction, too. So they're very well protected," he said. "We can tend to our own affairs."

She smothered a laugh and settled into his arms.

Far beyond, Michael could see a herd of elephants silently grazing in the moonlight, the big, torn-eared bull on the outside, near but not within the herd. Night birds of prey soared above, and a dry breeze blew briefly by. Michael picked up the scents of lion and leopard, but they were quite distant. He also picked up the scents of the two pairs of lovers, and in the darkness a slight smile crept over his lips.

CHAPTER 26

Counting Elephants

Somewhere in the eighties of the last century the idea got about that Physics, and those sciences that might be conceived as derivatives of Physics, held a monopoly on Reason; aesthetes had therefore to eschew Reason.

William Empson, *Seven Types of Ambiguity*

The true man of science will know nature better by his finer organization; he will smell, taste, see, hear, feel, better than other men. His will be a deeper and finer experience. We do not learn by inference and deduction and the application of mathematics to philosophy, but by direct intercourse and sympathy.

Henry David Thoreau

Early the next morning, Johnny, Bruce, Horst, and Paul left for the airstrip and a day of elephant counting. Michael stayed behind in charge of security and the camp. Davie, at Michael's request, had agreed to be a lookout for the people outside the camp doing fieldwork. The morning was still, the air calm. Only the continual call of African doves disturbed the quiet. A hawk soared on the rising air, then disappeared to the east. Aromatic plants perfumed the air. Yet there was an urgency to their actions.

Johnny and Bruce pushed the Cessna 182 out of the shade and onto the grass strip. "Gonna take a while to refuel and check out this 182, Horst," Johnny said, "so you're free to wander about for a while. Best to stay on the runway, though, considering Cecile."

Horst nodded his head, filled his pipe, lit it, and wandered down the runway.

"Refueling out here in the bush is a bit of a trick," Johnny said to Paul "You and Bruce can hand me the Jerry cans, one at a time, and I'll fill up each tank. Got to be very careful not to damage the wing." He took off his boots and climbed carefully to the top of the Land Rover and then onto a wing.

While they were doing this, Paul looked around to see where Horst had gone. He seemed quite a distance away and next to him was a man on a horse.

"Jesus, who's that?" Paul asked. "Maybe my eyesight's going, but he looks like he's dressed in leather — out here — and he's got a rifle and another long thing . . ."

"A sword, would you believe it?" Bruce said. "Well-known character. Been wandering around all his life. All my life as well."

"Always gives me the creeps," Johnny said from on top the plane's wing.

"We Maasai call him 'Shetani — devil," Michael said. "Old Shetani — the old man on horseback. "Some say 'watch out if you see Shetani. Something bad going to happen.' Sometimes when they see him they cry out 'enkeeya, enkeeya' — our word for death."

"Phooey, he's just a lonely old man living in his past," Bruce said. The Maasai elders say you only see Shetani inside Tsavo, never in the deep, beautiful green forests outside the park.

Michael responded, "Not that I believe it. Just a little of my 'anthropology studies,' as Elizabeth tells me I do."

Horst returned. "For God's sake, Horst, put out that pipe," Johnny shouted. "We don't need a brush fire."

"That man on horseback — that strange guy — what did he say?" Paul asked.

"Asked what were we doing here. Why did we have to use an airplane. That sort of thing," Horst answered. "Talked like to owned the place, tell the truth."

"Some Kikuyu and Maasai think he does," Michael put in.

After they fueled the plane, Johnny did a standard safety walkaround, Bruce and Paul watching. "I've been taking flying lessons back home in Oregon," Paul said. "Love it. So I know a little about these airplanes." Johnny seemed pleasantly surprised.

"Mostly trainers — 172s, small Pipers," Paul added, "Never got to these bigger 182s. But everybody back home loved them — said if you can stuff it in, you can fly off with it, no matter what the weight."

Johnny patted the cowling of the plane. "Just had her repaired, annual checkup, engine, overall. Look at the beautiful cushions — even prettied her up."

It was time for Bruce and Johnny to explain their elephant count procedures to Paul. Paul thought Johnny looked liked a British public-school graduate trying to dress like an American hippie. But as fun-loving, adventurous, and unpredictable as Johnny was about life in general, he took his research seriously. Johnny showed him an aluminum rod that stuck out horizontally just outside the front passenger's window. He handed Paul a stopwatch and a mechanical counter, a round chrome-plated device about as big as a large pocket watch. It had several buttons on the edge. One said START and the other said STOP. "Start the watch at the beginning of each flight leg when I tell you to," he said. "We'll fly outbound for half an hour by your stopwatch. When it says thirty minutes, tell me and I'll turn back on a parallel track just alongside the one we followed out. After you tell me when to turn, start the watch again. Each time the bar crosses an elephant, you click the hand counter.

He explained that Paul did not have to look at the counter, just keep his eyes on the ground. The whole operation had been calibrated so Johnny knew the area the bar covered for each hundred feet above the ground. "The other people doing this use just one rod and one counter, but I've had two installed, one for the right front seat and one for the right rear seat." He smiled, pleased with his airplane's outfitting, Paul thought. "They've been separately calibrated," Johnny continued. "Bruce will handle the rear-seat counting — that's a little harder to do".

Paul asked how they had checked the accuracy of what they were doing. "Every way we can," Johnny replied. "Comparing counts of the same herd from the air and on the ground. Counting houses on the outskirts of Nairobi. Counting cattle over ranches where we knew the total number." He told Paul that Bruce had done this with him many times, and that Bruce and Paul would take separate counts and compare them. "Today I'm going to take Bruce's counts as correct, but after today we'll take the average of the two. We'll keep an eye out for signs of poaching, too."

"We're going to do transects," he continued, "starting along the Galana River and then flying back and forth on parallel lines. Better take a leak now if you need to, because we'll be up two hours at least." He looked at Paul. "I'm guessing that since you're working on a pilot's license, we don't have to worry about airsickness with you."

Paul nodded.

""I'll navigate and mark on the flight map where we've been. We've got a lot of ground to cover in the short time we're here, especially if we have to cut our time even shorter to make the trip to Voi." He brushed back his long hair. "I think you guys brought along enough fuel in the trailers. It's the time I'm worrying about." He looked at Bruce, and was surprised to see that Bruce didn't seem to hear him and was looking down the dirt runway. Always the silent thinker, Johnny thought. Now what's bothering Bruce?

Michael mentioning Elizabeth put her on Bruce's mind, and he'd been thinking about her a lot. He was torn between how much he liked her and felt they were well suited for each other, and how much he needed to be free to pursue the elusive nature of this wilderness. It was good to be with just these men and away from Elizabeth for a little while, even if he had to put up with Horst sitting next to him, tight in the back of the plane.

Johnny pushed the throttle forward and the plane accelerated fast, bouncing over the rough ground and lifting quickly into the air. Almost immediately he put the plane in a left-hand turning climb, quick and exciting. Commiphora trees and thornbushes fell away. Tsavo looked drier and drier as the plane rose. Bright green faded within the dust to a light brown with a garnishing of green from the scattering of grasses.

Paul got his first look at Tsavo from the air. Along the Galana River he saw dead trees, some fallen and some standing, done in by elephants as they starved to death during the big drought ten years ago. Along the river he saw live shrubs and young trees that were a darker green, creating a meandering highlighted line against the plains.

The plane was buffeted in the updrafts and downdrafts. Soon they were a thousand feet above the terrain. Johnny shouted over the engine noise. "I'll set us up on a line along the river. We'll use our campsite as the starting point. I'll call out 'Count' when we pass that point, and you two go to it! We'll begin a thousand feet above the ground. It'll give us a wider view, and we're less likely to spook the animals." Horst, looking at the window to his left, paid little attention to what the other three said to each other.

Johnny leveled off, and the plane bumped along. "Turbulence is an experimental error up here," he said, then moments later shouted, "Count!"

Paul clicked his stopwatch. Below, only a few hints of their campsite were visible. One tent, wisps of smoke. Mary, a tiny figure, waved gaily, and Elizabeth moved her arm like a semaphore. The men were harder to identify. Their entire islet of civilization was a mere few specks within Tsavo. Still, Paul wished it were even less visible to any unwanted visitors. But these were quickly passing thoughts, as he felt that he was competing with Bruce to see who could count the most elephants.

Disappointingly, for the first twenty minutes on the stopwatch, they saw no animals, just more of the bleak land empty of animate life, a tawny lion-colored landscape as Paul had seen it when he first looked out over Tsavo's plains from Lugard Falls. Then a few elephants came into view. One, two, three clicks. A wandering group of males. Five more minutes passed. A large herd appeared ahead, and as the bar crossed the images of the animals, Paul clicked his counter as fast as he could, hoping he wasn't missing any. At exactly thirty minutes, Paul called out the time and Johnny turned the plane 180° and flew back on a compass heading that kept them flying in the opposite direction from where they had come, with the aluminum rods on the north side, away from the river.

Like so much scientific observation, the work itself was tedious and repetitious; it was the male companionship Paul was enjoying, and the competition as well. But he found, as usual, that the requirements of exact counting made him aware of details of the countryside that he otherwise would have missed, and these took his mind off all his concerns. They passed over an oryx, then another, and saw a smaller animal, probably a bat-eared fox. He would not have noticed these lone animals as a tourist on a flight from one park to another, he thought, nor the sad vegetation. A casual traveler would have found it simply dull and turned to a book or a magazine to pass the time. Tsavo's many stories and its surface, the face of a wounded world, would have been invisible to them.

It's one of the contradictions of the late twentieth century, Paul thought. The technology of flight, the realization of one of humanity's greatest fantasies — to hang like a hawk, soar like some ancient wide-winged dinosaur — was now considered interference with nature. Noise pollution. Yes, indeed it was. To most people, he thought, an airplane is just a kind of cocoon — they sleep in it, watch movies, pull down the window shades and wish the flight were over. But, he thought, it gives me, Johnny, and Bruce an insight into Tsavo, lets us observe in ways we never could have in an earlier time. He took a quick glance to the back. Now even Horst was watching everything out the window.

Oops! His attention was slipping. A lone elephant passed under his aluminum bar. Click. Then nothing. They continued to search the landscape and click the counters. Then they were crossing over very devastated land, barren, harsh. Paul's spirits fell like the plane's sudden descents in turbulent downdrafts. They were wrapped in the aluminum skin of the plane, packaged as it were, isolated, protected, separated f rom the drought of life below them. Paul glanced to the horizon. Awful emptiness. The ancient mariner could not feel more desolation, greater sadness.

"Hell of a view!" Johnny shouted. "Depresses the shit out of you, doesn't it? Your face is as long as a giraffe's neck. I felt that way myself when I came here right after the drought. Still feel that way." He stuck a chocolate cookie in front of Paul's mouth while he flew the plane with his left hand. "Sugar'll bring your spirits up till we can get a drink." He gave Paul a friendly pat on the shoulder. Paul heard Bruce's counter click and looked down. Several more elephants passed underneath. Click. Click.

* * *

Casually tossing his hand grenade from hand to hand as if it were a ball, Joseph, standing next to his Land Cruiser at the edge of a woodland facing the devastated land, watched Johnny's airplane make its long transit one way and then back the other. He snuffed out his campfire, probably visible from the air. The usual jealousy about the airplane wasn't on his mind. Instead he was preoccupied with Horst's suggestions and the idea of Horst getting in contact with one of the big international wildlife groups. It seemed a golden opportunity for him, to finally become somebody as important as Bruce and Michael. And it might get him into a position where he could make more money. He could move to the other side of all of this, become one of the conservationists. And he'd have a chance to be a good guy finally.

He watched and waited until the plane flew away to the east and circled over what he knew would be a landing strip. Sure enough, the airplane noises soon ceased. He decided it was time to make his move to find his guys and get them started just searching out the jumbos, no shooting.

* * *

After two hours, Johnny marked their location on the flight map he held between his knees, and shouted, "Stop counting!"

They flew across the strip and followed a standard rectangular landing pattern. Johnny brought the plane to a surprisingly smooth touchdown, then taxied over near the trees where he had parked the plane before. They climbed out in silence.

"Not many," Bruce said.

Paul looked at his counter. "Two forty-two."

"Two forty-eight," Bruce said. They both noted the two numbers in their notebooks. Paul felt embarrassed, outdone by the experts. "Pretty close," Bruce said, patting him on the back, "Not bad for a beginner."

"We'll have you up with the best of them in no time," Johnny said. "Not many jumbos," he said. "They used to be everywhere fifteen years ago. Hope we find them on our next flight."

They ate lunch, and made two more flights in the afternoon. Johnny again approached the landing strip.

"And now on to Voi?" Horst shouted from the back of the plane.

Johnny turned briefly to look at Horst and said, "Sorry. I got so caught up in the elephant survey that I completely forgot about your trip to Voi. But we've got plenty of fuel, but it's getting late to fly to Voi today. We'll take you there tomorrow."

He turned the plane and headed back to the landing strip, circling the strip to check for stray animals and checking the wind direction by looking at the way grasses leaned toward the ground and leaves blew on trees.

Horst nodded. Actually, he would be glad to get out of the small airplane. It had been cramped and almost claustrophobic. But it was helpful for him to have seen what the scientists actually did. He was sure he could use it one way or another to push his own agenda. And one more day didn't matter.

As they drove the Land Rover back to camp, Paul was filled with a mixture of strong emotions: elation over contact with the air and the view of the terrain and the time with Johnny and Bruce, two of the world's experts on elephants. They were famous among Paul's colleagues, and here he was spending time with them, flying with them. At the same time he felt an immense sadness over the forlorn countryside. He did not know whether he wanted to smile or cry.

"Hell of a place, isn't it?" Johnny said. "Moves you every which way. A little Scotch'll cure it. I know how you feel — it grabs me every time." An oryx passed in front of the Land Rover, and Johnny veered off the track and charged after it over low scrub, grinning like a kid playing with a pet dog. "I love to see them running!" he shouted over the sounds of the Land Rover's metal screeching against the shrubs. But he soon tired of the game and turned away.

Through it all, Bruce remained silent in the backseat, lost in his own thoughts, thinking about Elizabeth and why he had come back to Tsavo. Too many painful memories, that was for sure.

At camp, Johnny parked the Land Rover, jumped out, and strode jauntily over to Mary. While they chatted, Paul sat down with his data book and made some calculations. Later, he spoke with the rest of the group.

"Based on our first counts, there are twenty thousand elephants, give or take ten thousand," he said.

"Give or take ten thousand!" Horst snorted. "But that means — according to you, that is — there could be, um, as few as ten thousand elephants in real trouble or as many as thirty thousand." He walked over to Paul, put an arm around his shoulder, and looked at Paul's notebook. "For God's sake, isn't that how many there were before the drought? I apologize for repeating myself, but this is just a waste of time. In the time we have, you'll never get a number that means anything."

"I said based on our first counts. It's just the first day."

"We may as well sit around and drink and throw dice — the winner writes whatever he wants in the report, or get the hell away before the poachers find us again."

"What we're doing — it's the only way," Paul said.

"We'll get a better estimate," Bruce said.

"We're using the amount of grazing and browsing on the plants, too," Mary pointed out, "to see whether the elephants are overeating their food supply."

Horst lit his pipe and walked away, shaking his head.

CHAPTER 27

Voi

Cities give us the illusion of self-sufficiency and independence and of the possibility of physical continuity without conscious renewal.

Historian Lewis Mumford

Johnny, Paul, and Horst reached Voi in midmorning and walked up a dusty street that led from the airstrip into the town. Paul found this sudden return to a town disorienting. A mangy dog crossed the street, squatted, and relieved itself, leaving a pile of turds in the dirt road. The light seemed different, hazier, probably from the dust that a town full of people stirred up, he thought. They approached the town market, a dusty square with a few stalls and people hawking wares, some sitting on sheepskins on the ground, some holding sheepskins up to sell. Paul was distracted by them, and Johnny and drifted away. Suddenly Paul was surrounded by a group of children, each carrying one or two things to sell and all shouting at him at the same time.

"Sir, buy this basket from me! Please, sir!"

"Sir, buy this woven hat from me! Good for the sun! Shouldn't go out without a hat here! Please, sir!"

"Sir, buy this basket! My sister made it, specially. See? Well made! Buy it!"

Johnny was suddenly at his side, guiding him away and speaking to the boys in Swahili, making them laugh.

"They would have sold you something for sure," Johnny said, "at an exorbitant price, probably ten times what it was worth. They always do."

Paul, feeling uneasy in the surroundings, was glad for Johnny's intervention.

Johnny guided Paul and Horst to the Tsavo Park office. Johnny opened the door and called to the park ranger inside. "Mac?" A tidily dressed man with a neat mustache emerged out of nowhere. Johnny smiled to himself as he introduced Horst and Paul, making a point of noting Horst was representing the IESC.

"So," was all the ranger replied and curtly motioned to a side office. "There's only one phone line available to visitors. Keep it short, please." Horst darted for the desk and phone. Somewhat off put but also oddly amused by Horst's haste, Paul said he'd help Johnny get supplies while Horst finished his phone calls.

Horst, wiped the dusty desktop with some paper towels from a stack he retrieved from a corner table, then took out his handkerchief and wiped his face. He took a small address book from the inside pocket of his corduroy sport jacket and laid it neatly on the desk, glanced around the room. Paint was peeling from the walls. A poster, torn and creased — from some safari trip Horst guessed — showed a huge elephant. Another poster showed Victoria Falls. He was crowded against a dirty brown four-drawer file cabinet. The desk he sat at was bare and the drawers scratched with peoples' initials. Pathetic, he thought.

He picked up the phone and tried dialing the international operator. There were crackles and hums and several false starts, but he finally got through to the headquarters of the International Endangered Species Coalition in Washington, D. C. But the president, his old friend Jim, was out of the office. Horst described the urgency of his call and the assistant said he'd try to find him — to call back in fifteen minutes or so.

He tried the second number. He heard an intern brimming with good cheer announce, "International Ecological Fund!"

"Is that Gibbons? It's Horst here in Africa. Get me Gary Anderson, if you will, please." He sat back in the chair and didn't have long to wait.

"Anderson? Horst here. Well, that's what I was calling about. Things are going terrible back here, truth be told. We've been under attack by poachers, lions, elephants, you name it."

He listened, then interrupted. He had a lot to say.

"I need you to make some calls. Get us out of here. This scientific team you helped assemble, to put it broadly, is inept — useless really — don't understand the big picture. Not a clue. Intent on staying, they are, when some international big-time poachers are killing elephants all round us and worse, shooting at us. As if this was a kid's sandbox and they could just go ahead and play their science-in-the-sand game, counting elephants, picking leaves off the trees and shrubs, digging in the soil to see what it's made of."

He listened, his face becoming more set.

"Yeah, well, they're naïve. Bruce Airley might suspect the government is involved but he doesn't have any specifics. Yes, *that* Bruce Airley. Real son-of-a-bitch." Horst paused while he listened to the man at the other end of the phone line. "No, no. Can't say Bruce is stupid. No, more, well, infatuated with the jumbos and this barren Tsavo landscape. Can't quite explain it. Like he's seeking something. . . . What?" Horst paused again, listening, "No, not piles of ivory or evidence of the poaching. Nothing physical. Something a little more weird than anything else. I told them I'd get the IECS and other allies to help by contacting the powers that be, send in some troops or such, assure shelter for Bruce and gang 'til they get their damned data." Horst paused. "Even though you and I know that's not going to happen.

"We'll have to handle this whole situation very carefully. I have a lot to tell you. Maybe you should take some notes since I don't know when I'll get to a phone again."

* * *

Johnny and Paul wandered through Voi, making some purchases to resupply the team — fresh meat, vegetables and fruit, and a few other things that the team had begged them to get. They finished with time to spare, so Johnny suggested they have a cold drink. They bought six bottles of Coca-Cola in a little store, no more than a shack, and sat outside on two dingy chairs in the shady overhang of the roof.

"Twelve hours from bottle to throttle — that's the rule. Otherwise I'd have a beer," Johnny said, his usual jaunty self. He tipped his chair back and put his feet up on another one. He looked around, then settled his eyes on Paul, who sipped at his Coke quietly, thinking about what he would say on his phone conversation. Without ice, the drink tasted flat. The town seemed the worst of all possible worlds. It was neither city nor Tsavo. It was poor and dusty, without beauty, neither civilization nor nature.

Paul was uneasy about the phone call he needed to make. He finished his Coke and stood. It had been close to an hour since they left Horst.

"Horst has had enough time," he said. "Let's get going."

Surprised by Paul's sudden urgency, Johnny took his Coke, hoisted his backpack with the remaining bottles of Coke, and followed him down the dusty street. "You got it, team leader."

Soon they were at the park office. Johnny went in to check on Horst, who was sitting back in the rickety chair, his feet on the desk, pulling on his pipe.

"Need to make another call. They weren't there but should be soon."

"Let's give Paul a chance, then you can try again," Johnny said, not waiting for an answer. Horst reluctantly stood and took his time leaving the room, bumping into Paul on his way out.

Johnny was sitting on a bench in front of the camp office. He motioned for Horst to join him. Something told him it would be best if Horst wasn't poking around in Paul's business. He'd known Horst too long as a capable gatherer of information that he would use in various ways, usually to his own advantage. Better safe than sorry, he thought.

Horst joined him and motioned to the Coke. "Got any more of those?"

"Yep," Johnny said, pulling one from his backpack.

* * *

Paul called Billy, his closest colleague at the International Ecological Fund, who was also one of his best friends. Billy's voice sounded distant and cold. "We've been hearing you're having some trouble," he said.

Trying to keep it as light as possible, Paul took a breath before responding.

"Big trouble. The poachers are heavily armed, which means there's got to be some big money behind them."

"Gossip is that the problems are your fault, Paul," Billy said, "and Bruce what's-his-name too."

"What? *My* fault? That there are big-time poachers out here?"

Billy told him there were other things being said — that he couldn't run an expedition; that there was confusion; that he was wasting time. "They're saying that the answer's obvious but you're doing all these unnecessary measurements and risking everybody's life."

"Are you saying we should pull out now?"

"Do you have enough to write a report?"

"Not the way I see it."

"Gossip's against you on that. What I hear is 'if Paul can't write the report now, he'd better stay.' Not very nice. Tell you what. I'll do what I can. It's terrible, really. I mean your life's on the line and what are people saying? You should stay there and get killed over a bunch of data? Over a bunch of elephants? But it won't look good for you if you return empty-handed. Would anybody want to fund you after that?"

"And to think we went into this for some kind of truth. Right now I don't even remember what that was all about."

"Don't get that downhearted, Paul. It was about science and knowledge and nature. Kant and the limits of knowledge applied to ecology. That was what you used to talk about."

"But I didn't expect to get killed over it. People are shooting at us. This is not backyard cops-and-robbers — they're *serious*. Are you asking me to get killed over a research report?"

"No, of course not. It just doesn't sound as dangerous as you make it from this end. Your decision. But with the talk around here, if you come back without a good story my private advice to you is, it won't be good."

"You came to *me*. This was *your* idea. I just suggested how we might do it. At the time you liked it."

"That was then. Now there's bad news circulating about you. You can guess the source — name beginning with 'H'."

Paul needed only a few moments to digest that. He nodded bitterly and said that if they were to stay, they would need more money, equipment and protection. He asked for two more vehicles and some armed guards. "I've got a list —"

"Paul, you know I'd really like to, but I can't buck the establishment. Too much is going against you."

"*I've* got almost a dozen people who could end up dead through no fault of mine, and you're not going to help out?"

"I'll do what I can, Paul, but Washington politics, New York money — you know how it is. Hardball stuff back here."

"Not like being shot at."

There was a long silence. Then, "I'll do my best. But to be honest, I don't see much at this end. Call me at the end of the week."

"Don't you get it? Three of us flew to Voi to call for help. We have to go back to the others and we don't have a phone booth out there. We have some kind of two-way radio, but you can't reach us on that."

"Isn't there somebody we can reach? Maybe at the museum in Nairobi?"

"Then what? He'll fly down to give us a phone message? I don't think so."

"Look, Paul, I've got to go. I'm late for a meeting. Like I said, I'll do my best. You can come out if you want to. Try to let me know what you decide." The line went dead.

Paul put down the phone and looked out a dirty window to the barren plains beyond. He'd heard of the politics different scientists had faced, but this seemed extreme. They were facing real dangers and the choices his colleague framed were no wins. Had to get a good report. Had to do it while trying to stay alive and with no help. And what was Horst up to? Could whatever he said in his phone call already be circulating? He was ashen when he joined Horst and Johnny.

"You look like a ghost," Johnny said, with a start. Horst wondered if his report to the International Ecological Fund had traveled that fast.

"News is not so good," Paul said, ignoring Horst. "I need to think." He walked down the street as Horst hopped up and headed into the building.

Johnny stood and followed Paul. Never a dull moment, he thought, can't even come into town to resupply without some sort of drama.

Horst picked up the phone and tried the number again. This time the assistant, quite pleased with himself, put on Horst's old friend Jim, who asked how things were going.

"Just what I expected," Horst said. "The whole area's devastated. They're all out there trying to count elephants. You and I know we have to grab any numbers we can and use them to our advantage and to the advantage of the elephants. It's all perfectly clear. Vegetation destroyed. Don't see many animals of any kind. It's a political issue — yes, yes. They want to find out if the number of elephants is up or down from the time of the drought. Imagine trying to do that now. Believe me, a one-day fly-over should be enough. We've already done that. But they think they have to have some kind of statistically valid estimate, and all that technical garbage . . . What?" The line crackled.

Outside, Paul suddenly turned from his head-down meandering on the outskirts of Voi. Johnny was a short distance behind him. "Horst is talking to someone else, spreading some sort of crap. We need to know what it is."

He started to run to the park office, Johnny following along at a leisurely pace. Whatever was happening wouldn't be changed by his hurrying along. Horst was probably up to something. Nothing particularly new. They'd have to talk with Bruce about it.

* * *

Jim asked what Horst thought they should do. He replied that they should have the entire area declared a World Wilderness Preserve, that the whole matter was politics not science. "Get the aides on the Hill behind the idea; get an article in the *New York Times*."

"So, what's the approach?" Jim asked.

"For one thing, there are poachers out here and if anything they are more of a threat to the elephants than the stupid scientists. . . . "

"Christ. Poachers on top of the rest?"

"You better believe it. And I can't leave the group. I need to be here to protect the elephants and be in a position to report Bruce Airley's ineptitude. Paul what's his name ineptitude, too. I need you to make some calls. The government here may be worth something to us. Bruce thinks they may be funding this new round of poachers. They've got a new twin-engine plane, bigger than anybody's ever seen out here, for Pete sake, and those new Toyota Land Cruisers. Clearly, they can be bought. And we may be able to leverage media and public sentiment and possibly our own government. Could be a great way to get coverage of what we've been doing for the last ten years or so. It's almost hand cut for us."

Jim sat up in his chair. Suddenly it became clear to him. Horst, as always, had found a way to move their agenda forward. Butchered elephants would make great front-page coverage, with the IESC reporting the slaughter and providing the answer — a wilderness preserve to protect them.

"Horst, you're a genius. Even when you're out camping in the dust, you figure out a way to work the system. But it sounds dangerous. Better look both ways."

"It's dangerous, but you know me," Horst said. "What we may need is to partner with the government here, corrupt as they are. I'm working this local guy — a small-time poacher who knows his way around Tsavo. This guy can help position us and provide the inside information we need. Ironically, he went to school years ago with Bruce and the Maasai he works with. Doesn't much like them and could use some money. So he can help once we get rid of them. ....
The team is almost laughable."

He described each of the people with great derision, chuckling as he did so. This was much better. Talking on the phone to his colleague in Washington made him feel like he was back on his home turf, away from Tsavo, from this depressing, drought-stricken land.

Paul reached the outside window to the room Horst was in and quietly stood to the side. Horst was such a blow hard, it won't be hard to hear, he said to himself. And he was right.

"And Paul's brought these two women – useless, completely useless . . . What? . . . Oh not useless for that, no. In fact, do you know this Mary what's-her-name — Weaver? Looks like Marilyn Monroe with freckles . . . Yes, yes, well too bad you aren't out here."

Somehow Paul wasn't surprised. Elizabeth had mentioned Horsts' reputation. Still, it made him a little sick. He'd like to go in and give Horst a good whacking. But now wasn't the time or place. Maybe he could get enough evidence to get Horst removed from the expedition. Clearly, Horst had been spreading some sort of self-serving bullshit. He needed to know what it was.

Johnny came round the corner of the building and motioned for Paul to move away from the window just as the ranger was coming out of the building. It wouldn't do for the ranger to see team members spying on each other. Paul did as asked, indicating to Johnny that it would not be for long.

"What made you name Paul to lead a study like this? He's weak and easily manipulated by Bruce," Horst said and then listened for a minute.

"Get Paul removed, and Bruce, too. That needs to happen for any of our agenda to move forward. Put me in charge. We'll do a quick survey and be back in a week with all the ammunition you need to get international protection for Tsavo, and some money in here for restoration."

Jim cut in and told Horst that some people in California working on the condors had used Davie as an expert advisor. Horst thought Jim was joking. But Jim said he better go easy with Davie. "On second thought, Davie could be a big help," Jim said. "He knows Tsavo well, is the word. Could replace Bruce as your guide around the park. Pretty good shot as well, they say, killing game and putting them out for vultures to feed on. Could be your personal guard, if it came to that."

The ranger out of sight, Paul moved back to the window, motioning to Johnny to join him. They heard Horst tell Jim where they were camped.

"Yes," said Horst. "Credibility. That's the ticket. Once everything is in order, they can pick me up and I'll get out of here. Yes, that Johnny has a radio — his wife'll know how to contact him."

Outside Paul whispered to Johnny that he thought Horst was setting them up. Clearly he had no respect for the team. He was hoping to get an idea of what tact Horst was taking so he could report to Bruce.

"What do you have on Elizabeth Esker?" Horst asked.

There was a pause and soon Anderson was back on the line.

"She's solid but known to be feisty."

"Feisty, you say. I'd say no shit Sherlock if it wasn't such a cliché," Horst said. "What kind of contacts does she have?"

Paul had had enough. He motioned to Johnny that he was going in.

Seeing Paul at the door, Horst quickly finished his conversation, hung up and turned to them. He smiled and apologized for not being able to help with the supplies. "Had to keep in touch with the people in Washington. Let them know everything's going well. Keep the money flowing."

Johnny was uncomfortable — he disliked these political types and Paul might be right about what Horst was up to — but he just smiled at him. "That's your end of it, isn't it? Our international representative."

Paul looked around the room. Horst was clearly lying, holding something back, he could feel it. What had he told the international groups? What kind of trouble was he brewing?

Johnny walked into the main area and thanked the ranger. Horst shook hands with the ranger, thanking him for the use of the phone and telling him how much he appreciated the facility.

Outside, the sunlight blinded them and the heat blasted them. Once they had put on sunglasses and their eyes had adjusted to the light, they saw that the open plains were visible beyond the end of the street. Brown soil, scattered trees and bushes seemed to stretch to the end of the world. A wild emptiness. Paul felt a sudden strong desire to get back to the camp, back into the wild. It seemed safer than being stuck near Horst, and the telephone. And what would he find back at their camp? In spite of Bruce's belief that the poachers would not be bothering them, perhaps they had come anyway. Perhaps this time they had killed someone?

It took a while for them to load the airplane with groceries and Jerry cans of fuel. Johnny seemed his usual carefree self. As soon as they finished, the three were back in the air, Paul looking out the window all the way back, squinting in the bright sunlight, trying to see their camp.

CHAPTER 28

Music in the Night

What will happen to this earth depends very largely upon man's capacities as a dramatist and a creative artist.

Lewis Mumford

The discovery of prehistoric flutes made of animal bone in France and Slovenia, ranging in age from 4,000 to 53,000 years old, demonstrates that ancient civilizations devoted considerable time and skill to constructing complicated musical instruments. . . . Many different types of scales can be played on reconstructed prehistoric flutes, and the sounds are pure and haunting. . . . It is quite possible that humans have been making music for several hundred thousand years.

From an article in *Science* magazine[2]

Horst strode into the tent to the meeting he had convened. Best to appear upfront and get to his news as soon as possible. Mary and Paul were sitting comfortably close to each other on folding chairs, Paul's arm around the back of Mary's chair. Horst tried not to let that annoy him. The others were spread around at the camping tables, chatting amiably after their dinner.

"The news is good," Horst said, as he lit his pipe. "Talked with both IESC and Ecology Fund. They understand the danger we're in and are commiserating with each other about how they can help. There's talk of making this an international wildlife preserve, but of course, that would only happen down the line. Now they are seeing what they can do to get a handle on these new poachers. They do have some inroads to the government here, so if there's any connection, they will do their best to convince the government that being involved with these exploitive types isn't in their best interests. First order of business, they made clear to me: control those damned poachers. And they trust me to get that done. Said they'd provide support I needed."

"Like what?" Davie asked.

"Whatever we need — money,"

"Guns? Artillery? Bigger airplanes?" Davie asked.

"Well, this is international treaty stuff. Involves nation-state independence. We can't have our non-profits arming people down here without some official approval."

"More damned talk," Davie said.

"So what about our interests? Are they going to do anything to help us finish our work?" Paul said, trying to remain calm.

"Of course. These groups want to protect the elephants. They appreciate science and sound reports that help to protect the species. They'll do what is necessary to accomplish that."

"So when will we know more about what they will be able to accomplish?" Bruce asked, wondering what was going on with Paul. Clearly, something had happened to him on the trip to Voi.

"I'll need to make another trip to Voi in a few days to find out," Horst replied, filling his pipe and lighting it, pacing back and forth behind the tables like a general in charge. "Hopefully, Johnny will be able to take me." He looked at Johnny.

"I'll be 'mazed if those groups lift a finger ta help," Davie offered. "From what I've seen, they've got their own agendas, the S-O-Bs — stuff that don't align with us Homo sapiens. Some bureaucrats in a Washington office, never been out in the wild, prob'ly never even walked off a goddam sidewalk into a park's woods. Jesus Christ almighty."

"Actually, Jim had good things to say about you, Davie," Horst said, glad to have the ammunition.

"That so?"

"It seems you're known widely for your condor work," Horst said and smiled broadly at him.

"Well, they got one thing right, I guess. Well, do your thing Horst. Whatever," he said, walking out of the tent.

"We'll continue our work then, taking every precaution we can," said Bruce, getting up to follow Davie. "And hope for the best."

He looked back to see Paul talking quietly to Mary. He'd have to check in with him soon. As expected, Horst likely didn't achieve anything that might actually help them. But he'd had his chance to establish his place in the group. Maybe that would satisfy him for a while.

Outside Howie was sitting quietly by a small campfire. Others joined him.

As darkness fell, Davie left the campfire, took a black plastic box from an aluminum suitcase he had set on the hood of a Land Rover, and put it carefully on the ground. Horst watched with concern as Davie opened the box. Damn, it was a record player! What next out here? Davie opened another compartment in the aluminum case and withdrew a record.

Elizabeth and Bruce were now watching Davie, too, and Horst walked over near them, standing as if he was still in charge, as Davie took a clean cloth from a pocket inside the case, sprayed a little liquid on it from a plastic bottle, and delicately — lovingly, Elizabeth thought — wiped the record. This must mean a hell of a lot to him, she thought. It's the only neat and clean thing about him. He turned and she saw him in profile. Beneath the grime, he actually had some fine features. Grecian nose, well-proportioned face, high cheekbones. Clean him up and he wouldn't look bad at all.

In the darkness just beyond the glow of the fire, Davie put the LP on the spindle, turned on the machine, and placed the needle on the edge of the spinning record. Cicadas called in the night. A lion whumped its husky roar in the distance. Wind rustled the fever tree leaves. The campfire crackled. Suddenly, loud music came out of Davie's record player: a piano and a saxophone. Modern jazz. It seemed mournful on the Tsavo plains, Elizabeth thought. Without anything to echo against, the music fell on the soil and was absorbed like rain on the waterless plains. Annoyed, Horst beat a quick retreat into the darkness.

When the record ended, Davie rejoined the campfire circle.

"What the hell was that?" Horst asked, returning and again lighting his pipe.

"Jazz," Davie said. "Dave Brubeck. Piano, saxophone, an' drums." He walked over to Mary, who was sitting on a small tarpaulin on the ground, writing in her notebook and examining column after column of numbers, the data she had gathered. She smiled up at him, then returned to her numbers.

"Like a graveyard 'round here," Davie said, sitting down next to her and lighting a cigarette. "Nobody talkin' except about trouble. Nobody doin' nothin' for fun. Pretty sad. I say, ta hell with it, at least for a little while. Little good music get your minds off your troubles." He kicked at the sandy soil with his boot and stared at the group.

Mary looked over to him. "Davie, that's a nice thing you've just said. How'd you happen to have that record player on this trip?"

"I carry that thing everywhere," he answered. "Listen to it whenever I get a chance. Not many chances out in the bush studyin' bloody vultures." He looked at Mary longingly, hoping that the music would charm her. Then he saw Horst staring at him.

"Is it safe to make all that noise when there are poachers about?" Horst asked.

"Ain't noise, first of all," Davie replied. "And if they're int'rested at all, the poachers know exactly where we are."

"Here we are in this huge wilderness, surrounded by nature," Horst said, trying to be polite. He hated this kind of music.

"Horst thinks your music is spoiling the wilderness," Elizabeth explained.

Davie took a drag on his cigarette. "Sorry, Horst. I woulda thought you'd like a little culture out here, since you're a cultured city person. Jazz. I like it — warms my heart. Tell the truth, it's a break from this godforsaken, dried-up graveyard — no rain, no bars. I'm out here in the wilderness, as you call it, all day long an' all night long. Sometimes I need a little break."

Horst puffed on his pipe. "Well, my good man, I can understand the need f or a break." He sat down next to Mary, separating Davie from her. There was nothing Horst would have liked better at that moment than to be in a restaurant in Geneva sipping a good wine with Mary next to him, dressed nicely, short skirt, tight blouse. For a few moments that was all he could think about.

"An' anyways, people been makin' music of one kind or another out here for thousands of years — maybe hundreds of thousands of years," Davie answered.

"Probably sang before they talked," Howie put in. "My theory anyway. Heard the birds. Think about them Neanderthals wanderin' around here. Men trying to court the women. See them listenin' to these birds and lookin' at them. One of them starts whistlin' and singin' and the good-likin' girl — to a Neanderthal, mind — turns around and smiles. Yep. Didn't need words back then." Howie grinned and pulled his multi-colored hat down low over his head, something he did when he knew he was pulling somebody's leg.

Horst had never thought about music that way. He thought of Tsavo as a place whose only sounds were the wind and wildlife, a romantic notion, he thought.

"When did the first girl dance?" Davie asked, looking at Mary. She listened in silence. "When did the first man take up two rocks an' bang out a rhythm?"

"I gotta record from West Africa, some great percussion, moves my soul. An' y'know what it is? It's one guy singin' an' scratchin' a rock with a tin can. He gets more music outta that tin can than you get science outta that bottle of gin, Horst," Davie continued.

"I would never would think of a rock scraping a tin can as music or natural," Horst said. His words came out a little slurred. He took a swallow of gin from his canteen. It was the lowlifes, like Davie, and the blacks — he looked at Michael — who thought that sort of thing was music, or culture, but he was careful to say nothing.

"I heard that in one of them caves in France there's a fourteen-thousand-year-old cave painting of a man's leg dancing," Davie went on, enjoying his own reverie. "There musta been music with that dance. Is that old enough — long enough — to be natural?"

The male hornbill, disturbed by the strange calls coming from the phonograph, flew from his tree and circled Davie. Mary caught the beat of its wings flickering in the campfire and saw it settle on a tree limb away from its nest to watch Davie.

Before Horst could reply, the music ended and Davie rose to walk back to the Land Rover and take the record off the spindle. Wiping it again, he put it back in its sleeve. He moved away from them, farther into the darkness, and suddenly a beautiful voice began to sing.

> *Where do de blues come from?*
> *Where do de blues come from?*
> *Come from de lowlands*
> *Where my folk are from.*

Elizabeth could just make him out. He sings too? All that dirt and he can sing?

> *Gotta save de blues*
> *Blues never done nobody no harm.*
> *Goin' back to the lowlands,*
> *Goin' where de blues is from.*

Davie came back to the dying fire and sat on the ground. Elizabeth asked him where he had learned that song. A blues aficionado, she was not familiar with it.

"That song tells it all," Davie said, sitting again near Mary. "The blues come from the lowlands, the lowlands bred the blues — music in nature, nature in music."

"That's just some dark, muddy river song," Horst corrected him, "written by some guy in a city ghetto. What'd he know about nature?"

Bruce surprised Elizabeth by going over to Davie and saying, "Play something we can sing to — what is that Irish record you have?"

"Clancy Brothers," Davie smiled, and soon Bruce and Davie were singing harmony to a song new to Elizabeth, about fishing on the high seas.

Howie joined in, then Johnny. More gin was poured, and they sang more songs. Singing eased Bruce's yearning, quieted him.

Horst disappeared, probably back to his tent, Elizabeth thought.

Michael contributed a Maasai warrior song, Elizabeth and Mary sang too, several ballads, and finally Bruce and Davie sang a song about whaling — "The Greenland Fishery," they called it. Elizabeth would always remember that moment, with the campfire behind Bruce and Davie, spotlighting them as they sang about a failed attempt to catch a whale.

Davie went back to the Land Rover and put another record on the phonograph. Elizabeth smiled, recognizing Fleetwood Mac's *Rumors*. Rock-and-roll filled the campsite. The group had finally coalesced, Bruce thought, not surprisingly over music.

Paul had enjoyed Davie and Bruce's singing, and he hated to put a cramp in the moment, but he needed to talk with Bruce. He followed Bruce and Elizabeth as they made their way to Bruce's tent.

"Bruce?" Paul called out.

"Yep," Bruce said, "I've been meaning to talk with you as well." He gave Elizabeth a quick smile and turned back to Paul.

"See you later," Elizabeth said with a wink.

"Over this way," Paul indicated. He wanted to make sure they were out of hearing distance.

"I take it you weren't too pleased with your trip to Voi."

"For one thing, the Ecology Fund seems not to be willing to help us, despite what Horst says."

"No shocker to me."

"They've been getting negative reports about the science and what we're likely to accomplish. Seems like I'm taking the blame. Horst had talked with them before me, I bet. There wasn't much I could do to change their minds. And I heard him deriding members of the group to whoever he was talking to."

"What members?

"Mary, for one. Then he asked what contacts Elizabeth had."

Bruce's eyes went steely. He didn't speak for a while.

"We'll see about that."

"I'm sure he had words about all of us. I couldn't listen to all he said."

"I'm afraid we'll have to put up with him for a while longer. My hope is he'll tire of the conditions here and leave. I'm actually surprised he's lasted this long, considering the poachers and all. Way beyond his pay grade. The son-of-a-bitch."

They had made an arc around the outskirts of camp and were back near the tents.

"Get some sleep," Bruce said, giving Paul a little hug around the shoulders. "Things have a way of working out." But as he turned and walked toward his tent, Bruce wasn't at all sure he believed it himself.

CHAPTER 29

Mung Beans

It is easy to be brave from a safe distance.

Omaha Indian Saying

The next morning Howie emerged from his tent wearing a brightly patterned Hawaiian shirt that flapped gaily in the morning breeze. In his right hand he carried a machete and in his left a large plastic bag filled with light brown pellets. A nylon cord hung around his neck. One end of it was tied to a plastic laboratory graduated cylinder and the other end to a plastic funnel. He came over to the fire and sat down. Paul, Mary, and Elizabeth had seen Howie's strange collection of equipment before, but said nothing. Johnny asked what it was, and Howie told him it was soil-science equipment,

"You look like a circus clown," Johnny joked.

"Some people aren't sure it's so funny," Paul said. "Once, Howie and I were working together in the Bob Marshall W ilderness in Montana — you know, that's a place people go to get really away from it all and to commune with nature. Well, we would go down one of the trails with Heck carrying his machete in one hand, his bag of beans in the other, and that laboratory stuff hanging around his neck. When we'd see another hiker — you know Heck by now — he'd smile and wave his machete and say, 'Hi! How're you doin'?' And you know, nobody'd ever said 'Hi' back."

Everybody laughed, but then Johnny asked Howie what that equipment was for.

Howie answered that they were for measuring the amount of chemical elements in the soil. "You can't just dig a hole and take out the soil and weigh it, because soil has a structure. Most people think of it as just packed dirt, but it isn't like that at all. Worms and small mammals dig tunnels in it. If it's formed by blowing wind or flowing water, it's laid down in layers with air spaces. If a plant root grows through it and dies, another kind of hole is left — a little tunnel. Dead leaves and twigs decay on the top and form a kind of intricate structure. If you were a little mole running through the soil, you would think you were in elegant caverns."

"Soil's got an architecture — a design," Elizabeth explained to Johnny.

Davie listened, too, interested.

Howie went on to explain that if you dig out some soil and weigh it, you don't really know what its density was — all the structure's lost, you just have a pile of dirt. So we cut out a rectangular hole and we weigh the soil. He pointed at a small pack, indicating that a scale of some sort was inside it. "Then we measure the volume of the hole."

"What's the machete for?" Davie asked.

"To cut the hole. It's the easiest tool to carry and use."

"So how do you measure the volume of soil?" Johnny asked.

Howie told them that the usual way was to carry water along and push a plastic bag into the hole, fill it with water, and measure the amount of water that it took to fill the hole. That's what his graduated cylinder and funnel were for.

"But water's heavy to carry, so I invented another way." He held up the plastic bag. "Mung beans. Small, uniform, light. For the accuracy we need, they work just fine. I push a plastic bag into the hole and fill it with the beans. Then I pour the beans through the funnel into the cylinder, so that's how I measure the volume that they took up."

Johnny laughed. "Mung-bean measurements. And you call yourself a scientist?"

"It may sound silly, but it's darned practical if you're the one carrying the gear. Besides," Howie said, grinning, "when you're finished measuring, you can sprout the beans and eat them."

"Edible science or worse," Paul joked.

"We call this bulk density," said Howie.

Johnny laughed again. "Come with me when I go behind the bushes and I'll give you some bulk density to measure."

"You got it," Howie said. "Participating in biogeochemical cycling, that's what you're doing."

Howie then got serious, saying that he wanted to make some measurements of the soils, and that Paul had promised that he'd have an opportunity to do so. Davie volunteered to drive him. Bruce said he, Johnny, and Michael needed to stay behind but would try to join up later. Mary and Elizabeth said they were busy with other things, although Mary looked longingly at Paul, and almost decided to go along. To tell the truth, most of the team were a little curious about what Howie was up to and wanted to watch him at his work. Horst had gotten up with a nasty headache, so he was glad that the camp was clearing out.

Howie took out his little book of random numbers, and following Howie's instructions, Davie drove on a line perpendicular to and away from the river, so that Howie could sample the soils near the river and then into the savannas and grasslands on the farther uplands. Their random number route took them north across a junction where two dirt roads came together A vehicle was parked at the intersection, facing them and blocking their route. They saw Joseph in the savannah off to one side, seeming to be searching for something on the ground

"Joseph an' his Toyota Land Cruiser," Davie said. "What's he doing out here and why's his Cruiser blocking our way?"

"We've heard some not too good things about him," Paul said. "What'll we do now?"

"I'll find out," Davie said, getting out of the driver's seat. Joseph looked up and waved at Davie, and motioned him to come over and then returned to searching on the ground. Howie was immediately curious. Not many people he had met so far were all that interested in what was on the ground and underneath it. "I'll stay with the Rover, just in case," Paul said, but Howie and Davie were part way over to Joseph by the time he finished. Paul saw that he had no weapons and seemed relaxed and casual.

"Greetings. I certainly didn't expect to see any of you guys out here," Joseph said when Davie and Howie got near him. "Watch where you step. Elephant prints all around." He pointed at the ground where they were standing. "That big jumbo was here. Zamani Baba. Digging in the dirt. Young jumbo with him, digging as well. They do this sometimes. Always wondered what they were after." He was glad that he had put his rifle back in his Land Cruiser before he started his careful search and didn't dare mention that actually he had stopped because he thought he finally had a chance to kill the biggest of the big and make a whopper of a sale of his ivory.

Howie got down on the ground next to one of the places the elephants had been digging and began to shift some of the soil in his hands. "Must be a sort of mineral dig for them," he said. "Most of these big planter-eaters don't get enough minerals from their food, so they have to dig it out and eat the soil."

"Sort of their vitamin-mineral pill, eh?" Joseph said. "You know much about this stuff?"

"That's 'bout all he knows," Davie cut in. "This here's Howie the soil expert. Don't think a guy dressed like him is some big time wildlife hunter do ya? He's been tellin' us all about dirt and how important he thinks it is."

"Soil," Howie said, still sifting the sandy soil. "Dirt is soil out of place. Like that stuff all over your face, Davie," Howie quipped.

"This stuff they've been diggin' a different color — darker —." He took a little plastic bag and a pair of plastic gloves out of one of his many pockets, put on the plastic gloves and hand fed some of the mineral soil he had touched into the plastic bag."

"See. He treats this stuff like he's in an operatin' room and doesn't want his dirt ta bleed ta death," Davie added.

"You're actually an expert on this stuff?" Joseph asked again.

"He's got us spendin' the day samplin' his 'soil' as he calls it, all over the place, at places he chooses off a map at random. Gotta be a little weird in the head," Davie continued.

"Is that why you're out this way? I'm surprised Michael or Bruce isn't with you, what with all these poachers and their big guns wandering around, not to mention the big cats, the rhinos, and the jumbos."

"Well, Paul's gotta a pistol back at the Rover. An' I'm pretty used to Tsavo," Davie said.

"Even so. Not smart these days." Joseph had gotten interested in what Howie was doing. Something entirely different than he had ever come across, but possibly a clue about where to hunt for elephants. "Tell you what. I'm free today. Let me go along with you. I'd like to learn more about this dirt — 'er, soil — stuff you're studying," he said to Howie. "I've got a good rifle in my Cruiser and I'm a pretty good shot. Least I can do is help you out."

"Gotta ask our science boss," Davie said, and guided Joseph over to Paul, still sitting in the Land Rover, Howie following behind.

Paul listened and looked off in the distance. It wouldn't be a bad idea to have that added protection, he decided, and it was probably a good idea to get to know Joseph a little better as well. If he knew so much about Tsavo, maybe he could be a help, an addition to Michael, Johnny, and Bruce, even though they had told him Joseph was a small-time ivory poacher who had been in jail just for that. Still, who knows? Seems calm enough and pleasant today. Davie seems comfortable with him along. That's something. What the hell, everything was a risk out here, and Joseph's right. We're probably not doing the smartest thing out here with just my pistol.

"Okay. You're on. Welcome. You're the guest of the day."

"Just won a roundtrip diggin' in the soil," Davie said.

"The truth is where you find it," Howie put in, "sometimes where you look for it, but you got to know where the looking is."

Davie looked around. "Isn't this the place they used to call 'Elephant Bone Corner?' he asked. "Yessir. Probably 'cause poachers shot so many elephants, but also 'cause someone found a few elephant bones here. You know the old stories — never can find an elephant graveyard, must be in a secret place. Maybe they found a few here," he said.

Paul and Howie asked if he thought it was true about a hidden elephant graveyard. Davie broke in, " Used ta be a grave digger, remember, so I guess I know a little 'bout this."

"Yep, I agree," Joseph said. "What I believe is nobody finds elephant graveyards because live elephants pick up bones and carry them around for a while and then scatter them. Somehow elephants can tell their kind of bones from those of other animals — maybe even tell bones of individuals from one another. Can you beat that?"

"Takes a lot of intelligence to link elephant bones to an elephant that used to be walking around," Howie said. "Now there's smart if you want smart. We think all the smartness is up here," he pointed at his head, "but maybe with the elephants a lot of it's here," he touched his nose.

"Cut it out, Heck," Paul said. "You guys have to get used to Howie. Always saying the weirdest things."

"That, or the smell reminds them of an elephant," Howie said.

"I think it's more 'an that," Davie replied. "It's like they're in mourning."

Joseph followed them for a ways, then parked his Land Cruiser off to the side of a dirt track and got in their vehicle. The day progressed, with Davie using the odometer and stopping at distances Howie read him from his now well-worn book of random numbers, and then the group would hike to a point where Howie would make his measurements. The work went slowly, so they did not reach the far uplands until late in the afternoon. At their last stop, they were in an area of very tall grasses, about four feet high, taller than they had seen so far and stretching for a long distance, as far as Howie could see. It seemed most unusual to Howie, especially because it was little grazed.

Before they got out of the Land Rover, Davie opened the glove compartment and took out a pistol, which he hadn't shown the others he had with him. Then he checked the sharpness of his knife.

"What's up?" Paul asked.

"Tall grass, big cats — old Chinese saying," Davie answered. "Lions 'specially like to lie in tall grass, either to rest or to hide while they hunt. Good idea to have some protection, 'specially this time a day."

"Why this time of day?" Paul asked as they started walking down a narrow trail between the grasses.

Davie reminded him that during the daylight lions could easily see people and generally avoided them, "'cept, of course, for your 'casional Tsavo man-eater," but that at dusk, the lions couldn't tell people from other wildlife, and generally hunted at that time anyway. Paul wondered aloud how primitive people would have survived around the big predators. Davie replied that he had a theory.

"Most predators avoid us 'cause we stink." he said. "That's how primitive man survived. Not by his wits at first, but 'cause he smelled so bad no self-respectin' predator could stand him." He wiped his dirty hand across his shirt, leaving a diagonal line of reddish dirt.

With you along, we'll be pretty safe, Paul thought, smiling a little to himself. Joseph motioned that he would move back enough so he could look around and watch out for any poachers or other dangers, taking his rifle with him. Paul, uncomfortable that Joseph was now well armed and could easily shoot them, looked at Davie, but Davie seem completely unperturbed.

He was enjoying spending time in the field, a relief from Horsts' politics and worries about new big-time poachers. He could relax a little with Joseph along. Whatever Bruce and Johnny had said, Joseph seemed okay.

Joseph decided that these two guys, Howie and Davie, were not upper class rich guys, not like Johnny or Bruce, and not specially treated like Michael. They seemed just working class guys, more like himself. What did Davie say? He was a grave digger? And this Howie. No nose in the air upper class guy. Not dressed like that, like clothes some clown had thrown away. It was one of the first times he met scientists who seemed to have grown up like him, poor, not cared for, not elite. And they were doing something highbrow in spite of that. He felt a connection with these two. Paul wasn't all that bad either, although he came across more like Bruce than the others. And what this Howie was doing interested him, not just because it might help him track and find elephants, but it just seem different and interesting to him, having spent his life out in places like Tsavo, but always searching out the game and only using the ground to help track them. This Howie stuff was a new twist.

The grass became taller as they went forward, reaching five feet. They passed one patch of six-foot grass. The patch of grasses seemed ominously quiet.

Howie was already digging in the soil with his machete. It took much longer for Howie to cut a hole into the soil in the tall grasses than it had anywhere else.

"These here bunch grasses. The tufts are so stiff an' tight, take you forever," Davie said. "Got another machete? I can help."

Howie shook his head, and spent half an hour cutting away several tufts and then digging the hole. The sun was casting long shadows from the trees in the distance when Howie looked up. Insects buzzed, and Howie had to keep waving them off with his right hand, the one holding the machete. The machete moved so quickly that Joseph, from his distance somewhat away, could see only a blur and thought Howie might cut off his own nose.

"Better not spend much longer out here. Twilight's the time of the big cats, 'member," Davie warned again. Just as he said this, they heard a rustling and saw a big male lion moving toward them through the grasses. They froze. Davie slowly reached for his pistol. The lion seemed to pay them no attention. He came within fifty paces and settled himself down in the tall grass about two paces from the path they had followed.

Without taking his eyes off the lion, Howie whispered to Davie, "You know, in this light, that male is a kind of sterling brown rather than the tawny yellow you see during the day."

"Good camouflage for hunting at dusk," Davie whispered. "Betta finish up now, quick an' quiet."

"King of the beasts. Sure looks like the king now," Howie whispered. He put a plastic sack into the hole and poured mung beans into it. The falling beans sounded like rumbling thunder in the silent countryside with the lion waiting between them and their Land Rover. They cringed, expecting the lion to jump at the noise, but he did not. A bird made a coughing sound. In a stand of trees to the north, some grazing animal replied with a similar cough.

"Best we wait a bit," Davie whispered. "Maybe old simba will leave on his own. Let's hunker down. Talk quiet, an' don't move."

Joseph motioned to Davie toward the lion, so the rest would know he also understood what was happening. He pointed out his rifle and moved his hand to point a little behind himself, hoping at least Davie would understand that he meant to follow along at a distance, watching out, but not interfering. This was just the kind of trouble these guys were likely to get into, he said to himself. I knew they needed me along. He decided to let them try to work things out for themselves. He didn't feel especially comfortable with the lion in the tall grass, truth to tell. And what would a rifle shot bring out if he did have to use it? Maybe those goddamned bigtime poachers, which he wouldn't be able to handle alone or with Davie. Best to let those guys try to deal with this big guy. He'd seen too many people come to Voi badly mauled by lions, some by hyenas. Let it be, yup. Best if I just watch and get involved only if the worst happens.

"Can we try to circumvent him?" Paul whispered.

"Uh-uh. You move away from a lion, even slowly, at dusk, an' he thinks you're fleein'. An' he's built to chase anything that flees. If you take that long walk, even slow like, he's gonna come after you. Can't walk away from cats. That's what Cecile did an' you saw what that got him." Davie thought for a minute. "Y'know, we're gonna have to walk right by him to get back to the Land Rover."

"He'll smell fear on you, sure as I'm hidin' here, so you damn well better *be* confident and *act* confident," Davie said to the others. He paused, thinking. "Look, I got this pistol and Joseph's back there somewhere with his damn elephant gun. I say we try ta walk out very calmly. Won't take out the pistol because he'd know then I'm a threat. Having a weapon out changes you, makes you strut. Lions can tell. I'd shoot him from here if I could, maybe Joseph could better'n me, but in that tall grass, it'd be a tricky shot by either of us. Nothin' worse than a wounded lion in the tall grass."

Howie, who had kept quiet, made a decision. He opened a small pocket on his backpack and took out his precious yo-yo. "I'm going for it. Follow me," he said. He stood up, put his pack on his back, his plastic funnel and cylinder around his neck. With his machete and sack of mung beans in his left hand, he began to whistle *When the Saints Go Marchin' In* and started down the animal trail that would take them within a few feet of the lion. As he walked, he casually did a series of tricks with the yo-yo, whistling all the time.

Like children behind the Pied Piper, the others trailed along nervously behind him, Davie at the rear. When Howie came even with the lion, still lying in the grass, he made the yo-yo do an arc in the air and, continuing to whistle, walked past, maintaining a slow but steady pace. As Paul passed, the lion yawned and turned toward him, mouth open, huge, sharp teeth shining. Then it wiped its face with a forepaw and watched Howie ahead. After Davie passed him, the lion yawned again, rolled over, stood up, and walked away in the opposite direction. Paul exhaled deeply.

"Don't relax yet," Davie said. "Them lions sometimes circle 'round an' meet their prey head-on. He could be between us an' the Land Rover again before we get out." Joseph rejoined the others, keeping his rifle out, and they walked out quietly, nobody talking.

But nothing else happened on the way back.

When they reached the Land Rover, Howie opened the door and Davie applauded loudly. With a grand sweep of his hands and a little bow, Howie tossed his equipment into the back of the vehicle.

Joseph smiled, feeling at home with these two. He patted Howie on the back.

"You guys aren't the complete amateurs I thought you were," he said. "Got to admit, Howie, you know some stuff I've never thought of, but it's interesting. And Davie, someday I've got to join you when you go after those vultures."

"You're not so bad yourself," Davie said, shaking Joseph's hand. "Don't know what you used to do. Course everybody gossips 'bout everybody else out here. But what the hell, I always take people as I see 'em and see what they do. You'd be welcome to join me, get vulture crap an' vomit all over you any time. If you think Howie's soil hang up will get ya dirty, you ain't seen nothin' yet."

Paul went to talk with Joseph while Davie and Howie stowed their gear in the back. They all crammed into the Land Rover, and Paul talked with Joseph as they drove him back to his vehicle. "Thanks for your help, Joseph," Paul said. "You're right. We weren't the smartest being out here without more of a guard. Nice of you to fill in. Come along anytime."

"Well, thank you," Joseph said. "Truth to tell, I enjoyed finding out what Howie did. Sort of crazy in one way, but fascinating in some others. Hadn't seen that kind of science in action. Wish I'd known about it years ago. Maybe would have helped me stay out of some trouble. Maybe I could learn about this stuff and find another way to add to my income. Always seemed to me only those rich upper class guys got to do the science and the well-paid jobs. But you two seem to be doing okay. Got me thinking." And with that, he stepped out of the vehicle and walked to his own.

CHAPTER 30

Baker

The exceptions to any rule are most interesting in themselves for they show us that the old rule is wrong. . . .The scientist tries to find more exceptions and to determine the characteristics of the exception, a process that is continually exciting as it develops.

Nobel Laureate physicist Richard P. Feynman

I n the near twilight As Paul, Howie, and Davie were getting ready to get into their Land Rover, a dust-spreading vehicle approached.

"Think it's poachers?" Paul asked. He rummaged around in the back of the Land Rover, hunting for another weapon. Davie unlocked the safety on the pistol he still had in his pocket. The minutes dragged on. The dust cloud grew larger, but the vehicle was still too far away to identify.

Howie continued to look through the field glasses. "I'll be damned," he said.

"What?" Paul asked.

"Take a look." Howie handed him the binoculars. "It's a goddamn VW bug." Howie said.

"If a poacher's driving one of those, he's a little loony," Paul said.

Davie grabbed the field glasses from Howie, took a look, and nodded in agreement. He put his pistol safety on and stuffed the gun into his pants pocket. The three went out into the open and watched. The VW beetle was going along slowly but steadily, bouncing over shrubs like a small rowboat in a rough sea. Now they could hear its characteristic engine sound, a rhythmic metallic banging, which Howie attributed to the way the valves of the small engine moved in the parallel cylinders.

Now he could make out that the VW was a rusty brown, and as it drew near he could see that there was just one person in it, driving along slowly. The driver waved, pulled alongside them, and stopped. He opened the window and looked out. He was a balding man of indeterminate age.

"Howdy," he said. "Nice to see a fresh face." He opened the door and climbed out, seemingly unconcerned about whom he had run into. He was wearing old U.S. Army fatigues and an Eisenhower jacket, which Davie thought strange given the warmth of the afternoon.

"Name's Baker. Baker Kingsley. Pleased to meet you." He stuck a hand toward Howie, who introduced himself and Davie.

"Thought you might be a poacher," Davie said. "Good thing you ain't. At least I *think* you ain't."

"Poacher? Hell, no. I'm just out here botanizing — looking at plants. It's my hobby, so to speak. Sometimes I even make a living at it. I've been roaming around Africa for a while now. Seen some of the strangest plants, I'll tell you. In fact, let me show you." He opened the door of his VW, pushed the front seat forward, and leaned into the back, digging around. Howie peered in through the dusty side window and saw that the back seat was filled almost to the top with old-fashioned cigar boxes. Baker dug down and brought one of the cigar boxes out and set it on the ground.

"Now this is a rarity," he said, opening the lid carefully. Inside was crushed newspaper, and inside that was a smaller box, which contained a carefully dried plant. "Welwitchia," he said. "Got it in South Africa. One of my favorites. This is part of a leaf — this darned plant just has two leaves, the ones it was born with, so to speak, its cotyledons as we botanists call it. In other plants, these just f all off, but in Welwitchia, that's all the plant gets, and they grow and grow, sometimes getting fifteen feet long, and looking torn and tattered. They grow right on the ground, this weird plant doesn't make a stem worth anything. Of course, this is just a small part of one. One of the strangest plants in the world. But you know, if you plant this piece of it, it will grow just fine. Looks like hell, doesn't it?"

"Where'd ya get all them cigar boxes?" Davie asked. By this time Paul and was strolling over to take a look.

Baker was carefully rearranging the plant in its box. "My uncle in New Jersey used to run a cigar store. He died a year ago, and I had to go down and take care of his affairs. I was the closest relative. Seemed too good to throw out, so I just loaded them in my VW and took off."

He pulled himself out and turned to look at the others. Small pieces of newspaper stuck to his Eisenhower jacket, and one large piece had stuck to his balding head. "Then I got this great deal on a freighter. Took me and my car and my cigar boxes from New York to Africa real cheap. And you know what? These boxes have turned out to be kind of useful."

He ducked back into the car, rummaged around some more, and brought out a canteen. He took a long drink of water, then tossed the canteen back into the pile of stuff in the car. Howie noticed that it ended up in a different place from where Baker had found it. There seemed to be no order to anything about Baker or his car.

"You just travelin' out here by yourself?" Davie asked.

"Oh, yes. Always do. Don't like too much company — talk, talk, talk. You get so interested in what the other person's saying you forget to look at the countryside. You miss everything that way. Might as well be on the subway in Manhattan. I'm out here to learn about the plants. I like to watch the birds and other animals, too. I don't mind meeting up with you fellows, though — it gets lonely sometimes. Hey, how about a snack?"

After some more rummaging among the boxes in the back seat, he extracted a sack of M&Ms, which he placed on the sloping front hood of the VW. Then he leaned in again and came up with two large bottles of Coca-Cola. "Care for some candies or a Coke?" he asked, opening one of the bottles and taking a long swig. Then he opened the bag of M&Ms and offered it around.

"How far'd ya come?" Davie asked, wide-eyed with disbelief. This Baker character was even weirder than Howie, he thought.

"You mean today? Or since when?" Baker leaned back against his car and took another swig of Coke, then reached into the front passenger seat and pulled out an old World War II army officer's hat, smacked the dust off it against his thigh, and put it on.

"I mean how long ya been out here in Tsavo?"

"Oh, so that's what this place is! I've been wondering. I've read about Tsavo. No wonder I keep coming across artesian wells. Been a blessing, I can tell you. It'd be mighty hard going through this dry country without those wells."

"How'd ya find the wells?" Davie asked. He looked even more bewildered.

"That's easy — you can tell from the vegetation around them. It's like they're marked with signs. You can see them from a mile away. Look over there — there's one." He pointed. Sure enough, there was a different kind of vegetation in a clump.

"Ya know the whole story 'bout Tsavo?" Davie asked.

"Well, if you put it that way, I'd have to say no. Does anybody?"

"I mean d' ya know 'bout the big elephant die-off an' the drought an' all that?" Baker looked puzzled. "I heard something about a place where that happened — about ten years ago, wasn't it? You mean *this* is that place? Hot dog. Got to see me an elephant graveyard."

"There are poachers out here. It could be dangerous traveling all alone," Howie said.

Baker laughed. "Have to be a pretty dumb poacher to attack a rusty VW with one old guy in it."

"Hell, they might just shoot first an' ask questions later. Only you wouldn't be able ta answer. You'd be D-E-D," Davie said.

"You've got a point there, I'll have to admit. But what about you folks? What are you doing out here if you think it's so dangerous?"

"We're a research team tryin' to find out what's happenin' to the elephants an' their habitat," Davie told him.

Baker's eyebrows rose. "That a fact?"

"Yup, that's a fact," Davie said.

Paul watched the two of them with amusement. Here was somebody even stranger than Davie, and Davie couldn't figure him out.

"Where's your camp?" Baker asked Davie.

"Headin' back to it. You want to join us for the evening, you're welcome."

"Maybe I will. I could use a little company now and again — with the emphasis on *little*. Tell you what, you fellows go on ahead of me. I'll follow your dust trail but stay back far enough so I can see what's passing by. I'll make my own camp close to yours. I'd invite one of you to ride with me, but you can see for yourself. . . ." He waved toward the VW.

Howie glanced in again. There was absolutely no room in there for another person. He looked more closely. On the dashboard was a nice, slightly rounded fur piece. "What's that, if you don't mind my asking?" he said.

"That there's my old tomcat, Jimmy. Jimmy and me, we've traveled the world together. That's just a saying, you know — we didn't really do the whole world. But then one day, old Jimmy just up and died. I couldn't bear to part with him, so I skun him, buried the rest of him — nice little ceremony — and fixed his hide so the fur would keep well. Keeps me company. He doesn't talk much, but when I get lonely, I just reach over and pet him, know what I mean?"

None of them knew what he meant. "Not exactly," Davie said.

"I'll explain later," Howie said to the others.

"That a fact?" Baker said.

"That I'll explain later? Yes, it is. At least, it's a fact of the future," Howie said.

"Yes, that's accurate. I like the way you put that," Baker said. "Care for some more M&Ms?" He extended what was left of the bag to Howie.

"Not just now, thanks. Maybe later."

"That a fact?" said Baker.

"Maybes can't be facts, Jimmy," Howie said.

"I'm Baker. Jimmy's my cat. *Was* my cat. That fur piece, that's Jimmy."

"Right. I'm sorry. *That's* a fact," said Howie.

"What the hell you two talking 'bout?" Davie asked.

"Facts," Howie said. "Isn't it obvious?"

"Oh, sure, obvious as hell," Davie said.

"Davie, don't start again. It'll never end."

"That a fact?" asked Baker.

"Mr. Baker, I think you ought to stay close to us on the way back. We've been having some troubles with poachers and we expect more. You may need a little protection yourself," Paul said.

"Well, I certainly wouldn't mind some company for a while," Baker admitted. "Let's go along. As I said, you lead, I'll follow. Don't worry about me, just put your lights on as it gets dark and I'll follow you."

"Careful also about gettin' outta your car at dusk an' after dusk. We just met up with a big male lion out here," Davie said.

"Will do." Baker said cheerfully. He took a last sip of his Coke, screwed the top back on, and laid the bottle carefully between two boxes in the back of his VW. As soon as he turned around to get himself seated, the bottle fell off the seat onto the floor.

Davie and Howie walked back together, Howie grinning to himself.

"Now that's a weird dude," Davie said.

CHAPTER 31

Botanizing

The notion of looking on at life has always been hateful to me. What am I if I am not a participant? In order to be, I must participate.

Antoine de Saint-Exupery

The next morning, the oldest of the Land Rovers would not start. Bruce was working on it when he heard the sound of a Volkswagen engine and Baker drove up. Even though it was Baker's first visit to the camp, he had looked at it for a while before arriving and as a result carefully skirted around the tents by a wide margin so as not to disturb anyone still sleeping. He stopped his car within a foot of the front end of the Land Rover — about three inches short of Bruce himself, who still had his head under the hood and didn't realize how close the car had come to him. Mary, watching from the center of camp, held her breath until Baker stopped.

Baker got out and peered under the Land Rover's hood from the other side. Mary could not quite make out conversation between them, but soon Baker was digging around in the back of his VW and tools of all kinds started to appear. She wandered over to listen, curious because of what Howie had told her about Baker the night before. At first she stood about ten feet away, just watching. An unbelievable number of tools were coming out of the Volkswagen, and every once in a while, in addition to a tool, Baker would emerge with a Hershey bar, once with a bottle of Coca-Cola, which he propped up on the sloping hood of his VW. Other things flew out of the Volkswagen when Baker was almost hidden inside it: an army officer's hat, a brown T-

shirt, an apple (an apple? thought Mary), several paperback books, a frying pan, a camping stove, a small hatchet (Mary noted it was in a leather case, thank goodness), a first-aid kit, and various objects she could not identify.

He and Bruce were having an animated discussion. After a short while, Baker took two small wrenches and started to work at something on the top of the engine.

By the time the sun had risen completely over the eastern horizon, Bruce nodded to Baker, got into the Land Rover, and started it up. A puff of foul smoke belched from the exhaust, and then the engine settled down, running smoothly. Bruce let it idle and left it running. Baker began to put his tools back into his car — tongs, books, a hatchet went flying into the backseat as haphazardly as they had come out. Then the two men headed over to where Michael was frying bacon and eggs. As they passed her, Bruce stopped and introduced Baker as a botanist, "but he also appears to be a mechanical genius. He fixed the Land Rover."

"A botanist? So am I," Mary said. She offered her hand.

Bruce introduced Baker around and smiles emerged from several faces after brief exchanges with him.

Horst stepped forward and held out his hand. "G.H. Grobben's the name. Member of the National Academy of Sciences, U.S. Received the League of Discoverers' award from the New York Athletic Club. Member of the board of the East African Wildlife. Past president of the Ecological Society of America. Out here representing major NGOs interested in the elephants," he said.

"That a fact?" said Baker, pulling a bag of M&Ms out of his pocket and handing it to Horst.

"Which?" asked Horst.

"Which what?" asked Baker.

"Is *which* a fact?" asked Horst.

"That's what I was asking *you*," Baker said. "You just told me all this stuff about yourself and now you're saying you don't know if any of it's a fact or not." He shook his head. Elizabeth grinned broadly but said nothing. Horst noticed and made a point of ignoring her.

"Hey Baker," Howie said. "Do you happen to have any plastic funnels. Mine got too close to the fire last night."

"Well, now, Howie. Good chance, my man, good chance. Let's take a look in my vehicle."

Baker smiled broadly at Mary. "Ready for some botanizing little lady?"

Mary's face brightened and she nodded yes. Baker suddenly turned and started to stride away from camp. She hurried to keep up with him. Soon they were comparing notes and plant identifications. Their strolling brought them back to Baker's Volkswagen. "Hold on a minute. I'll get one of my plant keys — I found a key to plants of East Africa in Nairobi. " He opened the car door, bent into the back, and rustled around once again among the cigar boxes. He opened one and brought out two books and another Hershey bar. "Care for a candy?" he asked.

"Not this early in the morning," she said sprightly, amused. Then she turned around and looked at the vegetation and pointed to one plant, telling him that she hadn't figured that one out, although it seemed to be pretty common and the gazelles liked to eat it.

Horst, watching as he sat finishing a mug of coffee, was irritated. Another weirdo to add to the collection, he thought, and the one really good-looking woman on the trip seems to find him fascinating. Son-of-a-bitch.

Baker bent over and took a small hand lens from the pocket of his Eisenhower jacket, which he seemed to wear all the time. He picked a leaf and then a flower, opened his book, and sat down on a nearby log. Mary joined him. Horst could see they were sitting very close, looking in a small book and taking turns staring at the leaf and flower through the hand lens. Their faces were close together. Horst could only think about Mary's body, as he sat in the morning light, in the brightening sun, sipping his coffee and watching.

Howie joined him. "How ya doin' Horse?" he asked. "I'd say it's another great day out in the wilderness."

"In the middle of nowhere," said Horst.

"One and the same," Howie said, sipping coffee from his mug. Horst and Howie listened in on Baker's and Mary's conversation, which they could just pick up.

Baker handed the leaf, flower, and lens to Mary. "We might as well go through the key, step by step. Not making any progress otherwise."

Baker thumbed through the book, a small field guide to plants.

"'Leaves needlelike or flat.' That's easy. Flat. Not a conifer out here. Leaves simple or complex."

"Simple," said Mary.

"Leaf veins parallel or spreading."

"Spreading. It's definitely a dicot."

"Right. Flowers individual or complex, in groups."

"Individual."

After a few more minutes of this, Horst grew bored, stood up, and walked away. Howie decided to join Mary and Baker, who began to walk up a steep rise. Howie soon began to tire.

"How're you doing, Howie?" Baker asked.

"I am a bit spent, a meter more will do me in," said Howie. He puffed. "But I could go along a little farther if you want."

"Nah. It's time to take a rest, you're right," Baker said.

They sat down on the rise, and Howie looked wistfully up at the sky. "I could use a beer," he said. "And a burger."

"Would'n mind them myself," Baker said, half listening while he looked through the field guide.

"Imagine. All this dust, like Egypt. Sitting here for two thousand years, and people wishing for beer all that time," Howie mused, looking up into the sky and off into the distance. "And what do we have? Cats and cockroaches, is about all. W hat this place needs is a Good Humor Man."

"You're quite enough," Baker laughed.

"I mean the little man with the white pushcart full of ice cream."

"I thought it was beer you wanted," Baker said, poring through the field guide, then stopping to point at a plant. "That's it," he said to Mary.

"Yup, that's it all right," said Howie. "Beer. If a Good Humor man selling beer came over that rise, I'd be as happy as could be."

"Some wilderness experience you want," Mary said.

Howie groaned. "I think I've been wildernessed to death, or dust — can't tell the difference between them anymore out here in Tsavoland. We ought to get Disney here, call it Tsavoland, with Mickey Mouse selling cold soda, in between the elephants, that is. Some kind of light rail for people to ride on, or maybe golf carts, with drinks and sandwiches."

Mary and Baker ignored him, engrossed as they were trying to figure out the name of the plant they had found.

"Then again, there are probably things like peyote out here. That'd make the trip a lot more fun. Have to catch a poacher and ask him what they eat or sniff on their days off." Howie got up and wandered around the top of the rise, Mary and Baker paying no attention to him. Baker pulled a Boy Scout knife out of a pocket of his jacket, cut a small twig off a shrub, and looked at in through his hand lens. He passed the lens and the twig along to Mary, and soon they were in a discussion about which plant this was.

But now Mary found her mind wandering. Should she have let herself become involved with Paul? She had promised herself not to let it happen. It was so unprofessional. I should have controlled myself, she thought. I can botanize with Baker, and I can do the research I was sent out to do. Now what will Paul think of me? And what will the others think, if they know, or when they know? She moved away from Baker, as if looking at a grouping a plants a distance away. She needed time alone — to put her thoughts and feelings into perspective.

* * *

That evening Horst wandered over to the meeting tent, and seeing no one inside, went in, filled his pipe, lit it, and sat down to watch the sun set over the plains. He was thinking of Baker. Everyone seemed to find him entertaining. Horst categorized him with Davie and Howie, another weirdo that somehow needed to be tolerated. His eyes settled on Mary, who was sitting by herself near the campfire with her clipboard on her lap, looking serious. She seemed like many other young women he had seduced, usually graduate students, occasionally young faculty members at the colleges and universities he visited to give lectures, or ambitious young staffers working in government offices.

Seduction was a habit, a kind of addiction. Often he hated himself for the way he treated women. It was like his drinking; he would vow to stop, but never could. And out here in this desolation, gin and the possibility of going to bed with Mary were his only reliefs. He thought about his wife, a tall, striking blonde with bold blue eyes. Intelligent, too. Why wasn't she enough for him? Thoughts of her troubled him; she knew about his seductions. She had stayed with him, not forgiving him, but putting up with him.

Sometimes it wasn't even fun, it was just too easy for him to seduce these young women. Many of them were impressed with his accomplishments; they were like groupies, he thought. He puffed on his pipe and brooded.

Yes, he felt a strong urge to seduce Mary; just thinking about her and what he might do took his mind off Tsavo's emptiness and his regret at coming along on this trip. He did have a purpose here, he reminded himself: to protect Tsavo and its elephants from the likes of Bruce and the poachers, whom Horst saw as simply two sides of the same coin — both intent on killing elephants and interfering with nature. Oh, he wasn't sentimental about elephants as Cecile had been. No, in fact, he didn't really like animals, had no pets. It was the purity of Tsavo that appealed to him.

He had to find a way to take over this group and put a stop to their silly measurements. Mary was the worst of them that way, with her funny forester's clipboard and her love of counting things and taking notes. Mary and her boyfriend, Paul, too, measure, measure, measure. Horst would give Mary something to measure, right between her legs.

If he couldn't take over from Bruce directly, he would still find a way to win. Bruce, whatever his intimate knowledge of elephants, his familiarity with plants and animals, his feeling of oneness with Tsavo, could never outmaneuver him on that world stage where he excelled. Never. He would show Bruce up, and screw Mary along the way. He watched Mary intently, planning his next move with her.

Mary, unaware of being watched, still sat alone with her clipboard, but actually she was thinking about Baker. A lot of his comical statements had a kind of wisdom. He was so spontaneous, so free. She enjoyed him, but how she envied him. And Howie. The two of them were odd characters. But ideas just rolled out o f Howie's mouth, like the plains outside of Tsavo greening up quickly after a rain. Often kooky ideas, but sometimes fascinating ones. Why couldn't ideas rise up within her as easily? In contrast to them, her creativity was no more than a few craggy shrubs and dried out grasses along their route. Maybe she was just too serious. She and Howie had done some work together in the deep woods of Minnesota, and he'd said some of the oddest, funniest things. Remembering, she couldn't help but smile.

Horst saw her smiling, off by herself, and decided that he had waited long enough. Besides, he'd soon be gone. He slung his corduroy jacket casually over his shoulder, smoothed back his hair, and approached her nonchalantly with a winning smile that had raised tens of millions of dollars, put him on the board of a dozen leading environmental organizations, and helped get him elected to the National Academy of Science.

He walked over to her and greeted her. Mary, deep in thought, literally jumped up, then apologized. "My mind was a thousand miles away. Actually, about eight thousand."

"I didn't mean to startle you," Horst said soothingly, melodiously.

"I was just thinking," she said.

"Must've been a nice thought. You had a charming smile on your face." Horst put his binoculars up to his eyes and pretended to search the darkening landscape and the evening sky for birds, giving Mary a moment to collect herself, and unconsciously drawing her attention to his face, his best feature. "About the birds out here, I'll bet."

"I had a good idea, if I do say so myself." She looked away, embarrassed to have made such a bravado statement to a famous scientist.

Horst assumed a serious expression and turned his blue eyes directly on her, saying that he'd be most interested in hearing what she had to say, because science could always use good ideas. He invited her to stroll with him to the edge of camp so they could watch the sunset while she told him about her idea. She blushed and said that she was afraid that he would laugh at her because she was just a beginner as a scientist. But Horst said on the contrary some of the best ideas came from the freshest minds.

Mary took a deep breath and opened up to Horst, talking about how the elephants overgrazing and trampling and digging in the soil might have made Tsavo's soil infertile. Horst found what she was saying boring, but he continued to smile and nodded encouragingly. Let her talk. It always worked.

She told him about an idea she had f or a new way of thinking about elephants and their habitats, based on her measurements. Words cascaded from her. For the first time, she had the attention of a member of the National Academy of Sciences standing beside her. She stole a glance at his profile. He was handsome, too, in a rugged sort of way, like a bit of granite, New England granite, and he could be charming. Maybe he wasn't so bad. And maybe her idea was a good idea.

He urged to continue, turning to look into her eyes, his blue eyes trained on her, entrancing her; she did not see their danger, did not recognize the soul of the leopard behind those eyes.

"Well, I was just thinking, maybe elephants in Tsavo act like the worst wildfires in America, making long-term changes in the *soils,* not just removing the vegetation for a while but permanently changing the very ground we're standing on. If that's true, it may take much longer than people think for Tsavo to recover — if ever. Maybe the elephants are, you know, a geologic force like Elizabeth has said, a huge force."

He told her this was interesting, and he began to think there might be something to it. She asked if he thought her idea was worth pursuing. Horst paused. He reached into his jacket pocket for his pipe, trying to look as if he were thinking carefully. "I would say definitely." He stuffed tobacco into his pipe. "Perhaps, if you wouldn't mind, I could help to develop the idea."

"Mind? Of course not! Could you really?"

"Certainly. We scientists have an obligation to help one another." His blue eyes pierced her as surely as a leopard's tooth. She was elated.

"What we need to do is set it down," Horst said, lighting his pipe and puffing on it to get it going. He thought it made him look contemplative. Mary didn't see its red glow, nor perceive its symbolism. She saw only the craggily handsome rocklike face of the New Hampshire mountains, mistaking a surface for the deeps.

"You take a first crack at it as soon as you can," he continued. "Write it up. I'll read it, and we can talk about it on the rest of this trip. No time like the present." He touched her hand; she shivered.

There may be something to the idea anyway, as boring as soils are, he thought. Always good to publish a paper that makes you look like a broad-minded thinker. Actually, he was a *broad*-minded thinker. He smiled, liking his pun. Of course, as the senior scientist, he would be first author. If I play Mary right, I could get a great lay *and* another publication — two for the price of one, he chuckled to himself.

It was getting to be dusk. Howie had started a campfire and called over to Horst and Mary, suggesting they join him and they did. Mary fell silent. The trees, the soil, and the sky were silent as well. No breeze ruffled the leaves. A few wispy clouds hung in the darkening sky. Horst leaned back casually against a rock, letting his left hand and arm brush against her. As happens near the equator, the twilight sped past quickly, scattering stars, and it was dark.

"Nice campfire," he said. "Reminds me of the old days at school, summer camp, families gathered 'round, telling stories. The coast of Maine isn't so flat, of course, and there was the sound of the surf." He took her hand and sighed deeply. An animal rustled in the thornbushes as Horst waited patiently, patient as a leopard in the tall grass, planning his next move. Mary carefully removed her hand, smiling tentatively at Horst.

CHAPTER 32

Rendezvous

Forehead to forehead I meet thee.

Herman Melville, *Moby Dick*

The next morning Elizabeth and Mary enlisted Bruce in a quick field trip to explore a strange hill that rose out of the flat land near their camp. "A kopje," Elizabeth said, "also called an inselberg. It's isolated and lonely, but also intriguing."

"Yes, one of those strange isolated hills that you find now and again in Kenya and Tanzania," Bruce answered, turning his Land Rover toward it. Elizabeth had recognized it immediately from her readings, as did Mary, riding in the backseat, who added that kopjes have their own plants and small animals, which she would like to see.

"Small animals like those hills — they can hide there," Bruce said.

Both women wanted to stop and climb it, so Bruce parked the Land Rover at its base. Soon Mary was scrambling up the rocks, stopping often to focus on a plant.

Elizabeth and Bruce made their own way in a more leisurely fashion. Soon Elizabeth had her geological hammer out and was busy chipping off small pieces of the kopje's rocks and examining them with a hand lens. Nearing the top, she surveyed the plains below, noting with satisfaction that the Land Rovers and their trailers were not visible, so she had a view of Tsavo as if no people were present.

The dominion of the elephant, as she was beginning to view Tsavo, shimmered in the bright sun like a flat mauve sea, bluish at the horizon. The Tiva River lay behind them in sharp relief, where trees and shrubs painted a narrow meandering line of bright green. Far to the west, almost to the horizon, another greenish line marked the Yatta Plateau, the place where they had entered the park. It seemed to mark the end of one world and the beginning of another, the one they had come from — how long ago? The world of the twentieth century.

Near the summit, Elizabeth seated herself on a rock and pulled out a map, while Bruce viewed the plains below through his binoculars, looking for vehicles. But he saw none, and when he was satisfied, he sat down next to Elizabeth and pointed out the major landmarks and the route he intended to take to their nex t camp. He showed her that they could see, off in the distance, the Kimethena Hills marking the park's northern boundary.

"I've been looking at these kopjes all my life and wondered how they got here, " he said, putting his arm around her waist. "Tell me about it." She squirmed away, wanting to be listened to as a colleague, not as a girlfriend. "The kopje didn't exactly 'get' here," she said. "The land eroded away from it and left it here — it broke off in layers, like the way an onion peels." She held up a large rock chip. She explained that the kopje was made of ancient rocks — those left behind — as the surrounding, softer rocks, eroded away.

"Some of these rocks are nearly three hundred million years old. Ancient times, even for geologists — the age of reptiles, before dinosaurs — the time of the first truly land-adapted vertebrates," she said. "None of us so-called rational beings wandering about. Even before the movie star *Tyrannosaurus rex* made his appearance."

She picked up another piece of rock and looking at it, said that three hundred million years ago was an important time for the land ancestors of people. Clumsy as they were, those ancient animals had evolved to the point that they could live their entire lives on the land — reproduce, grow old, die. "Hatched their young from eggs. Eggs kept the fetuses in water, so to speak — a new invention, watertight eggshells. No more amphibians. The time of the first four-legged footsteps on the land. Without these creatures we would never have come to be, in an evolutionary sense, that is."

She waved her hands as if casting a spell over waters. "You look out and what do you see?"

"Wildlife habitat," Bruce answered.

"Yeah, and something to eat, right? Just like a man. But that's only three-dimensional, is my point, just space. I look out and see great waves of history, of evolution, the world as it was a very, very long time ago, and then how it was much, much later — long after but still a long, long time ago, and then even long after that, nearer to now, but still way back from our point of view. This rock we stand on" — she kicked at it — "was at the bottom of some ancient sea. You see it as it is. I see it as it is and as it was, and as it will be. Those Tsavo plains with your elephants on them were an ocean's basin, and creatures we couldn't have made up in our wildest imaginations crawled upon it. Weirder than your jumbos." Elizabeth was up and moving around, pointing, touching stones. Bruce had never seen her animated in this way about her work, and he was impressed — a truly professional woman, but passionate and feminine too.

"Deep in the earth these rocks formed. From heat and pressure unimaginable to us. Yep. Slow changes that gave enough time for these crystals to grow."

She motioned to him and handed him the lens and a rock chip. Their hands touched as he took them. Bruce felt the touch as sharply as if the crystal had cut his hand. He wondered if that touch itself had as ancient a history, or was it the touch of this bewitching woman only? What was happening to him? He had seen brief romances blossom on many of his trips, but never involving himself. A casual fling, yes, but now strange thoughts were rushing through his mind, and those thoughts raced on, out of his control.

Irritated with himself, he looked through the lens and forced himself to focus on what he saw — tiny white crystals, some yellowed with age, or exposure. Dust to dust.

This kopje, this skin of the continent come to the surface, was eroding back to dust. He and Elizabeth were walking on top of an ancient story. They were merely the most recent chapter, yet unwritten. Worn away, he supposed, were the chapters in between the reptiles' age and modern times. This was not the Africa, the Tsavo, he knew so well. Elizabeth's view had changed it for him, perhaps forever. Before it had been an ancient land misused, but also a land in which he had felt at home, a place that had always been the same. Now it was new and changing — pages of an ancient book blown in the wind, wet by the rain, stained by the sun, and on this ancient outcrop Elizabeth and he stood, in their brief moment.

Bruce was uncomfortable with these thoughts. They stirred feelings he did not wish to confront. Feelings not unrelated to those he had felt after the great elephant die-off and his own elephant shootout; feelings of a longing for something he could not name, could not picture; hazy, fuzzy, melancholy. All because of this black-haired witch-woman.

What Elizabeth had opened up to him made him feel even more distressed over his past actions toward the elephants. He was now caught up in the story of an ancient Earth, whose surface and life had gone from one cataclysm to another; and on its eroding surface a parade of species had marched.

What then did it matter that on these Tsavo plains in some few decades some elephants had died? Why should he have killed so many in the name of doing good, in the name of prolonging a population, and prolonging the greenness of Tsavo's surface? So what if he was right about how to manage the elephant population in the short run? It left their blood on his hands; how he wished to wash it away. The sense of unresolved yearning came again, and he felt that the only way he could resolve it, to put those horrid feelings at rest, was to make his peace with Zamani Baba, the greatest of the greatest land mammals. Irrational as this feeling was, it dominated him. His turmoil had personified; Zamani Baba was, yes, a person for him. He could not stay still. No, like a medieval crusader he had always had to seek to do what he believed was morally right. How he longed at this moment to be more like Horst, to have no morality except to satisfy himself, or to be like Cecile had been and be fulfilled by a love of individual elephants, or more like Mary and delight in data. Better to grow fish in a pond for the market, better to live on Maggie's farm, as the American folk song his mother used to sing had said. For a moment, he was angry with Elizabeth, who had cast the feeling of cussedness on him. God help him. He could no longer sit still.

Bruce got up and began to walk around the summit, explaining to Elizabeth that he wanted to look for the kopje's wildlife. But soon, off on his own, he noticed a dust cloud in the distant plains. He lifted his binoculars and looked through them: it was an elephant herd and they were only a few miles away.

He hurried back to Elizabeth and showed her what he had seen. Bruce suddenly seemed agitated, motivated in a way he hadn't been for days. He gathered Mary and they hurried back to camp. Bruce called Johnny on the two-way and gave him the general location and told him to fly over the herd and check to see if any poachers were following them.

It wasn't long before Johnny radioed in. He'd seen a large herd of elephants moving toward their camp. He also had seen several vehicles to the east of his flight path that he was pretty sure were poachers — he thought he saw that the men had automatic weapons and were headed toward the herd. He thought the poachers were an hour or so away. He was also quite certain he had seen Zamani Baba with the herd.

Bruce told the others what Johnny had said, adding that this was a large herd and probably the last and farthest east they would find. He asked Michael and Baker to come with him to help count the elephants, and that Davie and Paul to stay at camp and oversee the safety of the others. Baker said he would go along in his own vehicle.

Elizabeth wanted to go and didn't want to. She was concerned about Bruce and wished she could help, but she was also afraid. Bruce urged her to go with him, telling her that he would leave her in the Land Rover where she would be safe and could watch what happened. He didn't tell her that he thought her experience with first aid might come in handy, but anyway, he just wanted her to be with him. Once in the Land Rover, Bruce could see the herd through his binoculars. He wondered if the poachers were going to ruin his last chance to tranquilize and examine the huge bull and perhaps learn his secrets. Fate seemed to be against him, what with his growing feelings for Elizabeth, and the poachers approaching. He looked again toward the herd and realized they were moving at a quick pace. They now appeared to be less than a mile from camp.

Meanwhile, Paul took over the safety of the camp. Elizabeth noticed the change in Paul, from the rather humble newcomer unsure of what he could do in Tsavo to someone who seemed to have matured and grown in confidence. She watched him as he asked Davie to maintain a lookout at the south side, while he did the same at the north. She tried to remember whether she had ever seen him act so confidently and authoritatively in any of the places she had worked with him before. She couldn't. Yes, no doubt about it, Paul seemed to be maturing. Perhaps he was the one she should be putting her trust in; he did not have Bruce's fixation on elephants, at least not yet.

Paul asked Mary and Howie to look out on the west side of the camp, and he positioned Horst to the east. It wasn't much of a crew for guard duty, Paul thought, but the camp was small and the land so open that he could see all of them easily. Elizabeth found her binoculars and got into the Land Rover with Bruce.

Bruce kept in contact with Johnny by radio as they drove toward the herd. Baker followed in his VW. Johnny circled and landed on rough grass just south of the elephants, jumped out of the plane, and joined the others in the Land Rover.

Michael and Johnny knew that Bruce had brought the tranquilizing kit with him. Michael had tried to dissuade him from using it, but Johnny was keen on the idea and said they had enough time to use it, take the measurements that Bruce wanted, and let the elephant recover before the poachers got near them.

Bruce drove slowly and purposefully ahead and into the herd, Johnny urged Bruce to go farther in among the elephants — for which Bruce needed little encouragement.

For Elizabeth, watching through binoculars, the situation was unpleasantly reminiscent of the morning when Johnny had first arrived and Elizabeth had just met him, and he had swept Bruce, Michael, and herself up in his enthusiasm. She wondered once again what she was letting herself in for — was she becoming attached to one of those crazy elephant lovers? Where was the search for facts and scientific understanding — the reason she had come to Tsavo? Instead, she was out with a bunch of wild adventurers, no matter how much they knew about the wild animals. What was it her major professor had told her when she asked about the adventures he must have had in his wilderness research? "Adventures — Hell, no, I never had any," he had said. "An adventure is the result of either bad planning or foolhardiness. No adventures. Never — mind yourself, girl."

Through her binoculars, Elizabeth was able to zero in on the big old bull, Zamani Baba where he was standing in the midst of the herd. She felt a chill as she watched Bruce steer his Land Rover around one of the other elephants in the herd and then around another, sometimes passing out of her view behind one of the huge creatures, until suddenly he was in front of Zamani Baba, who was standing with two other large males.

Johnny got out of the Land Rover, opened a backpack, and withdrew a small box. Then he lifted up a rifle. Was he going to kill the old bull? She wondered. Johnny took something from the box and handed it to Bruce, who inserted it into the rifle.

Paul peered through his own binoculars from the camp. Davie joined him, and soon all those in the camp were with Paul, watching Bruce and Johnny. So much for guarding all sides of the camp, Paul realized. But then the poachers were going to be after elephants right now, not a bunch of scientists

"Shit, that's a tranquilizin' cartridge," Davie said, throwing a cigarette butt on the ground and stomping on it with the heel of his cowboy boot. What was this, Elizabeth thought? Was Bruce going to put the elephant to sleep at a time when they might be under threat from poachers? For what?

Bruce moved slowly and as quietly as he could, aware that every sound was magnified by Tsavo's silence. Not even doves were calling.

Zamani Baba lifted his trunk as if to catch the scent of the two men. Bruce moved in close to the big elephant, aware only of him. In all the years he had studied elephants and even killed them as part of control programs, he had never been this close to such a big old bull. Walking slowly, closer and closer, he could hear the bull breathing, smell his breath — strong, heavily scented, like a warm organic wind, a kind of life-essence. He could see a wart just above the elephant's eye and several scars from the tusks of other bulls.

The elephant looked down on Bruce with that same old-man-in-bifocals look that Elizabeth had often mentioned. Yes, this was an aging elephant, past his prime. The two old Tsavo experts, Bruce and Zamani Baba, were facing off. He was so close to the old bull that he didn't have to aim carefully, and shot Zamani Baba with the tranquilizing cartridge while holding the gun waist-high. But the bull bolted, and the cartridge glanced off his thick hide. As Zamani Baba moved back a little way, he raised his left front leg, and Bruce noticed a long scar and saw that the big elephant moved that leg somewhat awkwardly, as if in pain. So he was old and suffering, was he? And was there some kind of inner turmoil in him as well, paralleling Bruce's? Was this to be a shootout like in an American Westerns, or the coming together of two sentient and wise creatures?

Zamani Baba put out his ears and fanned the air, the breeze almost knocking Bruce over. Had the cartridge penetrated a little way before glancing off? Was he hesitating intentionally or starting to stumble from the effects of the drug? Bruce heard a low stomach rumbling from the bull. They were so close to each other that Bruce could smell the air near the bull, a heavy organic scent like a cow barn, air laden with the scents of manure and urine and fermenting hay.

The bull opened his mouth; his lower right tooth was pushed far out and had broken near the tip. It looked heavily worn and yellowed. He waved his trunk, bringing it up high, and then trumpeted, shaking Bruce with the vibrating air as if the elephant and he were ringing together as part of the same melody. Bruce wanted to reach out and touch the elephant and he tried to. It wasn't a conscious movement. He was no longer aware of anything but himself and the old bull. Some vague thoughts arose in his mind. Was this him trying to make a gesture of apology for all his past actions? Was he trying to communicate with the bull, who had seemed to him to be the essence of all life?

Was this to be the moment when the truth he had so long sought would be revealed — the truth about Tsavo, about elephants, about himself, about his sufferings? What could the elephant tell him? What couldn't he?

Bruce was no longer aware of the complete irrationality of what he was doing, only of himself and the face of the big bull. He searched that face for answers, but he saw nothing magical or mysterious. Where was the truth that he sought, that he desperately needed to ease his turmoil? Where was the music of the spheres, the songs from a parliament of fowls? He looked for insight, for answers, in Zamani Baba's eyes, hoping to see something like the depth of a meaningful wilderness that the famous American conservationist Aldo Leopold wrote about seeing in a wolf's eyes — eyes of intensity, depth, and intelligence. But he saw only two huge watery globes, old eyes, mysterious only in their vagueness, not yielding any revealed truth. And so, Bruce's suffering intensified. If what he sought was then not in this world, perhaps it was in the next. He felt exhausted and wanted peace and ease, and wished that the elephant would take him there, at this moment only, and only this elephant, and he gave himself up to the creature, starting to fall, to faint, hoping, hoping.

Zamani Baba looked down on the man whom he had seen many times before, and took him up in his trunk. If only now, Bruce thought, the bull would throw him down and end his desperation. W here was his Morpheus who could teach him to see and write? Where was his winged chariot? Were there only vast eternal deserts?

The big elephant lifted Bruce up as on a swing, the elephant like a tall ship waving with a tide, perhaps all that Bruce needed to sail away. But no, no death awaited him; the big bull gently set him down on the ground and pushed him away, blowing at him, scattering him with sand, trumpeting at him one last time, deafening Bruce, who scrambling to his feet, then fell, fainting.

Elizabeth, watching, thought only: What the hell? Is this the great white hunter who had come into her life to save her? She shook her head. Shit, no. She was furious, mostly at herself, but also at Bruce and Johnny for putting themselves, and thereby her and her companions, into this dangerous situation.

After a few minutes, Bruce looked up and saw Johnny bending over him, his hand under Bruce's head. Then Michael appeared, also bending over him. Baker called out that he could see vehicles approaching. He hopped into his VW and sped off toward the approaching vehicles.

Having gotten Bruce on his feet, Michael brought the Land Rover over. Johnny helped Bruce in, climbed in himself.

* * *

It was a dreary group who came together in the camp. Baker returned, having followed the vehicles he had seen off in the distance for a while, but they had gone westward, away from the elephant herd, so they were no longer an immediate problem. Johnny said he'd take a look around in his plane to confirm the poachers stayed on course.

Michael told those who had stayed behind what had happened, leaving out much of what Bruce had tried to do, but giving the facts of the confrontation with the elephants. In the almost-dark of Tsavo's dusk, they spent the next few hours preparing a simple dinner. Bruce had regained his composure, but only looked at Elizabeth without saying anything to her, and otherwise seemed completely distracted. For himself, he had failed.

Horst lit his pipe and frowning, came over to Bruce to ask what had happened. Michael filled Horst in, Elizabeth listening. Horst then made an attempt to lead the group, trying to get them together so he could make a speech, but nobody paid him much attention, and he did not really know what they should do, only that he was certain they should be on their way out as quickly as possible. He asked Bruce when Johnny might fly him to Voi again. He needed to find out what his contacts had been able to accomplish. Bruce looked at him blankly, then said. "Soon." Horst decided that was the best he'd get and wandered off.

Davie and Michael lit a small fire and everyone gathered around. Paul saw that Bruce still seemed dazed and distracted, and so he took the lead and began to speak to the group, quietly but purposefully. He said he thought they needed a few days to get whatever data they had gathered into some kind of order, do another flyover and then try to do research on their way out of the park. He asked Michael if they had time for that. Michael replied that Johnny's last radio message was that he had followed the poachers for a while and they seemed to be heading west as Baker had said, toward the park's boundary, and were not an immediate threat. Based on this, Michael thought they could spend a day or two. He looked to Bruce for confirmation. Bruce nodded.

Elizabeth realized that a not-too-subtle change was taking place, with Paul rising to the surface, and Bruce drifting down, to put it in geological terms. It was as if, because he was freer of the old-time prejudices and beliefs and conflicts that tortured Bruce and Horst, Paul was lighter, less burdened.

Elizabeth was struck by the geometry of the group at that moment. Paul was out in front of the rest, looking toward them. Mary stood by Paul, her metal clipboard in her hand. Elizabeth moved out in front near Mary so she could look at the others, who were moving around as they talked.

Davie smoked a cigarette, now and then moving toward the front near Paul and then Mary, then back again, like a caged animal pacing. Howie, sitting on the ground in an almost lotus position, looking up at everyone, was just behind Elizabeth, Michael in front of Bruce. Last of all was Horst, who hung back from the rest, near the center of the small camp.

Baker, meanwhile, was walking over to his VW bug, away from the others. Each member of the group was acting independently, and each seemed uncertain, undecided. If indecision was a sign of intelligence among the elephants, then this small group of people were geniuses, she thought, smiling grimly.

Collecting himself, Bruce came forward and helped Paul lead a discussion about what needed to be done. Michael m oved off to one side, listening quietly. Eventually — it seemed forever to

Elizabeth — Bruce was left alone. Elizabeth approached him, still torn between sympathy and anger.

"What was that all about — your trying to tranquilize that old bull? Was that supposed to help you count elephants? Was he going to tell you the number and discuss statistical analysis with you?" She began, her anger getting the best of her.

Bruce desperately wanted to apologize, and he tried. He said that he was "so sorry," and that he must have appeared totally bizarre, totally crazy. He admitted that science had nothing to do with it. "It was me, trying to deal with myself, with my life. It sounds sophomoric, I know. I was trying to find the meaning of it all. There. I've said it. We're not supposed to ask such questions, search for such answers. We're supposed to be too advanced a civilization to probe those ancient questions. But I can't stop myself. These questions plague me, give me no rest."

He went on to say that he had watched the elephants for many years, with their calmness, placidity, their unwillingness to hurt other creatures. Especially the old ones. He repeated that he knew how irrational "unscientific for our times, our civilization, is a better way to put it," his actions seemed. "But many before us have believed that nature held the answers for us." Bruce's attempt to explain and apologize made him seem even stranger than the actions themselves.

"To what question?" Elizabeth asked.

Bruce looked surprised, stumped. "All of it, of course." He still looked confused. "Thoreau said it best," he went on. "He wrote that he heard impala meat emitted scents of the plants, the blossoms, that it ate and you could tell therefore what it had been eating. He wished he could achieve that deep a contact with nature."

"But surely you of all people knew better than that," Elizabeth interrupted. "And nature is all around us. We're plopped down in the goddamned middle of it"

"Yes, but Thoreau said it the best again — he said he caught a glimpse of a woodchuck and wanted to 'devour him raw; not that I was hungry then, except for that wildness he represented.'"

"So this was your attempt to devour the wilderness? Own it in a way? To understand it?"

"Something like that."

"But Bruce, nature's all around you — us — here," Elizabeth said. "Why did you think you could find it in some deeper way in an elephant?"

Bruce frowned. "It wasn't *nature.* It was myself and the meaning of my place in the world. I was hoping. I don't know how to put it. It's not just me. I feel we are all lost. We know more — have more facts about nature than any people ever had. But we don't understand how we fit in. It isn't just me. Look around you in the cities, in your hometown. We are all confused about where we fit into nature, into the world."

Bruce looked out over the darken plains, a taut, painful expression on his face, and, in spite of herself, in spite of her anger, her heart went out to him, and she walked over to him, hugged him, and kissed his cheek.

"So you don't hate me."

"Hardly," she laughed. "But I can't say I completely understand you either." He held her hand tight.

"Is your quest over, then?"

"Let's just say it failed. Or more to the point, I failed."

Beyond Paul and Bruce, but still moving toward them in their typical, somewhat individualistic way, came the herd of elephants. It seemed an ominous presence to Elizabeth, as if to tell them that this was their turf and they wanted the people to leave. It left her with an even more unsettled feeling. She feared the elephants might treat them like they had the Cape buffalo one of those days that now seemed long ago, and charge again and again until the people retreated. But how could they retreat with all their gear out and exposed? And what were they really going to do? How dangerous was their situation?

CHAPTER 33

Charm

All my means are sane; my motives and objects are mad.

Melville's Ahab, in *Moby Dick*

It was time for Horst to make his next move, as he had with so many young women. Tensions were high after Bruce's encounter with the big elephant and emotions were easily exploited at a time like this. The opportunity presented itself after the group discussion at the campfire. He was sitting at the picnic table inside the screened meeting tent, rifling through some papers in the light of a Coleman gas lantern. Mary, seeing him there alone as she passed by, stopped uncertainly, then stepped in, smiling brightly. But Horst only briefly glanced up and then turned back to the papers he was studying. What's wrong? She wondered. Had she offended him somehow? She reviewed all the events since their last conversation, but could think of nothing she had done that might have irritated him. She came nearer.

"What are you looking at?" she asked.

"A map," Horst grumbled, frowning and not looking up. Out of the corner of his eye he could see her face color. That was a particular advantage of her lovely pale skin — it was so revealing of her emotions. She could be read like an exposé magazine. Clearly, he had succeeded in throwing her off balance.

She stood awkwardly for several moments while he purposely ignored her. Then she sat down next to him. "What are you looking for?" she asked.

"Something on the map," he said tersely, still not looking up.

She was flustered, just as he'd hoped. These ambitious young women who wanted to be treated as equals in science. The more eager they were, the more vulnerable they were. First step: Be nice to them, encourage them to think you take them seriously. Second step: Attack, shatter their newfound confidence, make her cry. It was so easy — and, he had to admit to himself, it was fun. Third step, sympathize with her, and then screw her.

He continued to ignore her. He rattled the map irritably and frowned. He knew that his position as a scientist, his status, gave him power over her, as it had with so many other young women. They were attracted to the power itself, and felt they must be wrong and he must be right.

"Have I done something to annoy you?" Mary asked in a small voice. Horst scowled.

"Don't you see I'm trying to concentrate? Bruce can't be counted on as a leader anymore. We're in a bad situation."

"I thought we were working together," she said. "That's what we were talking about the other night. Don't you think I should know what you're thinking about and planning?"

"You young scientists are so arrogant. You think you know what I know and can participate in decisions the same way I can."

"I never said that or thought that. I only want to contribute, and I can't do that unless I know what's going on. Paul asked me to join this team because I know some things that could be useful. If that's not the case, then I shouldn't be here."

He was making progress. The key was to get her to cry, and he was almost there. "Well, what have you contributed so far?"

Tears welled up in her eyes and she looked away. "I thought I was contributing."

"Look, our situation's tricky, in case you haven't noticed, and I'm doing my best to figure out a good next step. That's why I'm studying this map. You want me to play daddy to you and pretend that you can help? Well, sorry, there isn't time."

Mary took a deep breath. Her very reason for being here was being questioned by one of the most important people in her field. Tsavo blurred, and in spite of herself she began to cry.

Horst smiled to himself. Time for step three: Turn sympathetic, become the friendly father figure she had hoped he'd be. She'd be so relieved and grateful to be back in his good graces, she'd do anything he wanted. It never failed.

"Mary, why, you're crying. I didn't know you were so sensitive. This is a tough place for a sensitive person." He patted her shoulder. "Of course you can help out. Here, come over and take a look at the map with me. I was so concerned about our situation that I was much too curt with you. Really, it's not you I'm angry at."

But Mary's fears about herself — that she might not really have the brains and the imagination to be an important scientist — were not so easily allayed. She couldn't help herself. Tears poured down her checks and she sobbed aloud. Horst was getting a hard-on watching her. He moved over and put his arm around her.

"Now, now, sweetheart, it's not so bad. This is your first real field experience in such a wild place, and you've seen some frightening things. Sometimes it's good to just let it out. You just have a good cry." He drew her into his arms, and she put her head on his chest, her tears wetting his shirt. He could feel her breasts heaving. Why was it that this moment was almost as satisfying — perhaps even more satisfying — than the actual ejaculation that inevitably resulted from his plan of action?

He was so intent on his conquest that he failed to notice Elizabeth quietly entering the tent. She marched over to him. "Horst, for God's sake, are you crazy? Leave her alone. Mary, get away from him. Don't you get it? He does this with every female graduate student and young faculty member when he comes to a university. He's famous for it. And he's got you at a disadvantage."

"What the hell are you talking about?" Horst said angrily, standing up. "Mary and I were looking at this map and she got upset and I was trying to comfort her."

"Sure you were. Comfort her between her legs!"

Horst turned red. "Don't you speak to me like that, young lady. Nobody speaks to G. Horst Grobben like that. I'll get you fired for this! Then sue you for defamation on top of it."

Elizabeth stamped her foot. "Mary, get the hell away from him. Horst, take me to court. Try it. I'd welcome it. I could get twenty-five witnesses to back me up. It would be the trial of the century in a college town, expose you for what you really are."

Horst turned on her. "You bitch, how dare you! I'll hold a hearing about this tomorrow morning. I'll get you out of this group if it's the last thing I do."

"Don't pull that crap on me. I can recite your methods step by step. The women's-rights lobby at my university has a secret poster about you, just you. Don't pull that status stuff either. Just leave Mary alone. Mary, get away from the sonofabitch."

Horst grabbed Elizabeth and pushed her hard. Her back struck the table, and the entire tent shook, almost collapsing. Mary watched in horror. Was she going crazy? Were they all going crazy in this crazy place?

Elizabeth started to pull herself up. Her back hurt where she had banged against the table, and for a moment she felt dizzy, but she forced herself to get up and walk over to Horst, who had turned his back on her. "There's just one more thing I want to say to you," she said, grabbing him by the shoulder and turning him around, even though he was a good five inches taller than she was.

"What's that?"

"Just this," and she kicked him as hard as she could in the groin. Horst doubled over and fell down. "You get the message, you goddamned sadist? Leave Mary alone. Go screw a gazelle." She yanked Mary out of the tent and pushed her toward her own tent, leaving Horst still writhing on the ground.

The noise brought others running — Howie, Paul, and Bruce. Through the screen, they saw Horst curled into a fetal position in the dirt, retching, clutching his groin. Paul rushed in. "What happened?" Then to Howie, "Get the first-aid kit."

Bruce recognized immediately what Horst's problem was. "Don't bother," he told Howie. "There's nothing in the first-aid kit for this. He'll be okay."

"But look at him."

"He just mistook a tigress for a lady. He'll be fine in a few minutes — that is, fine enough for most of the things we really need him to do in the next few days."

Paul looked puzzled but he was glad Bruce seemingly was coming back to normal. Howie looked from Bruce to Paul. "Paul, Bruce's trying to tell you that Horst made a move on one of the women, either Mary or Elizabeth or both, and one of them kicked him in the balls," he said.

"Christ," Paul said, shaking his head as he left the tent.

* * *

The next morning Elizabeth awoke with a single thought: I will not speak to that bastard Horst. I will not, I will not. Mary was still asleep. Elizabeth got up, made up her cot quickly, and threw on some clothes. Grabbing her towel, washcloth, and toiletry kit, she hurried out. There, standing in the midst of camp, looking through his binoculars, stood Horst. She kicked at the soil. Why the hell didn't Tsavo just take him out? Where was some damned rhino when she needed it? Or that big elephant? She tried to walk swiftly by him so he wouldn't notice her, but as she passed he let the binoculars drop down around his neck and turned to her with a cold smile.

"Good morning, Elizabeth," he said as if nothing had happened.

She hurried past without bothering to reply, so furious that she could barely think and barely see as she strode to the artesian well at the edge of the camp. She was beginning to wash her face when out of the corner of her eye she caught a movement in the thick bush. It was a lion, a big male, walking about twenty yards from her. She froze. The lion stopped and turned and gave her a long, steely look, eyes unblinking, reminding her of the leopard at Davie's vulture tent. But not till the lion crouched down to face her was she seriously afraid. Terribly afraid. She could not move. She had no weapon. Nobody else was up except that bastard Horst, who'd probably love to see her dead. If she cried out, it might cause the lion to spring at her. His face seemed huge. Goddammit, she had been so angry that she had forgotten the importance of being observant, of always being alert, always being wary out here in this wild country.

The lion, still staring at her, crouched lower, backbone curved downward in a concave arc, like a house cat getting ready to charge a bird. Elizabeth was the bird, and she realized she was shaking. From sleep to anger to terror. Was there no end to this frenzy of emotions out here? The lion edged a few feet toward her. Since arriving in Tsavo, she had watched this stealthy attack by lions on unsuspecting prey several times from the safety of a Land Rover. It had been simply fascinating, the great cat acting just like a kitten with a toy mouse, trying hard not to be noticed, moving slowly, slowly.

A bird in a tree saw the lion and let out that seemingly universal East African warning to alert the other animals, a sort of coughing sound. The lion relaxed its body, sank down and put its paws over its eyes, and feigned sleep, again just like a kitten at play. It was trying to make the other animals think that it was not hunting, that its stomach was full and it was sleeping lazily. But the ruse didn't work. Gazelles and wildebeest moved away. Birds flew off. The lion took its paws from its eyes and looked around, actually looked guilty. For a moment, she thought it looked like Horst and that maybe she could kick it in the balls too. But then the lion crouched down in its attack position again and inched forward.

She knew she might be dead in a few moments. She tried to think what she could do. She couldn't run — she knew that a lion, like all cats, instinctively views a running animal as prey. Maybe she could hide — wait, in the thornbushes — that would give her some protection, but they were maybe fifteen feet away, and the lion was within thirty feet. It would be chancy, but she didn't have much time to think. She realized she was still shaking, probably giving off whatever it is that predators can tell is fear — scents, motions, attitudes. The lion moved another half foot toward her, then suddenly jerked its head around to look at something else.

She looked too. It was Michael, huge, silent, his spear in one hand, his rifle leaning against his left side. Oh, *thank God*, she thought. He put a finger over his mouth to make sure she would be silent. He did not speak or look at her, but focused all of himself on the lion. He drew his spear back, ready to throw, a motion that got the lion's attention.

The big cat's back shifted from concave to flat. Michael took one long silent step toward the lion. The cat backed away, stomach touching the ground, slowly, slowly. Michael advanced again. The lion crept back farther, then farther still. Michael charged and shouted something in Maasai that Elizabeth did not understand, and the lion turned and ran, tail beneath him, disappearing into the bush.

Michael returned to her and leaned down to ask if she was all right. "You must always watch carefully at dawn or dusk when you walk outside of camp," he said kindly.

Elizabeth tried to stop shaking. She felt weak, almost faint, as both her anger and her fear dissipated.

"Thank you, thank you, Michael," she said quietly and leaned against him. "I was foolish, wasn't I? God, I was so scared! It won't happen again. But thank you very much." She wanted to hug him. Could she? She did. She held tight to him.

Michael held her and spoke softly. He told her that the first time he had confronted a lion he, too, had been frightened, terribly frightened, so she had nothing to be ashamed of. But she should, he reminded her again, stay alert.

"I'm sorry, Michael, but to tell the truth, Horst, got me so angry, I couldn't think about anything else." She held on to him, imbibing his smell, which seemed to be a natural extension of the desert brush, soil, wildlife, air. Was this what Bruce was looking for in his quest to understand nature? If so, maybe she had found it. She didn't want to let go.

Michael was struck once again by the forthrightness of Americans, especially of American women, and this one, most of all. He enjoyed her boldness, but also found it somewhat alarming. But he could not pull away. He looked down and soon saw Elizabeth turn her head to look up. Her expression seemed unfocused but with a strange sort of bliss. She was expecting him to kiss her, but he did not.

"Thank you," she murmured. Michael was deeply moved by his contact with her body, reminding him of his British girlfriends when he had gone to school there, especially the one he had lived with for a year. For a moment he wanted nothing more than an intimate contact with Elizabeth. But with Bruce not functioning as leader and Paul, although beginning to take charge, not quite ready, Michael decided this was not the time. Hoping there would be that time soon, he felt himself pulling away from her. He told her that he was going to follow the lion to make sure it had really gone away and was not hiding nearby. She would be all right, he assured her.

Elizabeth came back to herself, slowly. What was she thinking? Tsavo was driving her irrational too, capturing her in its wildness, which she had thought she had come to understand. She didn't know if she should apologize to Michael, but he looked so cool and composed that it didn't seem necessary. She squeezed his hand and thanked him deeply.

"I'll just get back to camp," she said, wishing she could believe the lion wouldn't stalk her. But then why shouldn't she? Of all the group, Michael knew Tsavo's lions best.

He pointed to her towel and washcloth, and left her to her toilette. She was sure that somewhere, just out of sight, he was watching and guarding her as she brushed her teeth, washed her face, and brushed her hair. When she was done, she walked slowly back to camp.

Horst, seated on a camp chair, bird guidebook open in his hands, sipped a cup of coffee. As she passed, he gave her that same cold smile, then returned to his guidebook. She did notice, however, that he was sitting somewhat awkwardly, so that certain body parts were not in direct contact with the chair. She smiled. He can fake it from the waist up, but the truth lies below, she thought. Got the bastard just right. She stopped and turned quickly, and caught a glimpse of Michael at the edge of camp, making sure that she was safely back. Then she went into her tent and collapsed on her cot. As she drifted off to a quick nap, she wondered how in the world Mary and Horst would be able to stay together on the same team. And she wondered why she had had so much trouble letting go of Michael.

CHAPTER 34

The Shootout

Force, no matter how concealed, begets resistance.

Lakota Indians saying

A few of the others were stirring when Paul stepped out of his tent. Michael was outside, starting a fire, his rifle and spear nearby as always. Bruce was doing something, over at one of the Land Rovers. One Land Rover was gone — Johnny had probably taken it to the airstrip, Paul assumed, to check the plane.

As Paul was brushing his teeth, his mouth full of toothpaste, he heard a motor. Assuming it was Johnny returning, he paid no attention. Then he heard gunshots and saw men with guns emerging from a Toyota Land Cruiser. Caught without any weapon, he froze, unable to move. He watched Michael slip quickly behind a tree as five men carrying automatic weapons came out of the Land Cruiser and moved toward the camp. They seemed in no hurry, as if they expected no opposition. One wandered to Paul's right, putting himself in view of Bruce, who lay behind the Land Rover and shot him immediately with a pistol. A bullet ripped through Mary's tent. Bruce rose quietly from behind the Land Rover, aiming his pistol, but Michael got his shot off first. The second man fell, but in response the three others started shooting toward Bruce. Bruce went flat on the ground. With only pistols and rifles against assault weapons, they were doomed, Paul thought.

Then there was a loud burst from an automatic weapon. Paul dove behind a bush and tried to think. If he could reach the man Bruce had shot, he could get his weapon. The staccato burst continued for what seemed a very long time. One or two bullets whistled over Paul's head, but none came near him, nor, from his prone position, could he see any of them hitting near Bruce or Michael. Horst was nowhere to be seen. To his surprise, Paul saw that the shots were coming from behind the Land Cruiser. Another burst and the Cruiser's gas tank suddenly exploded, sending bright red and yellow flames and dark smoke skyward.

Through the smoke, Baker appeared, and to Paul's surprise, he was carrying an automatic weapon. Baker, not seeing any of the others, all of who had continued to hide, walked around the armed intruders, checking to make sure each was dead. One, whom he hadn't gotten to and was off to a side, raised up and, although wounded, slowly raised his weapon and aimed it at Baker. But another shot was fired from outside the camp, killing that last of the intruders. Paul looked in the direction that the shot was fired and saw Joseph appear. Seeing Paul lying on the ground, Joseph put his finger to his lips, clearly telling Paul to remain silent. Paul stayed on the ground, watching. He saw Joseph wave at Baker and join him, and the two cautiously approached each of the bodies on the ground. Everything was strangely quiet, just as it had been when Paul had started to brush his teeth; it was eerie, as if the shootout and the killing of five men had never happened.

Paul felt as if he were thawing, and tried to think what to do first. Mary. He rushed over to her tent. Davie was already there, calling to her and Elizabeth. Mary put her head out. She was unhurt but frightened. Howie came out of his tent holding his little book of random numbers. A bullet had grazed the cover and torn it off. Pages of random numbers were blowing away. Elizabeth, just venturing out, grabbed pages as they drifted by. Everyone slowly gathered around Baker. Bruce went over to the burned-out Land Cruiser and looked at it and Joseph joined him. Davie and Michael checked the bodies again, just to make sure.

Johnny raced up, on foot. "I was out watching wildlife," he said, panting as he surveyed the scene. "Heard some gunfire and came back. Before I could do anything, I saw Baker getting out of his VW with a submachine gun."

Horst stuck his head out of his tent. "What the hell? Now those poachers are coming and shooting us in our goddamned camp?"

"Jesus, Baker, you carry a an automatic rifle?" Howie walked over to Baker who was crouched next to one of the bodies. "I thought you liked peace and quiet."

"Oh, I do, yes, that's a fact," Baker replied. "But you gotta be equipped. I didn't come out here to get myself killed. Same with knowing about cars and motors — anybody who couldn't fix a car'd be a fool to *drive* out to a place like Tsavo totally on their own. He'd be better off walking — couldn't get so far from help that he couldn't walk back. And if he's on a horse, then he needs a spare pony in case his horse dies. In this case my spare horse was Joseph. Thank you very much my man."

Joseph smiled in return.

For the first time, Howie did not grin.

"I may be a little different, but I'm not a fool," Baker said, looking at Howie. "There's a long distance between those two, you know."

Davie bent to examine each body, going through the pockets, collecting knives and any identification. Two were from Somalia, the other three from Kenya. He piled up the knives and guns.

"And how come you were here as well?" Paul asked Joseph.

"Just good luck. Tell the truth, I like what you guys are doing."

Bruce got a Land Rover and hitched up its trailer. He backed the trailer to the bodies, and the rest of the men loaded them in. Bruce asked Johnny, Paul, and Baker to stay at the camp in case more poachers came, and asked Elizabeth to come along with him. She jumped in with Michael, Howie, and Bruce. Joseph got in his Land Cruiser, and Davie joined him. Bruce asked Elizabeth where the soil would be easiest to dig a grave. She pointed to the northwest and then told him where to stop. They buried the five poachers in a common grave. Nobody said anything. Nobody knew what to say.

* * *

It was mid-day when they returned, and they gathered in the shade of the tent in silence. Joseph was still with them. He spoke quietly to Davie as they joined the group.

"Guess you're invited. Better be. Saved one of us, at least — maybe more," Davie said. Mary stayed close to Paul, as far away from Horst as she could, and never looked at him

Horst, meanwhile, filled his pipe, lit it and smoked. He was thinking about what to do about Joseph. He'd thought he'd made an ally and now this. Was this the ruthless poacher he had thought he met? No doubt Joseph knew his way around Tsavo, about as good as Bruce and Michael. What kind of help could he be if he cozied up to the group? But maybe it was a ploy on Joseph's part. They definitely needed to talk. He looked over and Elizabeth caught his eye. He looked away. She had been trouble from the beginning.

Mary walked to the door of the tent and looked around; the hornbills, her favorites, whom she had come to think of as her friends, were nowhere to be seen. No animal called, not even the doves. She felt nature had abandoned her.

Bruce led the group in a discussion about their options. "The way I see it, we have two choices — either we quit what we came for and head back to the main road and go back to Nairobi, or we see what our opposition is and try to accomplish as many of our original goals as possible."

"If there aren't many, we may be able to scare most of them and get them out of the park," Johnny offered.

Horst cut in. "If I could get to Voi, I could call my contacts, even get to the media and get some international backing to stop these poachers. But there's no use doing that if there are no elephants left out here. Nature'll take care of herself if we just clear out," Horst said. "And if the poachers clear out, too, everything will be all right."

Mary inadvertently glanced at Horst, then quickly toward Elizabeth, who was staring, unblinking, at him.

"Come on, Horst, Mother Nature may take care of herself, but the poachers aren't going to just go away, and against poachers with machine guns," Bruce said. "How in hell are the elephants going to take care of themselves? We've seen what's happened everywhere else, and here, too."

"Well, the way I see it . . . " Paul began hesitantly. "The way I see it," he repeated, "we really don't have a choice. We either do the job we were sent for or send the money back. We've spent too much of the money to do that. And besides, I came out here to do a job and I want to finish it. I trust Bruce and Michael to see us through safely, or else warn us when things are just too dangerous. But unless they say so now. . . "

He paused again and looked at each of them. "We go ahead as efficiently as we can. We continue a survey of the park as we start back, or as much of it as we can — locate the herds, try to get a sense of the total number of herds and the pattern of their distribution. Do another air count if we can. From that, we can make at least a rough estimate of the total numbers. Count the bulls we see along the way. If we have enough fuel, or if we can get fuel resupplied . . ." He looked at Johnny.

Johnny nodded. Bruce was glad that Paul felt the same way he himself did. The group was deciding to stay.

"I'll go to Voi with you then," said Horst. "If you fools want to carry on, we'll need my contacts more than ever." Bruce ignored him.

"Can't we radio out for help if we need it?" Mary asked.

Bruce looked at her. "Or Johnny could fly back to Nairobi for help. Get the police or the army down here while we wait," Paul suggested.

Horst interrupted. "Nairobi even better."

"The government angle might work if we were in the States, but let's be straight about this — we're not sure who's funding these guys," Bruce said. "Poachers usually don't have the money to go out and buy the kind of equipment we've been seeing — airplanes, new vehicles, new guns. Somebody bigger and richer is backing them."

"What Bruce's saying is, this probably involves corruption in this government," Johnny explained. "Maybe pretty high up."

Bruce nodded. "Right. So if we radio out, we may just be talking to people who don't want us here and don't mind if the poachers go after us. They may even help them. That's happened before. For all we know, the people we go to for help could be the ones trying to get the ivory. And it could extend ever further — to some international group, and the government here could claim to be innocent."

"Oh, horse pucky," Horst sputtered. "You know my contacts, Airley. Totally above board. Of course they work with the governments of these countries. They have to. We live in the twentieth century after all. I'm offering a solution and you continue to ignore it. We get three international conservation groups behind us and we get out safely and protect the elephants. End of story. What about you, Joseph. Can you drive me to Voi? It's a ways but I won't take long once we get there. Just a quick phone call."

"I don't know why not," Joseph said. He had remained quiet through the discussion, so a few members of the group sat up and looked toward him, realizing he had joined them.

"Anything to help. I find I'm getting attached to you people," he said light-heartedly, a rare smile spreading across his face. He looked over at Horst, whom he was beginning to distrust and dislike, always talking down to him, treating him like some kind of go-to guy of no importance. The kind of upper-class person who had always treated him that way.

"Go and talk to your people, Horst," Bruce said. "But if their plan involves the Kenyan government in any way I'm not interested. Understand?"

"We'll see," Horst replied and turned to Joseph. "Can we go in the morning?"

"First thing," Joseph replied, sitting back and directing a well-intentioned look to the group.

Bruce directed a pointed look at Horst who smiled as if in agreement.

"But I'm not sure I get it, Bruce. If they don't want us here, why did they give us permission to come here?" Elizabeth asked.

"You forget that this is a National Park and an internationally recognized nature preserve," Bruce pointed out. "If all of a sudden some restriction came down for us as a group of scientists ..."

"And bloody well-known ones at that," Johnny interjected. "Bruce here is known all over, and Michael is famous as well. If they make it public they didn't want Michael in here, that wouldn't do much for their image in the international community. Wouldn't help tourism, or their reputation among the conservation groups."

"But you're saying they could be working against what the conservation groups want," Elizabeth responded

"Not in the open. Too many connections. The World Bank and other loan funds might disappear if the word got out," Bruce answered.

"Isn't the word out?" Horst put in.

"Now that's maybe a bit of irony," Bruce answered. "If it is out in fact, they wouldn't want it out officially. See what I mean? You have to think again about how much money is really involved in the ivory trade, at least in proportion to other sources of funds in a nation like this. Most of the ivory trade has been out of the low countries — Belgium especially. So if there were big backers of poaching, they could be from one of those countries, or from one of the Asian nations that value ivory so much, or — they could be right here."

Paul frowned. "So we don't know who we can trust and are more or less on our own, you're saying."

"Well, there's the international conservation groups — they're behind us. And UNEP — the United Nation's environment program. But there isn't an army out here ready to rescue us, if that's what you're referring to, no," Bruce answered.

Bruce put Howie in charge of designing a plan to search out elephants one last time so they could get an estimate of the number of elephants in the entire park. The group dispersed, Joseph nodding to many as he walked toward his Land Cruiser. Horst followed.

Howie spread a plastic poncho on the ground, laid out his notebooks, papers, m aps, and his book of random numbers, and set to work. Soon after, Baker drifted over to watch.

Howie drew the search plan — a series of zigzagging lines — on a copy of the maps of Tsavo's northeast, and Bruce, Paul, and Johnny watched with interest. Johnny was pleased to see where the path led and quickly pointed out that one of the lines crossed another airstrip, one that he had used several times. They agreed that they would have to work quickly and had to move to the next camp on Howie's map. They would pack up and go at first light the next day.

They talked long into the night, quietly, realizing that they had to leave soon and could take only the shortest time to gather the information they needed to take back with them. Bruce quietly took Paul aside and asked what he thought of Joseph becoming part of what they were doing.

"Not completely comfortable with it," Paul said. "But I'd say let's give it a go. It seems he's making individual inroads with members of the group. Horst, now Davie, and probably Howie. We've just got to get him away from being Horst's go-to boy. Joseph seems to know his way around Tsavo too well, and that's what Horst is lacking."

"We'll have to manage it. Horst no doubt has something up his sleeve."

"Yeah and who knows what he'll be up to in Voi tomorrow."

"We'll have to make it so it doesn't make any difference," Bruce said. "We get what we need and get out. Try not to let him get control of things. That's what he's after."

"You're right on that. If we do what we came to do he won't be able to insert himself in the dynamic."

"You got it," Bruce said.

"Easier said than done."

"Isn't about everything?" They laughed together and turned to walk back to the others.

Paul joined Elizabeth, Davie, Mary, and Howie at the campfire and talked about what data they had gotten and what, at best, it might show. Then he talked with Michael and Bruce about the fastest and most efficient way they could pack and leave; what they could leave behind and what they needed to take; who would fly out in Johnny's plane and who would travel in the Land Rovers.

Eventually Mary grew sleepy and began to doze off. She heard the mournful call of the hornbill and looked at Paul, wishing she were in a nest with him, safe. The fire dwindled to coals. Paul came over and sat next to her and then walked her to their tent. When he returned, only Bruce and Baker remained at the fire, talking softly, Baker resting his big gun on his lap as he listened to Bruce. Paul wondered where, among all those cigar boxes, Baker kept that big weapon. Then he, too, went to his own tent, feeling the dry soil beneath his feet, hearing the night sounds, muted in the open plain.

CHAPTER 35

The Economics of Ivory

His teeth are ivory so well known in Europe, some of which have been seen as large as a man's thigh, and a fathom in length.

Samuel Johnson's eighteenth-century dictionary

The noisy shootout the day before had alarmed the male hornbill, and he had flown away from his nest for the rest of a day. The next morning he returned and watched the people pack up their camp. Soon the ground was empty of human accouterments. But then the vehicles started up, and the noises alerted the hornbill. He flew down and circled the Land Rovers as they drove away. Once again, only Mary noticed him and heard his last, mournful cry.

Moving camp with three Land Rovers, an airplane and Baker's VW beetle was a bit of a trick, but Bruce and Johnny had worked out a kind of leapfrogging, moving the airplane short distances to rough but usable landing areas Johnny had found in his years working in Tsavo. On the way from one rough, grassy landing strip to another, Johnny followed the Land Rovers, circling them, sometimes buzzing them, telling them over the two-way radio about wildlife he had seen and occasionally landing nearby.

Baker had rapidly become an unofficial member of the team. He remained independent, always camping off by himself, but each morning he was there and ready to participate, to help wherever help was needed. Always curious, always asking questions. He was enjoying their company and learning about what they were doing. And now that the shootout had occurred, he decided that the team might need his help, so he decided to accompany the scientists when they moved to their new camp, farther northeast into the park. They stopped frequently, following Howie's instructions from his little book of random numbers, to make measurements, with Mary writing numbers and notes carefully on forms in her clipboard; Davie, attentive, helping her with observations; Paul making many of the measurements with her. They worked quickly, always with an eye out for signs of poachers, and listening for the noise of a motor vehicle.

On their way north they crossed the Tiva River — Tsavo's other big river, Michael explained to Paul. While Bruce, Michael, and Baker drove a ways downstream to some shallows, Davie headed straight across at a point where there was a sandy bottom and the channel seemed narrower. But his vehicle was soon stuck in the sand. Everyone got out to help push, but the stuck Land Rover simply spit water and wet sand over them. Soon they were all dirty, wet, and frustrated. Michael told them to stop and wait, and he went off and cut a large palm frond from a tree along the riverbank, and slid it under the rear wheel that had the least traction. With this done, the wheel rolled smoothly over the frond, and the Land Rover sputtered and coughed its way up the bank onto dry land, amid some cheering. After this effort, all were thirsty, reminding Elizabeth how dry and dangerous Tsavo could be.

After a short break, they proceeded on, and soon came over a rise and saw below them, spread out over the wide plain, a herd of elephants. The vehicles stopped and everyone got out and looked. Some of the larger elephants had huge tusks.

"If you were to harvest that ivory, you'd have a lot of money," Baker said. "I can see why poor people get into poaching."

"Rich people, too," Bruce answered. "A lot of money is made by a small number of people from that. You might control this whole country's economy if you could control the ivory trade. They trade ivory like they trade gold and diamonds — in a kind of stock market in Belgium. You can buy shares whose value is in the ivory itself, not in what it is made into. Just like with gold and diamonds."

"Why, if I got out my old rifle, I could be a rich son of a gun without even trying," Baker said with a sly smile on his face. "Seems the economics of it could be pretty interesting. I'll have to do a few calculations before I go to bed tonight and see what a balance sheet might look like. I bet it will look a hell of a lot better than cutting timber on the farm back home."

He positioned himself nearer to Bruce to see the big tuskers better, "Now that one — see it?" He touched Bruce's arm. "That one would be a whole month's salary in the States, let alone here, I'll bet," Baker mused.

"Ever shoot an elephant?" he asked Bruce.

"Yes mostly for scientific study, sometimes to manage the populations." He chose not to repeat the painful history that he had revealed to Elizabeth.

"It seems to me you could do some ivory farming and make a pretty good living off it," Baker said.

"Not likely," Bruce answered, thinking about his attempts to make sure the products from shooting elephants went to the local people. As he had told Elizabeth, that hadn't worked.

"That a fact? Why so?"

Bruce paused to think how best to explain it. "Look at it this way. Think about that herd as money — say, a million dollars."

"Okay, a million it is. On the hoof."

"Now suppose you want to stay in the ivory-farming business and keep your herd of elephants always about the same number. So that means you just harvest the excess growth — never decrease the size of the herd, just cull out the growth. Right?"

"Right. That would be the way to do it — once you figured out how many head you could run on your land."

"Sure," Bruce said. Running elephants on the land was both an amusing idea and a slightly disturbing one. He thought some more, quietly, and as he did, Baker saw a marabou stork circling high in the sky off to the side of the herd. Perhaps, from what Davie had been telling him, there was a dead elephant or some other dead animal nearby. Dust blew up from the elephant herd.

"Well, how fast do you think your ivory or elephants will grow?"

"I don't know," Baker said. "Don't they grow sort of like a Kansas wheat field?"

"Not exactly. You plant that wheat from hybrids, use a lot of fertilizers and pest-control chemicals, tend it, get a big yield, independent of what you grew last year. But with an elephant herd you're relying on the regrowth the herd can do itself. It's too expensive to import or buy young ones." He scanned the scene before him. "An elephant herd will increase maybe five percent a year, if you're lucky and plan right. Now, suppose you look at that money on the hoof and make another decision — decide to turn it into real money and put that money in a bank or CD or investment."

Baker thought for a minute. "I gotcha," he said. "I shoot all the elephants, every last one. Don't even want to bother keeping the little ones as pets if they're not making me money. So I take that million dollars of ivory and sell it. Put the dough in the bank. Let's see, a good CD could make me six, seven percent these days. I could buy myself the prettiest house in Nairobi and put my feet up on the veranda, live off that sixty or seventy thousand dollars a year income. Never have to lift a finger again."

"That's it," said Bruce.

Baker shook his head. "That does sound like a good deal. Why hell, there's more to poaching than I realized. Are we on the wrong side?" He laughed. "But you and Howie and I, we want the elephants. They're more fun to look at than a pile of money. So how are we gonna do that?"

"People have been trying to figure that one out for years. Probably a combination of things. Make money from tourism — that's the idea of these parks. Michael's people are trying that. Make money leading hunters and photographers — that's what I thought was a good idea until I tried it, couldn't get it to work. But maybe mix it up a bit, run a tour outfit. Popularize research and make a living from that. But you've got to love the animals and want to do it, want it more than money."

Baker nodded. "So that's why the poachers and whoever's paying them don't care whether there are elephants tomorrow. They just want that money in the bank today. They don't give a shit about watching elephants any more than I care about watching a pile of money."

"You got it," Davie said, joining in.

"Okay, let's look at it another way," Baker said.

"How many ways are you going to look at it?" Howie asked.

"Many's I can. Now, Bruce, suppose I buy myself a three-million-dollar herd. Harvest two-thirds of them — kill 'em off completely. Invest one million in a little house for me and the wife, invest the other million to pay for farming the last third. Then keep that third just to watch."

Bruce looked at the distant herd. If only such a scheme could be made to work, if only people weren't "so damned greedy," as his father, a longtime conservationist, often said.

"Sounds good to me. But first you have to persuade the conservationists that you really will save that third of the herd after you shoot the first two-thirds. Greed has overcome goodness before, you know, maybe they just won't trust you. And don't forget, you have to persuade the poachers to leave the rest of your herd alone."

"Well, we're doing that right now."

"No, we're *trying* to do that. We may not succeed."

"At least you fellows are trying, and you might succeed."

"*Might*'s a mighty big word out here," Bruce said, "especially looking the wrong way down an elephant gun."

Michael interrupted and said he thought they had stopped long enough and should be on their way.

* * *

Joseph had picked Horst up at dawn and as soon as he got settled, Horst said, "The poachers know we're here and don't like it. We've got to move fast."

"I'll be doing that all the way to Voi," Joseph responded, already annoyed and it was going to be a long trip.

Horst shifted in his seat, taking hold of a grab bar as Joseph drove the Land Cruiser hard, bouncing off rocks with dust seeping in from every gap in the vehicle.

"You see," Horst said, coughing out some dust. "Once I can talk to my people, we'll have an exit strategy in place. Those poachers won't know what hit them."

"Think they care about you?" Joseph asked.

"Well, they must have heard of me," Horst answered. "I'm an international expert on wildlife conservation, with all kinds of contacts that could cause them trouble."

"Yeah, shit, but they can walk their way around you never mind."

"Well what would you know about what I can get done? They seem to have the wherewithal to get what they wanted when they came into our camp."

"Sure, lots more ammo. But who killed who? What is this, Horst, you think us country fellows don't know nothin'? Can't do anything? Shit. Look at Davie. Pretty competent if you ask me."

"Seems like you're feeling pretty good about our group."

"Good about the group until you start to pull this shit on me about your fancy rich friends goin' to save the world. Maybe I'm better off working with Davie and maybe even with my old school chums, Bruce and what the hell even Michael."

"A Maasai? Don't think like us, I'm sure. How do we know what's in his mind, what he really wants."

"Educated at Oxford or Cambridge. Don't you think he knows as much as you or maybe more? Geez. You rich guys think you know everything. Why'd you bring me into this at all?"

"Well, we do need people who find can their way around Tsavo. But don't get uppity with me, Joseph. You're not the only one we could hire. And we know all about you. Hunting wildlife of all kinds, endangered or not."

Two impala dashed across the dirt track right in front of Joseph's Land Cruiser, and he was so distracted by what Horst was saying that he almost hit them. He slammed on the brakes, throwing Horst against the windshield — no safety straps in that vehicle.

"Jesus H. Christ, Horst." Joseph reached around and grabbed a rifle he had behind the driver's seat in a jerry-built mount. He got out the door and stomped around to the passenger side. Opening the door, he pointed the rifle at Horst.

"So you bloody rich bastards don't need me, eh? Well then find your own damned way to Voi. See if some rhino or leopard'll take your dollars instead of killin' yuh. I've had enough. Fought my way out of poverty you've never had to see. When to school best I could. Made a living the way I knew how, never killin' too many of anything. I don't need you rich fancy guys tellin' me what's endangered and who needs protectin'. I do it myself, and goddamned better than you'll ever do."

Horst had never had a gun pointed at him close enough so the end touched him, and he broke out in a sweat.

"Okay, okay, Joseph. I apologize. I got carried away thinking too much about what's been going on. I guess that shoot-out frightened me a lot more than I expected, and it just all came out. I'm sorry." He started to take a handkerchief out of his pocket to wipe his brow, but Joseph mistook this for his reaching for a weapon, and pointed the rifle at Horst forehead.

"Just need a handkerchief, Joseph." There was a pause. Neither said a word nor moved. Doves called. An animal in the bush made the coughing sound that Joseph knew meant a warning.

"Okay, Joseph," Horst said, "As I said, I'm sorry. Look, we're in this together and we both have to get to Voi. Let's just forget this argument and help each other. There's plenty in it for you."

"Sure, sure," said Joseph, lowering his gun. They got back in the Land Cruiser and drove in silence to Voi. But it was clear to both that the dye had been cast. They may have to work together, but neither of them could ever like the other.

* * *

Horst and Joseph arrived at the Tsavo Park office and were met again by the park ranger, Horst remembering his name. "Hello Mac. We're back to use your phone, if that's alright."

Mac nodded and ushered them into the back office where the phone was and left them alone. Horst walked to the dusty desk, wiped the seat and the desktop, as he had the time before, with paper towels from a roll on the top of a dirty four-drawer file cabinet. How it made him wish he was back in Geneva in a clean office. Surprisingly he got through immediately and in spite of crackling sounds on the phone was soon speaking with Gary Anderson, his close colleague at the International Ecological Fund.

"Good news, Horst," Gary said, "The Kenyan government's had a change of heart. We persuaded them there was more to gain internationally — development funds, appreciative world view of the leaders — if they worked to save the elephants rather than what they had been doing, supporting the poachers big-time. They agreed that they'd try to make a big show of saving the elephants by capturing the poachers, putting them on trial. They've already piled up some poached ivory in Nairobi and burned it to show they mean business."

"Good going," Horst said.

"One problem, though," Gary continued. "The poachers they had been working with, brought in probably by them — tell the truth — won't cooperate, won't stop. In fact they've told the government that they're making too much money and see no reason to stop. Since they're well-armed with good transportation — a

Beechcraft to spot out herds, Land Cruisers, four-wheel drive trucks — they're just going ahead. The government has had no choice but to fight back. So the government's brought in some of their soldiers — maybe they're outside mercenaries, who knows? And they're going to try to find the poachers and stop them."

"A little war," Horst mused.

"But they don't have a tracker — somebody who knows Tsavo well and could lead them through the park the fastest way to the poachers. Somebody who can search on the ground and find out where the poachers are operating. We can't use planes — that's just a giveaway. When they see the plane, they'll either immediately move on or get ready for a big shootout. Got to use a little stealth. Glad you've called, because we've been thinking one of those scientists you're out with can do it."

"Well, I've got just the man for you," Horst said, "named Joseph Kenjoy Spent his life working in Tsavo — hunter's guide, tourist guide, helped with game management, the works. Knows it like the back of his hand."

"Tell him we'll get a plane to pick him up. Name the day and location. Put him on the phone." "What are you going to be doing about getting me out, Gary?"

"Hmmm. Well, that's two planes, one for Joseph to get picked up and taken to the government troops, another to just take you the hell out of there. Put him on the phone."

Horst handed Joseph the phone, explaining that he should tell Gary where to have a plane pick each of them up.

"Hello, Gary is it? First good news. I've got a two-way radio for the aircraft frequencies, so your pilots can call me," Joseph said over the phone. "There are three gates into Tsavo East — the part of the park we're in: Buchuma, Voi — the main gate — and Manyani. Tell your pilot to fly to Tsavo's Manyani Gate. What? It's easy to tell, because it's the only place where there is a gate on both sides of the road, one going into Tsavo West, the other where we are, in Tsavo East. From that gate, tell him to fly East-Southeast — he'll follow a major road. That'll take him along a river. What? Called the Galana River. Tell him to follow the road on the south side of the river and he'll see the airstrip. I'll have my Land Cruiser so I should be hard to miss."

"When?" Gary asked.

"Well, can't be too sure. I say have the pilot call in the next couple of days, then we can decide the best day for him to pick me up." He gave Gary the specifics about contacting his radio.

"Now, for Horst, there's another option, depending on how things are playing out." Joseph listened. "Yeah, yeah, but things happen, you know? Good to have contingencies. Just listen. Not far into the park from that airstrip there's a big open space, just grasses, and just one huge baobab tree. Said to be the biggest in the world. Can't miss it. What? You don't know what a baobab is?" There was a pause. "What do you guys know? And you're goin' to do something out here? Look it up in a book. Tell you what. Looks like a huge tree turned upside down, like its roots are sticking up in the air. Its bark's gray as an elephant's skin and the base of the tree is about a far round as a jumbo. Can't miss it if your pilot knows East Africa. He can land there, grab Horst, and take off real fast." Another pause. "If your pilot can't do this, he can't do nothin' out here. Got the wrong guy. Hear me?"

Joseph handed the phone back to Horst, who talked for what Joseph thought was a long time.

"One other piece of good news, Horst," Gary said, "We're getting great PR for having persuaded the government to fight poaching — they burned the stack of ivory, as I've mentioned, are bringing in troops. Got in the major newspapers and even TV news. Might get a magazine article out of it as well. So thanks for your good work."

"Great," Horst replied, smiling and winking at Joseph. "What'd they say about me?"

"Oh, it was just a general PR news release, Horst. Didn't mention any names of anybody. Just what our organization is accomplishing."

"Didn't mention my name?" Horst shouted. "But here I am out here with a bunch of scientists with about as much idea of the importance of public support as one of their damned elephant friends, and with these other low-class guys, the type that couldn't make it in the real world if they tried. I'm taking on all these risks and what do you take me for? I want to do good for the environment, yes, but my reputation is also important to me. That's the kicks I get out of this work — being well-known helps me do my work. For Christ sake, couldn't you have at least gotten a sentence in about me?"

"Sorry, Horst, these PR things happen fast and have to be short and meaty. Just no room for it. You'll get your notoriety when you get back."

Horst was so upset that he forgot that Joseph was in the room and could hear everything he was saying. Joseph was taking it all in. So, Joseph thought to himself. That's what's this Horst is really after. Doesn't really give a shit about elephants or us who work here. Just using us to make a better, bigger name for himself. Calls me and Davie and Howie the guys that couldn't make it in the real world — *his* real world. And here I am helping the son-of-a-bitch find his way around, keep him from getting eaten by a lion, stomped on by an elephant, and shot by some well-armed poacher. Well maybe it's time I let Horst get around a little on his own, see if he can make it in *my* real world.

Horst, suddenly realizing that Joseph overheard everything, quickly changed the subject and asked Gary to look up information about Baker Kingsley. Gary told him the name was familiar, and that he would check *Who's Who.*" He was back in a few moments. "Let's see . . . yes, he's right here. Kingsley, Baker. Botanist. Member, National Academy of Sciences—"

"What!"

"Ummm . . . several plant species named after him. Let's see . . . 'Perhaps best known for discovering a chemical in a tropical rainforest plant that serves as a growth hormone and has been used in cases of dwarfism.' Here's an interesting bit. Member of the Marine Corps, 1968 to 1972. Heavily decorated for action in Vietnam. Purple heart, et cetera."

Horst was incredulous. "That can't be the same Baker Kingsley. The Baker Kingsley we met is a really weird guy driving a VW bug all by himself in the middle of Tsavo. And to call him weird in this group is saying something. He *is* a botanist, though."

"Hold on a minute. Let me ask around since you're on the phone."

Horst sat silently steaming. He had to take off his corduroy jacket and roll up his sleeves. There were some scratching sounds on the phone.

"Bob next door, our botanist, says Baker is well known for two things — as an excellent botanist, and as an oddball. Seem s the patents on his plant discoveries in the tropics made him pretty well-off. Not really rich, but enough so he doesn't have to work as long as he lives modestly. Also, some people think he suffered from battle fatigue. Here's a quote in an article about him Bob gave me. Let's see. . . oh, yes. Baker is quoted as saying, 'After the war, I realized what life was really worth — how precious it was. I decided to give up the game of science and make a science of games.' And here's one you'll like. When they asked him about his work in ecology, he said, 'I don't know any ecology. A plant is something I know about, I can touch it, pick it up. Ecology is just some vague idea without substance — a bunch of undefined terms looking for a meaning, actors in search of an author, so to speak.'"

Horst still couldn't believe it, but it had to be true. That absolutely bizarre person had won more prizes than he had, and had made a bundle, too. W as there a fair God in this universe or what?

"Bob wants to know if you met him, and if so, what you thought of him. And, oh, yes, what he's up to. Bob says to say hello to Baker for him."

"I met him, yes. It's a long story. Tell you when I get back."

Horst said goodbye, hung up, and the he and Joseph drove back to the research camp, an uncomfortable silence between the two.

As they neared the camp, Horst said, "Maybe it'd be best if I just go back alone and tell them about our trip."

"No, I think there's things I can add, like about the planes and how they're going to find us."

"No need to mention those yet. Let's let that stuff lie. I don't want them thinking that you or I am going to abandon them."

"But we are, for Christ's sake."

"Yes, time and place for everything. They've got enough to think about right now. We can bring that up when the time is right. Tell you what. Just leave me just outside the camp. I'll tell them you had other things you had to attend to."

"Don't want me talking to the rest of your team, eh? I thought you and I'd built up some trust."

"Not that, no. Not at all. Just don't want to upset them anymore than necessary. Here's the perfect spot." Horst opened the door as Joseph slowed the Land Cruiser, driving over some downed trees and rough soil. Afraid that Horst might fall out and injure himself, Joseph stopped the vehicle and turned to talk to Horst, who by this time was already standing outside, feet on the ground.

"Can't thank you enough for taking me to Voi, Joseph," Horst said. "I'll return the favor, best I can." Horst chatted a little more with Joseph, using what he thought was his best charm, mannerisms that had worked many places in the world. Then excused himself and walked away.

Everyone at the camp wanted to know what Horst had learned. They prepared a quick dinner and Horst passed around some Scotch he'd managed to buy in Voi.

"The good news first," he said, and explained to him that his organization in Geneva had gotten the government to stop supporting the poachers, and about the big ivory bonfire the government had set off as a show. "But then the bad news," Horst said, and explained that the poachers said no to the government — they were making too much money — and weren't going to stop.

"So we're gonna try to keep doing our measurements and move slowly out while these guys are armed and ready and might come across us?" Davie asked.

Horst decided not to tell them the arrangement he had made with Joseph to become the tracker for the government troops. If he did, then Bruce and Michael would want to jump in and do the tracking. He wasn't going to let these guys steal any of the glory.

Johnny pointed out that he could keep track of the poachers by air and warn the team which way they needed to move to keep out of the poachers' way.

"Yes, guess that would be okay," Horst said, "if they don't try to back track and figure out where you're coming from."

Paul, Bruce, Michael, Johnny, and Davie got into a long discussion about what route they ought to take, listening to Howie's need to follow his oddball random numbers to locate places to study. "Guys with loaded guns may not go for that random shit," Davie said.

CHAPTER 36

Baker Leaves

*Each man must look to himself to teach him the meaning of
life. It is not something discovered: it is something molded.*

Antoine de Saint-Exupery

B aker stayed with the group for another day, camping as
usual away from the rest, at his own tiny campsite. After the
attack by the poachers, he had tried to help the scientists sort
out what they might do. During the day he watched them trying
to organize their records, working with clouds over their heads, he
thought, subdued, serious, frowning. He decided it was time for
him to move on. He hadn't come to Tsavo to get killed, nor to stay
around other people for very long. He had helped the scientists
when he could, but it was time for him to go back to his travels. The
group seemed somewhat paralyzed. They had stopped doing their
elephant counting and botanizing, instead were spending their time
arguing about what they should do, and wasting time, from Baker's
point of view.

He was concerned about them, but knew that what happened
was not up to him. The group was in trouble, and it pained him.
Its leadership had been too dispersed, he thought, and had gotten
worse. There were too many personalities and too many agendas.

Baker had seen the effects of confused leadership too many times. When he got this feeling during the war, the next day there would be a firefight and he would find himself the only one left alive. Bruce ought to be providing the right kind of leadership, he thought, but his odd fascination with the old elephant was interfering — Bruce's mind wasn't sufficiently on the danger from the poachers. Johnny was too much of an adventurer to be in charge — Baker had seen enough of his kind in Vietnam, and watched them get killed, and learned to avoid them. Michael ought to be in charge, but was not. Elizabeth was probably the smartest of the group, and the most rational, at least most of the time — he detected her tendency to go off the deep end occasionally. But she didn't have the field knowledge to take care of a group in Tsavo.

Paul was — well, soft wasn't the right word. He was too kind, too inexperienced in this sort of situation, lacking in military training. But he did know his way around the field, a true outdoorsman, and was at least familiar with weapons. He was getting better as a leader, but perhaps not fast enough. Baker had talked with him many times during the past few days, trying to suggest to him what he needed to do to become a better leader of the group. Perhaps it was time for a new generation — Paul's generation — to take over; the older generation — Bruce, Johnny, Horst — had too much baggage. Paul was still relatively free and open to new ways of thinking.

Anyway, he had never intended to stay long with them, these elephant counters, as he called them to himself. Since Vietnam, it was no longer his nature to be that sociable. He had lost too many good friends.

So this morning he packed up his tent and gear and drove his VW over to what he had come to think of as the elephant-counters' camp.

"Time for me to be off. I've come to say goodbye," he announced to the group having breakfast around the campfire.

Howie protested, saying that they were just getting used to having him around, and that he shouldn't be leaving just when they really needed his help.

Elizabeth decided she would miss Baker too, especially right now. In spite of his weirdness, she was beginning to view him as one of the more rational and practical of the group. Who would she turn to once he left? Paul? Too weak, but maybe. Howie? Odd thought, but beginning to seem less odd.

"Baker, at least join us and have something to eat," Bruce said. He put out food portions of roasted impala from the day before, some crackers. Baker hesitated a moment, then sat down and helped himself.

Bruce was silent for a while, then turned to him. "I'm sorry you're leaving us. We've hardly had time to talk . . . And I've been wondering so much about you. It isn't easy to ask, but ... how'd you get so proficient with guns?"

"I sort of grew into it, you might say. Always hunted, since I was a kid. But this kind of automatic weapon, I learned about it in 'Nam." He took a swig of Coke from a big bottle, then chewed on a piece of jerky he had kept in his pocket.

"So how'd you get into 'botanizing'?" Elizabeth asked.

"I watched too many good young men get killed. Men just as good as me or better. Never figured out why I was spared. I promised myself if I survived I'd spend the rest of my life appreciating God's earth. I've been fortunate to be able to do just that."

They could not get him to say more. Bruce especially sensed that it would not be fair to dig any deeper. His own experiences in the Korean War led him to understand exactly what Baker was implying.

"So have you become some kind of environmentalist or antiwar activist?" Elizabeth asked. Mary, listening, slowly tore one of her data sheets into thin strips and wove the strips into a paper mat as Baker talked, a strange kind of idle activity — Baker mused. Bruce noticed it too and immediately thought about the weaver birds.

"Nope. Except for geology, biology, zoology, and all those other sciences - *ologies*, I keep away from *ists*, and *isms*," Baker answered. "I've seen the terrible effects that true believers in them have had on the world."

"You saved our lives, and we're all indebted to you. But how did you happen to come along just at the right time that day? Did you know something was going to happen?" Bruce asked.

Baker sipped at his Coke and thought for a few moments. "You know, I woke up in the middle of the night. I had this feeling — something wasn't right. Got out of my tent, still didn't feel right. I had that same kind of feeling in 'Nam sometimes. Something bad usually happened the next day. I couldn't sleep, so I got in my car and started to drive — lights off, of course. Stopped every once in a while, cut the engine, and listened. It wasn't long before I heard another vehicle. It was going along, off in the distance, with headlights blazing. I moved my VW behind some bushes and waited, nice and quiet. This vehicle came along and was headed toward your camp. I didn't like the look of it, so I followed, lights off, at a good distance. It was getting near dawn when they reached you. I stopped way back, grabbed my gun and ammo out of the trunk, and ran the rest of the way. You know the rest." Baker leaned back in his camp chair and took another chew of jerky. Everybody waited for him to say more, but he didn't.

"Well, we can't thank you enough," Mary said. "Isn't there something we can do for you?"

"Just keep living. Keep doing what you're doing. Keep looking pretty, acting nice to one another. Love nature. Now that you're in it, love Tsavo. And keep your eyes open. Those guys have tried to get rid of you. You'd better start packing before they try again."

Baker looked at the sky and then off into the distance and said he was sorry, but he'd stayed much longer than he'd planned, and it was time for him to go along. He stood up. "But I've brought you each something." He reached into his backpack and pulled out some items that he kept hidden in his hand. He walked over to Mary. "Here's something for you, to remind you of our botanizing," he said. Mary looked at what he had given her. It was seeds of a peculiar plant. The seeds had the shape of a cross on one side. They were from a plant they had identified together.

He walked around the group, handing out little gifts. Mostly, he gave out M&Ms, but when he reached Elizabeth he put a somewhat larger bag in her hand. "You may need this sometime," he said, and moved on.

Elizabeth opened the bag. It contained a small pistol and a smaller paper bag that held bullets.

He gave Paul a small but professional-looking compass, good quality. "You can survey your way anywhere with this baby," he said.

When he came to Howie, he put a packet of M&Ms and a smooth, cold object in his hand. Howie looked at it. It was a piece of obsidian.

"I found it out here. Always liked volcanic glass — it's been a good-luck charm for me. I want it to be the same for you. Keep it with you. By the way, I never asked where you're from."

"Where are *you* from?" Howie asked.

"Myland. Myland, Ohio."

Howie thought he heard Baker say "My land?"

"Yep. Spelled just like they do it in Europe. M-I-L-A-N. Every year they have the Milan melon festival. Best melons you'll ever have. You ought to come. Where'd you say you're from?"

"Riddleland," Howie told him.

"What state is that?"

"Mostly confusion," Howie said. "But sometimes it's in New York. Northern New York."

"Riddlelyn," Baker repeated.

"Riddle*land*," Howie said. "It's a small town. Very small town. Not even big enough for a raspberry festival, let alone a melon festival."

Horst, standing nearby and listening to this conversation, was once again totally confused. Baker went over to him and took his hands in his and put a hollowed-out bird's egg in it. Horst saw it was speckled. "I found this out here too, Horst," Baker said. "You're a diplomat, so I've heard. You handle delicate things, so here's something to put on your desk to remind you that someone appreciates the difficulty of what you try to do." Horst was surprised and touched. Baker turned to Michael and gave him one of the cigar boxes that filled his car, saying that there was some of that special plant, the Welwitchia, in it, and Michael should plant it and watch it grow for good luck.

In this way, Baker went around to all of them, giving each something personal. When he finished, he went over to his VW and straightened things a bit — that is, arranged them in a way made sense only to him.

"Where you headed?" Davie asked.

"Oh, wherever the plants take me."

He got into his car, started it up, and was about to drive off when Howie came over and leaned into the open driver's window. "We're really gonna miss you, Baker."

"That a fact?" Baker said. He smiled, waved, and drove off.

* * *

Baker's departure cast a pall over the camp. Something precious seemed to have left them, and they all felt vulnerable. If was as if Baker were escaping a sinking ship and they were the ship, floundering on a sea of sand. Elizabeth thought about the piece of obsidian Baker had given Howie, black as the blackest night, shiny as the shiniest day. Baker must have had a feeling that Howie needed a good-luck charm. What did that mean? What did he sense about Heck's future? Was he to sink with the ship? Baker had been so strange and yet refreshingly, so independent, without the usual cares of humanity, or that's at least how it seemed. Something important had gone out of their lives, and in the remoteness of Tsavo, each little something — each touch of a person, each piece of a personality, each segment of civilization — meant much.

Bruce missed Baker's weirdness more than he had expected. Not one to sentimentalize, he had nevertheless grown fond of the strange character who had turned out to be so competent in unexpected ways. And such a curious set of contradictions. A botanist who carried a machine gun and could lasso a gazelle or track poachers. A loner who was, in his own peculiar way, sociable.

Michael, too, had liked Baker. He liked any foreigners who took an intense interest in his countryside and wanted to feel it, experience it, learn about it. Michael stood at the edge of the camp for a long time, looking off in the direction the VW had departed, as if watching the car or its dusty wake far beyond the vision of any of the others.

Davie knew he would miss Baker's firepower.

Horst had mixed feelings about Baker's departure. Horst was tired of being surrounded by oddballs, and Baker was probably the oddest. What he had learned about Baker in his phone call from Voi had shocked and confused him and made him uncomfortable to be around him.

Johnny seemed unaffected as usual, whistling, teasing Mary and Elizabeth, but Elizabeth thought it was bravado. Bruce came over to her and said he wished they could talk, and she followed him away from the campfire.

Howie sat before the fire, watching the reflection of the flames in the obsidian that Baker had given him. He thought about Bruce's actions of the last few days, and Elizabeth's responses. Bruce had certainly fallen in love with Elizabeth, and she could be his salvation, Howie thought. The flickering reflection seemed to Howie to be his own spirit fading and reappearing, appearing and fading. He sat there without grinning, without puns, without tricks, and without his yo-yo, which he had given to Davie.

* * *

That day, Joseph rounded up his crew. He had been steaming mad all night and was still angry with Horst and what he had learned about him, but wasn't sure what to do. Still, he had to get together with his crews. There were three groups of three each. He contacted each and told them to meet him at a stand of tall shrubs near the huge baobab, and to make sure their vehicles were hidden in nearby shrubs and trees. He told them that Horst had hired him and the crew and were going to pay them all well and provide them with the equipment they needed. They had two main tasks — to find and keep tracking the poachers and to find and guide the government troops.

"The poachers probably know their way around Tsavo better than the government guys," Joseph told them, "but neither of them know much about the park. Once we find the poachers, we should have no trouble a'tall staying with them out of sight." He assigned two of his crews to do that tracking. "Once you find them, radio me where they are. Then you stay in contact but spread out on two sides of the poachers."

He explained to the third crew what Gary had told him about the likely location of the government groups, and said that the pilot with the science team would find them for them, radio him, and he would then tell this crew where to go. They were then to find the leader of these troops and guide them to the poachers. "But don't start looking for them until I radio. I'm thinkin' over how we're going to deal with them and haven't decided." Actually, Joseph was considering whether to help Horst and his international organization or not. But he'd let his anger get the best of him in the past and he didn't want that to happen again. It was to his advantage to know where the poachers were and find out just how well armed they were.

Maybe he could take care of the poachers with his own crew, and leave Horst and company out of the whole thing. Then, rid of the poachers and guiding the science team out of Tsavo, he and his crews could go back to what they had always done, careful small-time poaching. Well, he wasn't so sure anymore. He kept thinking about Howie, Davie, and Baker and how well he fit in with them. Maybe he could work with them, however they got their money to do stuff. He had always seen himself as an outsider whose only way to make a living was doing something illegal. Who would hire him and pay him decently otherwise? But these guys were doing okay, having a good time, and doing something worthwhile. Hell, he knew Tsavo better than any of them, well, at least as good as Davie. The more he talked with his crews, the more confused he felt deep inside, and he left them to go off on his own and think about what he'd like to see happen. No doubt the science team was likely to get into big trouble and could use his help. Bruce and Johnny knew where the money was probably, he was thinking. Maybe he didn't need Horst and could let the son-of-a-bitch find his own way out of Tsavo. But this was too much thinking for him right how.

*　*　*

The group decided to begin making their way out of the park the next day. Johnny would search for elephant herds to count by air and they would follow Howie's random numbers plotting to do fieldwork as they went. Around midday the Land Rovers came upon a green marshy area fed by a small spring, and everyone got out to look and to stretch their legs. Bruce had seen a reedbuck and was intent on shooting it for dinner. Howie emerged from a Land Rover and wandered over to a few palm trees near the marsh; their shade was a relief. He knelt down and felt the cool moist soil and seated himself contentedly in a lotus position, facing a small shallow pond. A small bird with long spindly legs and surprisingly wide feet stepped delicately from one water lily pad to another, exactly the kind of event Howie hoped for — something peaceful, to focus his attention. At first he felt peaceful and calm, but then he was overcome by a strange feeling, not only of deja vu, as if he had been here before, but a sense that he would be here again. He pushed away this foreboding thought and concentrated on the wading bird.

Suddenly something whistled past his ear. Then another, which glanced off one of the palm trees and landed by his side. It was a damned tiny arrow. He thought he fleetingly glimpsed a small, dark person on the other side of the pond, but he wasn't sure. He wasn't exactly scared, but he kept still. He might be a fool, but not that kind of fool.

Bruce was loading his rifle when an arrow whistled past his ear. He knew from past experience exactly what it was. He dropped to the ground and shouted to the others to do the same. Several more arrows flew toward them, coming from the dense bush. Though no one was visible, Michael threw his spear straight into the bush, then took up his rifle and started firing. Stretched out on the ground, Bruce did the same.

Howie was caught between the arrows and the bullets. He sat still, hearing a rustling sound in the bush, but no more arrows appeared. Bruce and Michael rushed past him, then he heard a loud roar and saw Johnny's plane fly low over the marsh, Johnny was on his way to the next campsite and was checking up on them, Howie realized. Anyway, that would scare whoever had shot at them, he was sure.

Meanwhile, not far from Howie, Michael found his spear in the deep bush. It had blood on the blade, which he wiped off with some leaves. Michael saw Howie and motioned Howie to go back to the others.

"What was all that?" he asked Bruce who had rejoined the group.

"Waliangulu — 'elephant people.' One of the locals. They use poison arrows to hunt." Bruce gathered his things and then told the others that he would stay with them while Michael searched to see if any of the elephant people were still about.

Elizabeth sat down next to Howie. She felt jittery and was concerned about him. She looked at her watch. Mary joined her and then Paul, and they sat in silence. It was more than half an hour before Michael came back. He said he had seen footprints, but they died out in the wet areas and he saw no other signs. Bruce suggested they take a short break and have some water and a snack. He wanted to talk to them about what had just happened.

"Let me fill you in," he began when they were all seated again on the ground. "As I said, those were the elephant people — they call themselves Waliangulu. They used to poach elephants with arrows and also used the arrows against their enemies, including the poaching patrol — including me, as a matter of fact." He took a long drink of water. "Sheldrick brought most of them over to his side years ago. Perhaps they've gone back into the poaching business. Since the big elephant die-off, so few people come here, and there are so few ways to make a living, perhaps they've reverted to their old ways. Anyway, they seemed intent on warning us that this is their territory, not ours. If they didn't mean to kill us outright."

"Wal-i-angu-lu" — Howie mulled the word over. "Paul, of course, never told us about poison arrows, either."

"Look, I'm as surprised to see them back as you are to see them at all," Bruce said. "Best remember this area. They may protect it especially, or they may just track us and try shooting us whenever it suits them. We won't know. We'll have to be careful. And there are other groups farther north who use poison arrows, too."

"Are they always deadly?" Howie asked, brushing dirt off his clothes.

"I don't know for sure. Some people say they have different kinds — stunning arrows, wounding arrows, killing arrows."

"Oh, God, why me?" Howie said, looking at Paul. They both chuckled. Bruce was glad to see that at least some of them were calming down.

"Some of the Waliangulu were famous poachers, famous for killing big tuskers with their tiny arrows," Bruce said. He got up and went off to the tall grass for a last look around. "The most famous was called Galo-galo Kafonde." He wiped his face with a handkerchief and drank more water from his canteen. "He was a legend even among his own, and a legend as far as Nairobi. They say he killed hundreds of elephants and knew every elephant path in the Tsavo bush. He also knew every water hole, the story goes — there's a lot of secret, hidden water holes that can be the difference between life and death out here. We know — or knew — some of them. God knows whether they've all dried up by now. But Galo-galo seemed able to go on through the park forever, in places where everyone else who tried died — usually just disappeared. So he must have known many secret springs."

"What happened to him?" Howie asked.

"In the end Sheldrick caught him. He proudly announced his name to Sheldrick because he thought of himself as famous and important."

"Well, to him, what we call poaching was probably an ancient way of life, and he was particularly good at it," Howie said. "I found the same sort of thing when I was doing some work in the southern Philippines. Those people had traded for centuries among the islands from the Malaysian Peninsula through Indonesia to the Philippines. I had a teenage assistant one summer and asked him what his father did. He said, 'He's a smuggler, and by the grace of God he's very successful.' We Westerners created the nation-state and made trading across boundaries illegal. It had never meant anything like that to them — *illegal* was a Western word anyway and a Western idea too. For them, land was land, ocean, ocean. People had territories, but not our kind of legal boundaries. Sounds like the Brits did something similar here — made Kenya a nation, created a park, and then called the native practice 'illegal poaching.' They overlaid the nation-state on top of the nature-state, so to speak."

"Good point, but it wasn't that simple," Bruce responded. "The time you're talking about—when it was no more than an internal native practice — that's lost in the shadows of the past. They've been selling ivory for centuries to other nations — other cultures if you prefer: to the Arabs, through them to Europeans, and from us and the people on the Continent to Asia. T here's a kind of hidden stock market in ivory in Belgium and Holland."

"Still, to them, it doesn't seem illegal," Howie said, "just the natural thing to do."

"When you have Somalian and some European tough guys sent down with machine guns in the pay of an undercover group, maybe connected to some African government or an international cartel, shooting elephants as fast as they can, it's not folkways anymore. It's called destruction of a species," Bruce said, raising the hood of one of the Land Rovers to check the engine.

"Anyway, after Sheldrick caught Galo-galo, he handcuffed him and tied him to a rope and had him lead them through the bush to his various hideouts and water holes. But he was a clever chap and took Sheldrick deep into the bush, w here the rope kept getting tangled. A ranger had one end of the rope when, all of a sudden, Galo-galo pulled hard on It — he was just out of sight ahead in the bush — and the ranger fell down and lost his grip. The ranger scrambled up and pulled hard on the rope, but by that time Galo-galo had escaped and the ranger fell over backward. Galo-galo got away."

"What happened then?" Mary asked.

"We caught another famous poacher and got him to show us poacher hideouts and many of their secret water holes. They had put water into deep holes in the volcanic rock — the pumice — and covered these with flat rocks so a passerby wouldn't notice them."

"Are they still out there?" Howie asked.

"Hope so," Bruce said. "We may need them one day before we're done." He closed the hood of the Land Rover quietly.

"Any antidote to their poisons?"

"Not that we know of," Bruce said.

CHAPTER 37

Poachers

What's happening to the elephants is outrageous, and the more so since we have been through these ivory crises before and should have found solutions by now. It is time for concerned individuals, NGOs and Governments to take action.

Ian Douglas-Hamilton
Testimony before the U.S. Senate Committee
on Foreign Relations

Flying out to scout for their next camp, Johnny saw poachers attacking an elephant herd. The herd was moving away from the poachers directly toward where Bruce had set up camp. This meant the elephants would likely crash through their camp with the poachers following close behind.

He flew over it once without descending, but the scene below angered him and he couldn't resist turning back and making one of his famous very low passes, first just over the scattered trees outside the clearing where the poaching was going on so he would surprise the poachers, then flying just above them, right at one of the men about to shoot an elephant, so low that the man ducked and tried to scramble away. Then he flew over a dead and bloody elephant straight at a man cutting off the tusks, so close Johnny thought the man must feel the wind generated by his plane's propellers, flying as close as he dared, almost hitting him and forcing him to duck and run.

Johnny climbed, made a turn and flew back over the herd, flying fast so to make a poor target for the men with weapons. Best he could do was a rough count, guessing there were no more than ten men, most with automatic weapons. There were at least 30 elephants, but just a few seemed shot at and dead. Most were still alive and trying to get away.

The poachers had a new four-wheeled truck and several other backcountry vehicles. Some of the men were using what looked to be chain saws to cut off the tusks — as he sped over Johnny couldn't quite tell. Others were carrying tusks and loading them into the truck. Reaching the end of the clearing, Johnny turned and made a third low pass, but one of the men fired at him, so he banked steep even though he was still only about 50 feet above the ground, then put the plane in full power and did a circling climb, hoping that the guy with the gun couldn't aim fast enough. And he hoped nobody on the ground was quick-thinking enough to memorize the airplane's registration number painted on the fuselage. He had to get away fast, but also needed to keep banking and turning, and his Cessna, which at best could climb 1,000 feet a minute was doing only 700. When he reached 4,000 feet and knew he would look small from the ground, he flew a wide circular path back to the camp and called Bruce on his two-way radio telling him what he had seen, insisting that Bruce meet him at the landing strip with Davie and Paul — that the four of them had to go divert the herd and the poachers before they reached their camp. He landed, taxied, parked, and climbed quickly out of his plane.

To Johnny's surprise, he saw Bruce with two, not one, Land Rovers. Bruce and Paul got out of the first, while Davie appeared out of the driver's seat of the second with Horst in the passenger side.

"You can't go pick a fight with these poachers, Johnny. I know that's what you want to do," Horst said. "I've got my Endangered Species Consortium involved — you know that by now — and since they've got the government on our side, we've just got to stay out of the way. And besides, it's illegal — you could be accused of a criminal act."

"By whom?" Bruce responded. "A government that has been involved in poaching and now wants to show it's anti-poaching?"

"Damn herd's going to run over our camp and kill anybody standing there, Horst," Johnny added. "And by the time the government gets troops out here and they manage to find the poachers, we'll all be dead, either trampled or killed some other way. Sorry, no way."

Johnny pulled Davie aside. "What the hell are you doing guiding Horst around? I thought you hated him."

"Man's gotta do what's right, Johnny," Davie answered. "Horst is determined to go talk with those bastards. I may not like him — don't — but I'm not gonna let him get killed just 'cause his head is swelled bigger 'an his ass."

Bruce and Davie drove off together, Bruce in the lead, but when they got within hearing distance of the poachers' weapons, Davie turned into the large clearing where the elephants and the poachers were, while Bruce drove ahead to much smaller clearing, which,fortunately, was near a streambed where water flowed during occasional rains, so there was a dense stand of thick grasses and mixed shrubs and trees. Bruce parked back of the grasses and led the way in, putting Paul right behind him and Johnny last. He knew Paul was experienced at wildlife hunting.

"Paul, follow me. We can come at them through this tall grass, just like we track wildlife we're hunting, and they won't see us at all," Bruce whispered. Johnny was getting their rifles ready.

Bruce walked along the tall grass and found an animal track that went into the grasses. He motioned to Paul to follow, pointing at the track, so that Paul could see that moving along it would let them go in without shaking the grasses. Johnny walked a little farther and found another track. Then the three moved slowly, staying low, almost in a crawl. Soon Bruce reached the edge of the grass and looked out, Paul next to him. Across the clearing, Bruce saw Davie's Rover had stopped near the large truck where a man wearing something like an officer's hat stood, who seemed to be in charge. Horst climbed out of Davie's Rover, and holding out a white handkerchief walked slowly toward the man. Davie stayed in the Rover.

Bruce watched as Horst and the man with officer's hat talked. Bruce heard the sound of another vehicle and, looking to his left, saw a Land Cruiser pulling up. It was as if he was watching a play performed before him, in silence. The poachers who had been shooting elephants stopped.

Three men got out of the Cruiser. Could they be one of Joseph's crews? If so, what were they doing there? Was there some plan going on between Joseph and Horst?

Horst and the man with the officer's hat seemed to begin an argument and the officer took out a pistol and aimed it at Horst, who put his arms up and began to back away. Davie opened the door of the driver's side of his Land Rover just as the man shot at Horst, who fell to the ground. Davie aimed his rifle at the man, but before he could shoot, Johnny fired and the man dropped. Davie rushed out and helped Horst to his feet. He didn't know how he was going to get him back into the vehicle but he had to try. He had his rifle over one shoulder, Horst leaning on him on the other side. Two poachers started toward Horst and Davie. Bruce and Johnny fired at them, and they fell to the ground.

The three men who had just arrived in the Land Cruiser were standing outside their vehicle watching the fight between the two groups. Joseph had told them to track the poachers, and they had, but now there were two groups shooting at each other, totally confusing them. One of them moved forward, his weapon out but a poacher saw him and shot and he was down on the ground. It all happened silently except for the sound of the guns. To Bruce, these shots seemed to be beating out the rhythm of all the motion; with each shot somebody moved. For a moment, it struck him as if he was watching an odd puppet show, but then he got his mind back on what was actually happening. Three down and most of the poachers had not seen or heard anything.

Davie and Horst had made it to the Land Rover when Davie saw a poacher a distance from the others take an automatic weapon out of a vehicle. Davie pulled up his rifle and shot him.

The poachers had not yet figured out where most of the shots were coming from, and in their confusion two more were shot by Bruce and Paul. The element of surprise had definitely worked in their favor. Being spread among the herd meant most of the poachers weren't aware of the first three who had gone down. But a poacher who had accompanied the lead man circled around and began reining fire on Davie's Land Rover as he helped Horst into the back seat. Davie got in and gunned the Rover into a nearby stand of trees. Smoke was pouring from the hood. He pulled Horst out and to the ground and away from the vehicle before it burst into flames.

One of the poachers pointed toward the tall grass where the men were. They fired toward the grass as they retreated to their vehicles.

They ran behind their big truck. Good, Bruce thought, they're going to leave. But one reappeared with a Jerry can full of gasoline, poured the gasoline on the ground near the tall grasses and started a fire. The wind was blowing the fire toward Bruce, Paul, and Johnny. Another poacher emptied a second can of gasoline. Bruce motioned to Paul to move back. The poachers, seeing that they couldn't outshoot whoever was attacking them, had started a fire as a way to fight back.

The elephant herd fled from the fire and the remaining poachers got into their vehicles and drove away from it, into the wind. As Bruce came out of the tall grasses, he saw the two remaining men who he thought were likely part of one of Joseph's crews loading the body of the team member into their Land Cruiser. Davie came out of the trees, motioning back to where he'd come. Bruce drove up to him and soon Horst was loaded into the Rover and they were on their way back to camp.

CHAPTER 38

Paul's Solo Fight

Free as the sun is free, that's how it's got to be.
Whatever is right for bumblebee and river and eagle is right
for me.
We gotta be free, the eagle and me.

E. Y. ("Yip") Harburg in *Bloomer Girl*

Elizabeth saw Bruce driving a Land Rover at high speed toward their camp. As she started toward the vehicle a strange wind came up, unusually strong, and she smelled a different kind of smoke from their campfire's — an acrid scent that she could not place at first, but then it reminded her of a grass fire that had burned near her home in Illinois — a fire lit intentionally to restore a prairie.

Elizabeth had almost reached Bruce when Johnny jumped out of the Land Rover and dashed by her, shouting, "It's a bloody grass fire! Those bastards started it to drive us out!" He rushed through the camp. "Everyone pack up," he yelled. "We've got to get out of here."

Mary and Howie emerged from their tents, confused. Elizabeth had had a little more time to process what was going on. She began stuffing gear into sacks

"There's a fire's coming. We've got to move," she yelled to Howie.

Out in the open, Howie and Mary could smell the approaching fire as well and soon were throwing gear into bags and taking down tents. Elizabeth shouted to Mary to gather their pages of data and field notebooks and store them in a large metal container they had brought along for the purpose. As Mary began the packing, and smoke floated in from the fire, she couldn't help opening several of the field notes book and looking once more time at her carefully written measurements. What would happen to these that had helped her get to know Tsavo's details in a way she had never expected. Would these survive? Would they ever be of any use to anyone? Tears came her eyes, but she continued packing.

She looked up some minutes later and saw Davie help Horst out of the backseat of the Rover. He was bleeding from a wound on his thigh. "Damn it, he's wounded," Elizabeth said to Mary. "Just what we need." But she went to help Davie with Horst.

"He'll make it," Davie said. "Packin' up is what's needed now."

"Water," Horst moaned, and Elizabeth brought him a canteen.

"I hate to ask … but you left with two Rovers." Elizabeth said.

"Right," Davie said. "We lost one."

"We've got to get my plane into the air, away from the fire," Johnny said. "Paul, come with me." He turned to Bruce. "You and me will need to drive the Rovers across the fire. I'll be back soon." Johnny and Paul ran to one of the Land Rovers, jumped in, and roared off.

As the Land Rover bounced cross-country, Johnny said, "Listen, Paul, the harder job here is getting the Rover through the flames. Bruce and I know how to do that. So you're gonna fly the 182 out of here and circle until the fire passes and then just land. Nothing to it. The rest of us will deal with getting the vehicles across."

"Right," said Paul, thinking over the few hours of flight instruction he had started in the States, and regretting that he had ever mentioned it to Johnny. "You know I've got about forty hours in a Cessna 172 and just ten in a high-performance plane like this 182."

"No sweat — you're ready to solo. The plane almost flies itself — just keep the prop full forward if you want to be really cautious."

He ran through a kind of checklist with Paul, scribbling as fast as he could on a piece of scrap paper. "Full flaps on approach. Got to do a stall landing on this rough grass. That's the only thing to watch out for. If all goes well, I'll meet you here at the strip in an hour. If you get a chance try to locate that large truck and they also had a couple of Land Cruisers."

Together, they had the plane pushed back and ready to fly in a few minutes. Johnny boosted Paul into the left seat and ran around to the right, giving Paul instructions for starting the 182's engine. It roared to life. Johnny looked at the approaching smoke, said a few more words to Paul, patted him on the back, and jumped out, closing the door. "Go, go, go!" he yelled, then dashed back to the Land Rover.

Paul saw the smoke approaching. Soon he would not be able to take off. No question about it. He pushed the throttle forward, keeping his feet on the pedals to brake the plane until the engine reached takeoff speed, then let up on the brakes but kept his right foot pushed down on the rudder pedal so the plane would not swing to the left. Damned centrifugal force, he thought, but at least he remembered about it. The plane bounded forward like an impala, leaping up and down over the bumpy grassland. Paul wondered if he would be able to hold on to the yoke, and if so, whether he could hold it steady in the takeoff position. The plane seemed to bound along the strip forever. Paul kept his eyes moving back and forth between the view outside and the instrument panel, watching for the airspeed to reach the takeoff speed. The trees ahead were getting very close. A gazelle dashed across the strip in front of him, fleeing the fire. Smoke was beginning to roll onto the landing strip. Fifty knots . . . sixty knots . . . seventy . . . Paul pulled back on the yoke, and the plane jumped into the air. He was over the smoke and the trees at the end of the strip. The 182 was climbing faster than any other plane he had flown in his short pilot training. A thrill went through him. Fun! At a time like this?

But as the plane climbed steeply, Paul had trouble keeping the nose steady. The plane skidded left and right, flying upward at an angle to one side and then the other. At first he overcorrected and made matters worse, but he kept the plane climbing. By the time he reached a thousand feet, he had the plane under better control, but he could feel his heart pounding and his mouth was dry. He leveled off at that altitude as best he could — the plane nosed up and down, especially when he looked outside rather than at the instruments. As Johnny had instructed, he looked ahead to scan the w ide swatch of blackened, burned grassland. He saw a large truck stopped a distance from the fire and armed men by the side of the truck looking up at him.

He was so intent on what he saw below that he failed to notice that the plane was banking more and more steeply, until suddenly the stall warning sounded. He would have jumped except for his seat belt. His attention leaped to the instruments. The plane was banked 35° and getting steeper, and his speed was down to 60 knots. He leveled off and pushed the throttle full forward. The 182 sprang upward, once again bounding, climbing clear. He let it climb to 2,000 feet, then leveled off and turned. He backed off the throttle, but not as much as before, and kept the plane in a shallow turn, shifting his eyes back and forth between the instruments and the ground, making sure that the plane kept a safe flying speed and did not wander too much from a banking angle of 15°, which his flight instructor had told him was a standard turn. Flight instructor? Seemed out of another world, another time.

He was now south of the fire and could see two more Land Cruisers looking like toy cars ahead. He flew toward them, this time remembering to scan the instruments and the view outside continuously. Now at a comfortable altitude, he pulled back on the throttle, put the flaps down 10°, and flew slowly. The smell of burned grass, a somewhat aromatic scent almost like the smell of overcooked meat, came into the cockpit, acrid but not unpleasant. Looking down, he guessed that the fire had burned a wide swath, maybe a couple of miles wide, but it was hard to tell with the smoke obscuring his view while he was also focusing on flying the plane.

By the time he came up on the two Land Cruisers, he had descended to 500 feet. He was looking around to see if there were other vehicles when something tore through the metal of the cockpit floor with a thud and then rattled around against the roof. He was being shot at. *Him.*

A bullet had passed through the passenger seat next to him. Without thinking, he shoved the throttle full forward and banked the plane sharply to the right to get out of the line of fire. Then he started turns left and right, climbing all the while.

Once he was back over the burned area and out of rifle range, he felt a great sense of relief. Except for the steady roar of the engine — a steadiness that was reassuring — the plane was in a peculiar way a silent place, a place in which he got a different feel for Tsavo's landscape than he had experienced any other way. Here, suddenly, he was on his own. No need to make conversation, no one to distract him from his contact with the land and the sky outside. He thought about what Baker had said about the benefits of traveling alone.

Several updrafts bounced the plane so that he could f eel the atmosphere tangibly in a way that was different from being on the ground in a wind — more active, more immediate, the wind almost animate. He and the atmosphere were one, with the plane their mode of contact, of communication. Below him, Tsavo spread out almost to the horizon. Now the fire was behind him, and for a few minutes he forgot completely about it, so immersed had he become in his contact with the wind and his view of the ruddy, empty vastness. It was hypnotic. No, contemplative. He was absorbed by it, into it, in a sense absorbed into all of Tsavo.

For the first time in days, he was able to relax. Bruce's fixation on Zamani Baba, came into his mind. It seemed that the elephant epitomized all of the park, all of nature for Bruce. The great elephant scientist, whom Paul had admired from a distance, was in fact lost. But a part of him could understand what Bruce was feeling. The image of that elephant came into his mind, as he saw it that first day when Davie was driving them to their first camp. In the strange calmness as he flew straight and level in the 182, he felt some kind of connection with Zamani Baba, almost an understanding. But nothing he could put into words. The 182 hit an air pocket and jolted up, and the understanding, if that was what it was, disappeared. He was back to flying the plane.

He flew on, farther and farther away from the fire, so distracted by the thrill of flying and his quick escape — and the very fact that he was alive — that he lost track of how far he had flown from camp. He saw a few elephants and some gazelles. Off to his right were two giraffes munching the top of a tree. Ahead he could make out the hills that marked the way to Nairobi. The topography was laid out below him like a map, and the relationships between the landscape and the vegetation were clearer than could be seen any other way: trees along the rivers and dry streams. *Man, I could do this all day*, he thought.

* * *

As soon as Johnny and Paul left, Bruce gathered the others and organized them quickly, telling Michael he would need to help him. They'd try to beat back the fire while the Land Rovers were being loaded up. When Johnny got back he and Johnny would drive a Land Rover and team members across the fire. He asked Elizabeth to lead the rest in putting what they could into the vehicles and trailers in the few minutes they had before the fire was upon them. Then he grabbed Michael, whom he knew understood how to do this kind of thing, and they ran toward the fire to see what they could do to create a safe path — beat out the burning grass if possible with shovels and rakes and brooms, perhaps light a small backfire. He guessed they might have half an hour before the fire was upon them, and hoped that this desolate part of Tsavo would provide little fuel — that the fire would be light and form a thin burning line that would pass quickly.

Bruce barely had time to think when he heard Johnny's airplane roar in takeoff and saw it pass overhead. He stopped for a moment to watch it, hoping Paul would be able to control it for his own sake as well as for the airplane's. As it passed over him, he felt sad. It should have been him — would have been him, ten, even five, years before, doing the wildest and bravest thing, roaring off in an airplane to save it from wildfire. The passing of the airplane felt like the passage of his own time; now he was an old man, no longer the primary actor. It was becoming Paul's era.

Elizabeth saw Bruce pause as the airplane flew away, and saw the look in his eye, and thought she understood what was going on in his mind. Then Davie grabbed her and pulled her to his Land Rover. She helped him cover its dangerous contents — its explosive charges — as best as they could and get the vehicle ready to make a dash across the fire. This gave her an idea, but she didn't have time to share it with Davie at the moment. Too much was happening — everybody running around, near chaos, tents coming down, gear being flung into trailers, as the smoke grew worse.

*　*　*

Vultures circled ahead of Paul, gliding lazily, floating. He pulled back on the throttle and raised the nose of the aircraft. Yes, he was sure he could do it. He put out 10° of flaps, then 20°. He pulled the throttle back more, let the nose rise higher. He picked out a vulture at his own altitude and banked the plane so that he circled with the big bird. Round and round. In flight, the vultures were almost beautiful, so different from the way they had looked when Davie had taken him to help catch them. The layers of vultures, some forming lines above him, some below, added to the three-dimensionality of his view. The landscape looked bolder, the atmosphere revealed. Maybe Davie wasn't so crazy after all to study vultures. The plane bumped from turbulence in the updraft, rose and fell, but mostly rose. He felt the atmosphere more than he had ever felt it before. Part of it. The wind and I.

The vulture next to him rose with him. They were in an invisible elevator together. He was freed from all the cares that had burdened him: no poachers, no responsibilities to the people funding this work.

He put the plane into a moderate left turn, watching the instruments to make sure the wings did not bank more than 30°, and circled 180° so that he was heading back to the camp and to the fire. Up ahead — way up ahead — he saw the line of smoke. But where was the landing strip? Where was the camp? The fire was burning along a great line, not quite from horizon to horizon but far to the plateau now on his left. He felt sudden panic. What if he had actually *lost* the landing strip? In what direction had he had taken off? The strip was headed 170°. Or was it 150°? He wasn't sure. Damn it, he really wasn't sure. In the rush, he had made one of the simplest and most basic mistakes of a beginning pilot — he'd forgotten to check his takeoff direction and to set the gyroscopic compass to match the direction on the magnetic compass. He also realized that he should have checked the gyroscopic compass in the air as well against his magnetic one, because the gyroscopic one drifted slowly. Shit! He was lost!

Don't panic. Fly the plane. The vulture soared serenely off his wing, calm, quiet.

Paul looked down and realized he could use the vegetation as a guide to his direction. North slopes had more vegetation on them, even at this very low latitude. He turned the plane so that he was flying at a right angle to the rows of denser vegetation — wherever he could find any. It was like looking at whitecaps on an ocean to determine the direction of the wind. He looked at his gyrocompass. If he was guessing right about the plants on the ground, the compass was off 20°. He checked the small magnetic compass. It bounced around like Howie's yo-yo as the plane tossed in the turbulence, and could best be read when the plane was straight and level. He got the plane straight and level, read the magnetic compass, and made an additional correction on the gyrocompass.

What if he still couldn't find the airstrip? Another moment of panic. Well, he could put this plane down almost anywhere, as long as he circled the area first. He could probably get it on the ground. At least a competent pilot could get it on the ground. But what then? He could fly to the fire zone and then search along it to find the camp or the landing strip. But what would the burned-out landing strip look like from the air? Okay, he would search along the first part of the fire zone for the camp. He looked at the fuel gauge. Half a tank. Enough. He could fly west to the highway, then turn 180° and fly back along the burned zone. If he flew at the right altitude — high enough to see across the burned area, but not high enough to miss the Land Rover — he could find the camp and then a place to land.

The burned area was fast approaching, as if the ground moved and the plane hung in the air. He pulled back on the throttle, settling the yoke so the plane slowed and descended slowly, and as he came up on the burn he began looking out the left window, this time remembering to keep scanning the instruments. He reached 500 feet and then, without thinking about it, pushed the throttle lever ahead just enough to keep flying straight and level. He saw a vehicle to his right and pulled the nose down. It was the Land Rover that he and Johnny had ridden out to the airstrip. God, he hoped Johnny wasn't dead. He had to be somewhere nearby.

He pushed the throttle full forward and climbed so he could get a good view, circling as he went. He saw the remains of their camp and located the intact Land Rovers. There were people waving to him. He dipped his wings from side to side so they would know he saw them, then circled, and saw, from 2,000 feet, that the outline of the landing strip remained visible through the burn. He had feared that once the entire landscape was blackened, he'd be unable to tell the airstrip f rom its surroundings, but in fact he could still make out shallow ruts from repeated touchdowns and takeoffs.

He flew to the southeast, then turned and lined up the plane parallel to the w heel marks, flying a standard downwind landing pattern. Just when he thought he could relax — he had found his companions and the airstrip after all — he realized that now he had to land the damned plane. This was the hardest maneuver of all in his short flying career, and the one he had practiced least. He could see that the strip was free of wildlife. And the one good thing about the fire was that it would have leveled the field even more than before, burning down the vegetation, so the landing would be easier. He looked for any flames still on the landing strip, but saw none.

From the palm trees he could see that the wind was now calm, so he didn't have to deal with a crosswind. Now he was turning onto the final approach to the landing strip. Look ahead. Pick your touchdown point. How was the plane's rate of descent? If the touchdown point doesn't move up or down in your view, you're going to land there. His instructor had told him that over and over again. He picked a point, the start of the tire tracks on the strip. It was sinking slowly down the windshield view. He was coming in too high. Full flaps. Pull off on the power. Now the point was starting to rise up the windshield. He pushed the throttle ahead. Gusts buffeted the plane, not just up and down but side to side. He was trying to correct, but he couldn't get the nose pointed just right. The landing point kept moving up or down. It wouldn't stay steady in his windshield view.

A big gust threw the plane way to the left. He corrected as best he could, but he was high and wide. Pull back on the power so that the airspeed was just down near the end of the white line on the dial. The ground was coming up fast. One hundred feet above the surface. Fifty feet. *Now, now, now*, pull back on the yoke, *pull*, cut the power. Use rudder and ailerons to keep the plane level. *Pull back. Pull back.* The loud stall warning blasted just as the right wheel touched down and then the left. Lucky. He pulled all the way back on the power.

The nose dropped and the plane bumped down the burned grass. Somehow he had done it; he hoped nobody had been watching his clumsy maneuvers. He let the plane slow of its own accord, then, when it had almost stopped, turned and taxied back toward the Land Rover.

Thank God, there was Johnny, pointing to where Paul should park. Paul stopped the plane, grabbed the shutdown checklist, ran through it, then cut the engine and opened the door. He had to pee like crazy, but Johnny was waving. When Paul climbed out, Johnny ran over to him and pumped his hand. "Great landing, Paul. Super. I couldn't have done better myself. You corrected for that last gust nicely. Thank God you saved my plane. I should kiss you on both cheeks." His eyebrows were a bit singed, but otherwise he was apparently all right.

To Paul's surprise, Bruce was there, too, with two jerry cans, a rifle, and a box of some sort that he held under his arm. He rushed over to the plane, climbed up on the wing, and Johnny handed him the jerry cans, one at a time. They filled the two wing tanks with gasoline.

"Go take a leak and get back. We've got a job to do in a hurry," Johnny said. Paul saw the two Land Rovers blackened from smoke and packed with gear, but no other people. Vaguely he wondered where they were. His mind was too full. He just needed to do what he was told at this point.

When Paul returned, Bruce was in the backseat and Johnny was waiting with the box by the front passenger seat. "Get in, fasten your seat belt tight, and hold this. I'll explain while we taxi." Whatever it was, it was heavy and awkward, rectangular with several taped protrusions, about the size of a small suitcase. Paul did as Johnny instructed. Johnny started the engine and taxied out for takeoff.

"That's a bomb in your lap," Johnny said, "You're going to throw it out the door when I tell you, drop it on the poachers. You won't really have to push it out. As soon as we take off, unlatch your door and just hold the box loosely. From what you said, they're not far from here. When we're right over them, I'll bank sharp to the right and the box will sail out. Bruce will be shooting to distract them — if we're lucky, he may even hit some of them. Now, where are they?"

"About twenty degrees to the right of the line of the landing strip, just beyond the burned area," Paul told them. "I saw them on my approach — actually, more than saw them. They shot at me and put a hole right through his passenger seat, right where I'm sitting, as a matter of fact." The thought didn't make Paul any more comfortable. In the rush, neither Johnny nor Bruce had noticed the small hole in the seat that the bullet had made.

"Right. We're going to stay low — at treetops — and surprise them. Hold on."

The plane was in the air immediately and Johnny put the nose over the trees and leveled off. They cleared the line of trees and descended, keeping low over the burned grassland. Paul felt they were skiing on Tsavo. Straight ahead were two Toyota Land Cruisers and a group of men with guns. It was all happening too fast to talk. Bruce began shooting through the plastic of the back window. One of the men on the ground fell and another picked up a rifle and aimed at them. Paul couldn't hear the shot. "Now!" Johnny shouted, and the plane banked hard right, the door flew open, and the box skidded across Paul's lap and out the door. Paul thought he could touch the top of the vehicle they passed over. He saw the frozen expression on the face of the man with the gun.

Over the roar of the engine, there was a loud *whoosh*. Johnny put the plane into a steep climb. Paul pulled the door shut,

"Jesus, what kind of bomb was it?" Paul asked, realizing things had happened so fast he had just done what Johnny told him and never thought about what he was holding.

"Something Elizabeth thought up and she and Davie made," Johnny answered. "They used Davie's explosive netting stuff and gasoline. You were holding a box full of explosive and gasoline. Good thing it didn't bounce on your lap too hard," Johnny said with a grin.

Then Paul heard the sounds of metal hitting metal and the engine misfire. He looked out the window and saw fuel coming from the wing. The bastards must have hit both the engine and the fuel tank. Johnny banked to the left and came around fast. Paul could see over Johnny's shoulder that the box had exploded — both vehicles were burning, and dirty brown smoke climbed skyward.

Bruce was shooting out the right rear window, through the transparent plastic. Another man dropped. The engine was missing badly, and Johnny banked the plane to turn back toward camp.

CHAPTER 39

Down to the Basics

He has to live in the midst of the incomprehensible . . . And it has a fascination, too, that goes to work upon him.

Joseph Conrad, *Heart of Darkness*

J ohnny flew the plane toward the landing strip. Paul saw a poacher fire directly at the plane from a Land Cruiser and saw and heard bullets hit the airplane's wing right outside him. Then he saw a poacher firing from a Land Cruiser approaching them and ducked for cover. Most of the elephant herd was moving rapidly away from the poachers, but two elephants — looked like young bulls to him — were charging the poacher's Land Cruiser. Good, good, he thought. They turned it on its side, throwing two of the poachers onto the ground and pinning another inside. One of the two who had been thrown out grabbed his weapon and tried to point it at the elephants, but they reached him first and stomped on him.

Paul looked ahead and saw that Johnny was just about to turn parallel to the landing strip and descend on the final approach. The young elephants below turned and pushed against the side of the overturned Land Cruiser with their tusks, shoving the vehicle along the ground into the shrubs. It stuck there, and one of the elephants reared up and came down with all his weight on it, crushing the cab and the two men inside. The fuel tank exploded and the vehicle burned.

As Johnny lined up the plane with the airstrip and began the final descent, Paul could see their two Land Rovers parked just along the strip and that the two young male elephants were running across the burnt ground. The smaller of the young bulls raced toward the landing strip. Uh oh, Paul thought, where's Zamani Baba when we need him, to keep these foolish young bull under control? Ears out, trunk up, the young bull charged Bruce's Land Rover and turned it over, then pushed it across the ground, destroying it. *God, we're down to one Land Rover*, he thought. Then he saw that Michael, standing a distance from the vehicle, was aiming at the bull. The elephant turned in a large circle and came racing back at the second Land Rover.

Michael fired. The shot hit the young bull, pushing back his head. He raised himself up one last time and crashed to the ground just short of the vehicle, raising a cloud of dust.

Johnny put the plane down on the runway, knowing he was lucky to get it to the ground. He and Bruce were quickly out assessing the damage.

Elizabeth and Mary emerged from a small stand of trees a half a mile from the landing strip and walked quickly toward the strip, watching Bruce go over to the young bull elephant to make sure he was dead. A third young bull elephant that no one had seen before came crashing out of the thorn bushes, pushing Mary over and knocking her out. Some time passed that Mary could not account for. When she came to, she was lying on the ground and Elizabeth and Paul were bending over her, offering her some water, clearly concerned. She assured them that all she needed was to sit quietly for a while, which she did, resting against Paul's backpack and seated on a blanket one of them had put down for her. She felt surprisingly well. Her head did not hurt; nothing else pained her.

She looked to her side and saw Horst sleeping fitfully a short distance away. Elizabeth had dressed his wound as well as she could and given him a strong dose of painkillers she had brought with her for emergencies. She wondered how long they would be hiding in this small grouping of trees and hoped they'd find a new and safer camp soon with good access to water.

* * *

Meanwhile, Bruce turned his attention to the remaining Land Rover. When he had last run it, its motor had been missing badly. Now he saw that the fan belt was worn almost to splitting, and he also found several small holes in the radiator. They would have to keep adding water to it, but water from where? Lying down under the Land Rover, he discovered that the front axle was slightly bent. The Land Rover was not likely to travel far — at best, it could go short distances, then be shut down to cool.

He and Johnny went over to the airplane. Bruce pointed out to Johnny where bullets had torn through the right wing, which was still dripping gasoline. He opened the cowling and saw that the engine was damaged. Bruce found that bullets had torn through one of the lines carrying oil, which was dripping out. It wouldn't be safe to fly the plane until it completely ran out of oil, and they did not have a way to repair this damage to the engine. Now they were without their fastest way to get to Voi to try to get more help. And they were down to one Land Rover. And a wounded man. They'd have no help in scouting poachers from the air now. Getting out of Tsavo just got more complicated.

Bruce, Johnny, and Paul brought the group together, told them they believed the bomb had been a success but they had probably lost the use of Johnny's plane. At best if would be dangerous to fly it. Bruce told them another piece of bad news: one of the Land Rovers probably would not make it to Voi, the nearest town. There was barely any fluid left in its radiator and they could only run it for short periods until they reached one of the artesian wells. He said that if they were divided up into small groups they would be easier targets for poachers. Best they stayed together.

"Can't you patch the Rover?" Howie asked.

Bruce shook his head. "Not likely."

"How far do we have to go?" Mary asked.

"Let's see. Twenty miles from the Manyara Gate to Lugard Falls. And we're east about sixty miles. I make it about eighty miles cross-country."

Horst was groggy, but awake. He tried to hold himself in a sitting position.

"I need to get out of here, obviously," he said to no one in particular.

"I've talked with Liz and she's had some emergency medical training," Bruce replied. "She thinks she can keep you stable and has plenty of pain meds, so we should be able to get you out in fairly good shape. You need to rest as much as possible."

"I've got other plans," Horst said, groggily

"You do?

"If that local poacher — what's his name … Joseph — shows up, he can contact my people. They're ready to fly a plane in to get me out when needed."

"That so?" said Paul, immediately standing up from where he had been sitting on the ground near Mary. He was fed up with Horst. By insisting that he talk to the head of the poachers and stupidly getting himself shot, Horst had gotten them into this jam. And now he was just going to waltz out of Tsavo through his connections? God knows what he'd told his people and what kind of reputation Paul would have — *if* he got out. And, as he suspected, Horst and Joseph had something going.

Bruce was having a similar reaction as was Paul. The years of betrayal Bruce had experienced with Horst were welling up in him. He had to get away from this conversation before he did something violent he would regret. He stood suddenly and went from their sheltered area to look out onto the Tsavo plains, hoping that the vast openness would help calm him as it had in the past. But a stream of dust blew in the distance indicating a vehicle was on its way. Just what he needed, somebody else to deal with. He hurried to get his rifle and indicated Davie and Michael do the same. As he walked quickly past Horst, he had a sudden desire to aim the rifle at him

— at least to scare him — and realized then how far this had gotten to him. The three took positions a distance from each other and stayed quiet, waiting for a signal from Bruce.

Bruce found binoculars in his pack and zeroed in on the vehicle. It was a Land Cruiser. As it neared, he could tell it was Joseph driving.

"Looks like you got your wish, Horst," Bruce said, barely keeping the sarcasm out of his voice. "It's Joseph."

Joseph slowed, seeing Bruce standing by a stand of trees and bushes, but he still brought a cloud of dust with him as he pulled up a short distance away. Bruce was motioning to him to drive closer. Then Joseph realized they were trying to stay out of sight of the poachers. He pulled his Land Cruiser into a sheltered area behind the group and strode to where they were.

"I've got a dead crew member. I guess there's some explainin' to do here," Joseph said.

Bruce was quick to respond, placing himself between Joseph and the rest of the group. "Yes. Saw it happen. Very sorry to see that man killed, Joseph. Wondered if he worked for you. But what were they doing there? You got some kind of thing going with the poachers?"

Joseph looked to Howie, who he could see was sympathetic. Davie looked angrier than usual, but his look said he was on Joseph's side.

"What a shit show," said Davie. "Real sorry 'bout that, Joseph."

"What was your guy doing there?" Bruce asked again.

"Horst hasn't told you? He hired me to have my guys track the poachers, that was all. They were just lookin' and tryin' to keep out of the way."

"What reason did Horst give you for tracking the poachers?"

"He said we needed to do something to stop the poachers. Said the government had sent in some troops to stop the poachers, but they didn't know their way around Tsavo and never would find the poachers. So Horst asked me to have some of my guys track the poachers, so we would know where they were, and others to guy the government soldiers, since they also wouldn't know their way 'round Tsavo. He told me that doing this would make me well-known and lead to all kinds of new work."

"Christ almighty!" Paul spurted, his face turning red, turning to Horst. "Hadn't you done enough before to make things difficult? Working behind our backs, then meeting with the poachers as if you were some kind of professional diplomat? Meanwhile helping them find out where we were and make us easy targets for them?"

Joseph saw that Horst's pant leg had been cut off and his thigh was bandaged. "You got a piece of it, too, I see. Guess that's fittin'."

Horst turned away from him and took another pill out of the bottle Elizabeth had given him.

"Sounds like Mr. Diplomacy thought he could reason with poachers and he's got us all into this mess," Joseph said, pacing into the brush and back to the group.

"No point in rehashing the obvious," Bruce said, giving a look to Paul, who was seething, barely containing himself. "We're in bad circumstances, as you can see, Joseph."

Horst pushed himself up to a sitting position. "No point in being coy now," he said, already feeling better from the medication. "I had a plan to get the government to bring troops in to save the elephants, save us, all backed by three powerful international conservation groups. But too much has happened," he turned to Bruce. "Your inept leadership has brought us to this crux."

Bruce, now himself under control, had to restrain Paul. It was clear what he'd like to do to Horst. Mary joined Bruce, giving Paul a look that somehow calmed him. She took his hand and pulled him to the side for a short walk back toward the bush. Elizabeth watched them, glad she and Bruce had each other.

"Seein' as how you were the one who had to talk with the poachers and get yourself shot, that don't make a lot of sense, Horst," Joseph said.

"And you — you send your crew at just the wrong time — and one of them is so dense he doesn't know how to duck," Horst said. "I thought you and your men knew their way around Tsavo and would know how to deal with some bad guys."

Joseph started toward Horst. "You bastard."

Elizabeth put herself between them and Bruce grabbed Joseph's arm.

"Know the feeling, Joseph, but he's injured. Can't do that."

"So you two had it all worked out, eh?" Bruce said, moving back to be able to take in the situation. Davie looked like he wanted to get in a brawl and stormed up to Horst.

"Son-of-a-bitch, Grobbins, you high-falutin' know-it-alls think you an' your money an' contacts an' smooth way of talkin' can solve every problem," Davie said.

"So what was the plan, Joseph?"

"Horst already told you about the troops being sent in for the poachers. I agreed my team would track them, provide info as to location — that sort of stuff. Then get Horst out when the time was right. Sounds like he never *shared* this with you," Joseph said, I didn't know that. Wouldn't have done this on my own.

"What did he promise you, Joseph?" Bruce asked, his mind racing.

"Said if I'd help him he'd get me more new vehicles and other equipment, and work out a way for me to be on a salary or somethin' with one of his organizations."

Horst looked away from the others, even though turning his body hurt his thigh where the bullet had hit.

Bruce felt the hairs rise on the back of his neck, but he was careful not to speak. He backed away from Horst and Joseph, trying to get himself under control.

"That reminds me," Joseph said, turning to Horst. "You said you'd be gettin' me two new Land Cruisers right away. Well, in this country, shipping in that kind of equipment requires a lot of legal stuff, and I've checked. Nothing's been ordered and nothing is on any of the ships due into port in the next few weeks. So what's up Horst? You cheatin' me?"

"Had a little trouble, I admit," Horst said, trying to lift himself to his feet. He fell back.

"So. Nothin's on its way and you didn't tell me. You expect me to do what you asked and once you're gone I get nothin'— that it? Just a double-cross.

"My international organization's been kind of slow," Horst answered.

"Shit. I don't believe you," Joseph starred at Horst and then started to move toward him.

"Haven't you noticed? I'm in pain here," Horst said.

Bruce needed to learn more about what they'd been up to, so he got between Joseph and Horst.

"Horst, you know that organization is honorable and reliable," Bruce said. "I know it."

"You can't call me a liar," Horst said, groaning as he changed position. His thigh was swollen and no position seemed to offer relief.

"Maybe, maybe not. But I can and *will* talk to your organization leaders when I get out of here and tell them what you did. They may not like some of the things I've done, but they've always been honest with me and never said they would do something and then not do it."

"And it's my man who got killed," Joseph added.

Horst looked away. "It wasn't my fault he got in the way."

"Had a wife and nine kids, he did," Joseph spit out. "Spose they're hurtin' more'n you."

Well, I'm sorry, but as I said, he made his move. I didn't even notice him."

"You don't really give a shit, do you?" Joseph tried to get around Bruce to reach Horst. Bruce kept him at bay.

"Joseph, Horst has treated us badly too. I'm just as mad at him as you are. But Horst can't be taking more of our time right now. I don't know if you've realize the predicament we're in," Bruce said, trying to keep himself under control. "Our plane is out and we've lost two Land Rovers."

"Well, ain't that just too bad. Maybe you wish now you'd respected me a bit all these years, huh? Always did it your way. Tellin' the law if I shot an elephant or two, while you've shot more than me and everybody I know put together."

It was all Bruce could do to keep calm. It didn't help that he knew part of what Joseph was saying was true. He saw Elizabeth come toward him. She indicated she needed to talk to him. He joined her a short distance from the others, while Howie and Davie came over to Joseph and talked with him.

"He's angry now, Bruce, and you can't blame him," she said, looking at Joseph. "He lost a man to this madness and apparently Horst swindled him into doing his work for him. We need Joseph, so you have to keep calm and work with him."

When they returned, Davie was crouched on his heels next to Joseph, who had taken a camp chair. Howie had moved away and was sitting cross-legged a distance away, his hat pulled down over his face, seemingly in meditation.

"Joseph, will you come and talk with me and Paul? This is important," Bruce said.

"I'll give you a listen, but only cause I like a few of your people. And you got two women stuck in this mess. No fault of their own."

Mary looked up to see Joseph and Bruce approaching. Bruce's look told her he wanted to meet alone with Paul. She squeezed Paul's hand and walked toward Elizabeth. She wondered who could pull this group together. Everyone was tense; everyone was mad. It didn't bode well for getting out alive, she thought.

Bruce indicated that Joseph and Paul move with him a short distance away, out of earshot of the others.

"Paul, what you just missed is that Joseph was hired by Horst's contacts to help in tracking the poachers."

"Oh yeah?" Paul said, staring at Joseph. "Why weren't we told?"

"I thought Horst would tell you. Guess he didn't. He's a slippery bastard," Joseph said. "I'm done with him."

"So why'd they need you?" Bruce asked.

"They needed someone who knew Tsavo. What he wouldn't have told you was he wanted to take over your operations. Couldn't do it without a good backup man who knew Tsavo."

"And you agreed to this?" asked Paul.

"Yup. Sorry to say I did. Can always use the money and well . . . I'm not proud of it. But it is a fact, as Baker would say."

Now Bruce saw the whole picture. Horst wouldn't be happy with helping to protect the group from poachers. He'd wanted to take over leadership, push Bruce out of the way, make him a laughing stock. He looked to Paul, who he could see was still angry but seemed to be focusing somehow as he stared at Joseph. He walked to the side and let Paul talk to Joseph.

"So, Horst had plans to take over, did he?"

"Yup. I figured it was a long shot, but the man's got ambitions. And he talked big, you know, like he had all these contacts and all this money. I got suckered, I guess."

Paul cleared his throat, trying to put things in a row in his mind.

"So, why are you here now?" Paul asked.

"Wanted to confront the bastard about my man. I want some money for his family."

Bruce almost snorted. "Good luck with that," he said

"And I wanted him to know *I know* he double crossed me. Wasn't ever goin' to pay me," Joseph went on. "That sort a thing don't work out here."

Paul saw that Bruce, pacing slowly, was coming to a sort of boil. Not good at this point. A distance away he saw Elizabeth watching the men. He motioned to her.

"Bruce, why don't you take a break, let me deal with this for a while," Paul said. Elizabeth arrived, indicating he come with her. Bruce looked at her for a moment, then strode in front of her as the two walked into some rough vegetation.

"Now I see the shape you're in," Joseph said, looking around. "That plane still fly?"

"Nope," said Paul, "and we're down to one Land Rover with a leaking radiator. It's not looking good."

"I see," said Joseph, and walked away to a clearing in the brush, taking a strand of grass from a nearby mound and chewing it. He saw Davie approaching.

"I hope ta hell these guys have been askin' for your help, Joseph," he said before he reached them.

"Can't say as they have," came Joseph's reply.

"We could use your help, obviously," Paul said, trying to keep his voice level.

"You plannin' on walkin' out of here?" Joseph asked.

"Don't see as we have much of a choice," Paul replied.

"Time ta ask real nice, Paul," said Davie. "The man's got a new Land Cruiser."

"Joseph, we could use your help and we would appreciate it. We've got one wounded man, two women, Howie, who is not a fighter. We're damned vulnerable at this point in time."

"No shit," said Davie. He spit on the ground.

"Wish it didn't involve Horst," Joseph said.

"Nothing we can do about that," said Paul. Maybe we have a chance of getting out of here, he thought. Funny that Joseph would be the ticket.

"Horst said something about you arranging to fly him out. Can that still happen?" Paul asked.

"I can make the contact for the plane that is supposed to pick him up. Might take a day or two. And we'd have to go out followin' the riverbed. We've already set the place for them to pick him up," Joseph said.

"Do it, then," Paul said. "The sooner we get rid of him the better."

"Well, if the plan still is to get him out of here, I'll do my best to make that happen," Joseph answered. "Be good to be rid of the bastard."

"What Paul meant ta say is thank you very much, Joseph," came Davie's voice over his shoulder. He was walking back to the others.

Paul, turning to Joseph, said. "We would really appreciate your help, Joseph. And it goes without saying I'm very sorry about the loss of your employee."

"Not really," said Joseph. "It needs saying." But he followed them back to the others.

Bruce announced that it was time for a group meeting and asked Paul to lead it. He walked to the side of the group. His head was thick with worry and recriminations. Why did he ever agree to bring Horst? Why didn't he monitor what the bastard was doing in Voi? His get-along go-along attitude had clearly been a disaster. Fact of the matter was he just didn't have the energy to constantly counter Horst's words and actions. He was sick of the whole thing.

He looked over to Elizabeth, who motioned for him to come and sit with her. He did, finally tuning in to what Paul was saying. *Joseph would help get them out; they would take turns walking and riding; Joseph knew locations for water, so they should be okay; they would need to stay out of sight as much as possible since the poachers probably would have access to another airplane soon; maybe they'd need to walk at night at some point, but they'd start tomorrow at dawn.*

After the meeting, each began checking and repacking their gear. Much of it had just been thrown in a Land Rover. Mary again carefully checked and then repacked the data sheets and field notebooks. Elizabeth watched her. It was the third time she had done that. Poor Mary, Elizabeth thought. How she loved the fieldwork. She was always that way, but now in this tight situation it was really getting to her. They needed to consolidate everything in one Rover, a trailer, and Joseph's Land Cruiser. They would leave at dawn, so they needed to do whatever they could before going to sleep.

Howie was the last to get his things together. As he put his little book of numbers in his pack, more pages fell out and a sudden breeze blew them about. Automatically, everyone grabbed at them, even Horst, but the pages fluttered away. Elizabeth ran after them but couldn't reach them. One sailed by Mary. She grabbed it and, without looking at it, handed it to Howie who, instead of putting it back into his book, which he had already put away, put it in his pocket.

Paul, who had quickly gotten his gear together, walked over and looked at the airplane while he waited for the others. It would probably never fly again, yet it looked whole, like a person who had died suddenly, painlessly, and looked only asleep. Left to itself in the Tsavo plains, the 182 would decay slowly, as any inanimate object would. But it would not stink. Rust, yes. And it was only yesterday that he had soared within it, as if with the angels. Hell, those were only vultures, Davie's angels, maybe. Now it was forever still.

Howie came and sat beside him. "Like Antoine St. Exupéry wrote, isn't it?"

"What?"

"The machine that brings us closer to nature. *Wind, Sands, and Stars*," Howie said.

"I don't know," Paul answered, "I'm kind of mourning the loss of the 182."

"Interesting, because now you're beginning to get it. Before this, you tried to be so rational. You thought that would solve everything. But now you're beginning to see that something is lost when you're so completely rational. You know what I mean?"

Paul did not know exactly what Howie meant, but he did understand the aircraft, and mourned for it, even though that too made no sense.

"Nothing makes any sense out here," he heard himself say.

Johnny opened the pilot's door, pulled himself up, and sat inside in the pilot's seat. Paul joined him in the copilot's seat. It was tidy and comfortable, den like. Johnny pushed and pulled the yoke. Paul looked on, wondering what difference was there between now and when it was flyable — sort of "alive"? How could he use that word?

"It's become your mistress," Howie said, rubbing his hand along the 182's skin. "Alas poor airplane, Paul knew you well."

"Sonofabitch." Johnny smiled in spite of himself. Elizabeth's face appeared in the plastic window. Then Mary's, as she stood on tiptoe. Neither Johnny nor Paul could hear what either of them said if, indeed, either said anything.

Paul focused on the 182, touching its leathery interior, as he thought about what they would face in the morning, glancing now and again at Johnny, who seemed to share his feelings. He felt sad more than frightened, and he could not tell whether he was sadder about what he faced, or what he was leaving behind — this airplane — that in a strange way represented safety, and now seemed to be an old friend.

CHAPTER 40

They Begin the Walk Out

Tuesday, October 2

What makes the desert beautiful is that somewhere it hides a well.

Antoine de Saint-Exupery

The group ate a cold breakfast so they could get moving as quickly as possible. Michael took advantage of this time and asked Bruce and Elizabeth to sit off to one side with him. "I hope you don't mind my talking with you about how we need to treat Horst," he said, looking at Bruce. "I just want to say, as you well know, the main thing now is getting ourselves safely out of Tsavo. I sympathize with how you feel about Horst, but in my years of contact with Europeans, Brits, and Americans, I've always been surprised at how this kind of disagreement — dislike — can disrupt what needs to happen."

"Aha, so Michael, as I told you at the beginning," Elizabeth said, smiling, "you're the anthropologist, reversing the usual, a Maasai studying us white guys."

Michael smiled back at her, but didn't comment directly. "Bruce, you know as well as anybody that getting out of here will only

314

happen if we don't get into internal squabbles that take all our time and energy. If you need to blow off steam about Horst, you've got me and Liz."

Bruce, looking at the ground and then far into the distance and then at Elizabeth, thanked Michael, got up and finished his cold breakfast.

They were all ready to leave shortly after dawn. Bruce and Joseph worked out a route that would be as straight as possible but with as much vegetation cover as Tsavo allowed — not much, but better than nothing. Listening to Bruce and Joseph, Johnny volunteered to walk ahead of the others and look out for any trouble, poachers, or dangerous wildlife. Michael, Paul, and Elizabeth started off on foot, following Joseph's Land Cruiser. Michael took large strides, his spear in his right hand and his rifle over his left shoulder. Behind him came the battered Land Rover. Bruce took the first turn driving, because the Land Rover was in such bad shape that he was concerned it would break down, and needed considerable care and experience to keep running. Also, Bruce wanted to limit the amount of weight it was required to move, so he decided Joseph would pull the trailer loaded with their gear.

Joseph's main stipulation in helping the team was that he wouldn't carry Horst, so Horst rode in the backseat of the Land Rover. He needed to keep his leg extended and Bruce thought one passenger was plenty. The others would take turns walking and riding with Joseph. As much as he loathed Horst at this point, he knew Michael was right about survival mode, which they most clearly were in, and personalities and grudges and betrayals all had to be put aside to keep a clear head.

They had drawn straws to see who would ride first and Mary got the shortest, so she was riding in the passenger seat with Joseph. Howie and Davie were in back. Mary began to enjoy the view as they drove along. Then she noticed a small animal running alongside the Land Cruiser, keeping up with it. It looked a little like a dog, but had great big ears and a kind of humped back. "What's that?" she asked Joseph.

"Looks like a bat-eared fox," Davie said. "What's he doing followin' your Cruiser Joseph? I thought they kept away from people."

Joseph laughed. "Usually do, but he's been following me around, I guess looking for scraps to feed on or insects me and my crew scared up. Usually eats insects, you know. Hung around so much I kinda got to like him and started throwing scraps his way."

Mary smiled. She was beginning to like Joseph.

Howie leaned over Davie, and they both looked outside to see the fox circling to the side of the Land Cruiser, pausing to dig an insect out of the hard ground. "Son-of-a-bitch," Davie said, a wide smile on his face. "Some people got weird likes."

Michael won the next chance to ride with Joseph, and Howie walked for a while with Elizabeth. She asked him what he thought their chances were of getting out alive.

"Each of us has our own idea about Tsavo, just as we do about nature in general, Double-E," Howie said. "In our modern world we think that idea is unimportant, no more important than whether one of us liked a certain movie, or a song, or a novel. But, in fact, our idea about nature and how we relate to it is going to affect which of us survive." Elizabeth found Howie's comment sobering and frightening. "It's like that about all of our life," he added, "but it's only when we're confronting survival directly that we realize it."

"I thought we were just fleeing the poachers."

"And they aren't part of our idea of nature?" Howie responded. "Even if they're just the force that makes us confront our reality, it's the reality that we are facing."

"Which of us are going to make it?" she asked. Howie just shrugged.

Elizabeth looked at Tsavo in a new way, once again. How many new ways could there be — were there going to be — for this place? she wondered. Then she thought of each of her companions, trying to decide who had the best chances.

Hours passed. They stopped to rest, sitting or reclining as best they could in whatever shade they could find. Joseph approached Bruce.

"I've got a good compass in my rig. Pretty sure we'll hit an artesian well in a couple hours."

Bruce nodded and attempted a small smile. "Thanks, Joseph," he managed to get out. It was still difficult for him to coordinate with Joseph but it was getting a little easier.

Mary fingered the pendant that still hung around her neck, comforted as always by the contact, as if her aunt who had given it to her were talking to her, urging her on. It was Elizabeth's turn in the Land Cruiser. Paul took over driving the Rover.

Mary walked with Davie and Bruce. Seventy miles now, based on what Bruce had said. That didn't seem too hard, she thought. Three miles an hour. Walk for ten hours and go thirty miles. She'd hiked much more than that in a day in worse country — mountains, flatlands full of bogs. They could be out in two, three days, but Bruce had said more like four, five days. Maybe you couldn't go as far in a day here. Oh, yes, it was partly about the water, she remembered.

The process of thinking about numbers and making a calculation cheered her. And she had her data, she had some new ideas, and she had fallen in love with Paul. Not bad at all. She decided to try to keep notes about the vegetation as they walked, and count the animals they saw. A scientific line transect — that would make a good story to tell! So much had happened here in Tsavo.

Bruce told the others to walk ahead of the vehicles so the dust wouldn't bother them. Mary led the way as spritely as she could, hoping to raise everyone's spirits at least a little.

Although the Land Rover sputtered now and again, it continued to run. Davie now walked far from the others, more or less parallel to Mary but off to one side. He looked at landmarks as he walked, as if trying to remember places he had seen before. Maybe there was a faster route than Bruce and Joseph had picked out for them.

Mary thought she could make out some vague shapes in the distance. Bruce had taken over the Rover and Paul was now at her side, briefly taking her hand. "There's some trees — palms, I think — so water and shade are ahead. Joseph was right," he said. "And w ay out there, one of those strange hills — a Kopje." He pointed. "We're making toward that patch of trees and we'll rest there," he told her. She looked exhausted but, under her wide-brimmed cowgirl hat, still beautiful. It pained him to see her struggling bravely. A welcome wind rose and whined organ-like through the trees, a sound seemingly from beyond their reality. They continued on, as if roped loosely together, swinging this way and that.

Soon they found themselves at one of the artesian wells whose water sprang sprightly and cascaded, forming a small stream around which palm trees and low streamside vegetation had grown up. They took mats and blankets from the Land Rover and put them on the ground. Mary sank quickly onto a blanket and was soon fast asleep. For a moment, all the men stood still around her, like the dwarfs around Snow White.

Elizabeth walked over to the small stream formed from the artificial artesian well. "Look," she called to Paul and Bruce. Howie, Davie, and Joseph came too. "See, it's formed a natural little perennial stream, and see how the vegetation is growing right down to the edge and protecting the land from erosion? The animals must come to this place. But this is what I was trying to describe to you, Bruce, about how the elephants and the other big grazers changed the streams — ate and trampled all the plants that grew alongside streams naturally, and left them like streams in cattle rangeland, destroyed and eroding."

Bruce looked at the streamside plants. He was amazed that, even exhausted, she could still be fascinated with geology in circumstances that threatened her life. Soon Paul, Howie, and Davie were discussing the little stream vigorously, so Bruce walked away to check on the condition of the others. He heard splashing; some of them were cooling off and washing as best they could in the flowing water.

He opened the Land Rover's hood and bent to peer inside. Michael, meanwhile, was walking the perimeter of the small oasis to keep watch. Howie was on his knees, feeling the soil, splashing water on himself, looking at the plants. Soon all of them except sleeping Mary had stripped to their underwear and were splashing and washing. Howie splashed Elizabeth, and a water fight broke out.

Hearing their laughter, Bruce pulled his head out from under the hood, and watched. He was pleased to see that the group was still spirited. They might make it back after all. And if they did, it would likely be Elizabeth who made the difference. Michael joined him, and they took out some food — jerked impala meat and a tin of crackers. Elizabeth, drying herself on a ragged towel, took one of the blankets and spread the food out neatly as if they were on a holiday picnic. She gathered everyone around and gently roused Mary. Mary rose up groggily and pulled her hair back with her hands, then went down to the stream with Paul and splashed water on her face. Elizabeth set out water from the well in tin cups. They sat on the ground and chatted away almost gaily, all but Horst who stayed to himself, pulling occasionally on his bottle of Scotch.

After they had eaten, most of them tried to nap. Elizabeth checked Horst's bandage and decided it needed changing. Mary walked downstream until she was out of sight of the rest, then stripped to her underwear and bathed. The coolness was indescribably refreshing. As she splashed water on herself, she noticed a crowned hornbill that circled above her, then perched on a limb and called its mournful call. Her hornbill, she was sure. Perhaps a good sign, representing home and safety. Maybe she would make it out.

Michael spoke quietly to Bruce and told him he could see another patch of trees at the horizon. Joseph confirmed it had water. They decided to shuttle people there in the Land Cruiser, agreeing that it would be best to make use of whatever help the Land Rover could provide while it was still running. Fuel in the tank was low, and they were down to one additional five-gallon can of gasoline.

Starting the motor, Bruce filled the radiator with water from the well and headed off with Horst. Joseph took off with Michael, Howie, and Davie. Michael would secure the campsite for the night and Davie would look for dinner.

Paul sat in the shade and updated his logbook, looking up frequently to see if Mary was okay. His heart went out to her. She was the most vulnerable of all the people on the trip. Her beauty and vulnerability seemed to Paul to symbolize Tsavo. For the moment, he saw the two intimately entwined, like vines grown together on the trunk of a tree. He got up and went to her, and gently touched her. He put his fingers against her lips, then caressed her cheek gently with those fingers. She looked up at him, her eyes sad, imploring, wondering. Something dwelt deep in her eyes, like gold coins at the bottom of the blue water of a well, something Paul could not explain. He wanted to comfort her, but not out here, exposed in their tiny society, like shipwrecked people in a crowded rowboat. Nothing they could do would be unnoticed in a land where there was almost nothing to notice.

They waited for Joseph to return. It was late afternoon when they spied the dust raised by the Land Cruiser. He'd dropped off the trailer at camp and they were next to go.

As soon as the Land Cruiser left the shade, Elizabeth felt the heat. Even as the day waned, a hot breeze blew in through the window. They reached the next set of palm trees near dusk. These palms grew by a natural spring. When they pulled up, the others already had a tiny fire going and were cooking meat from an oryx that Davie had shot and skinned when it came down to drink. The smell of the cooking meat seemed out of another world to Elizabeth, pulling her back to something — what was it? Civilization or the earliest era of human-cooked food?

Horst didn't mingle with the group. He ventured up to get some food, but then positioned himself a distance away from the fire, enjoying the last of his stash of Scotch.

Bruce worked on the Land Rover. He had turned it northwest so that the setting sun would give him light to work on the engine as long as possible. Howie sat a small distance from the campfire with his back to a tree, fingering his plastic funnel. He took some mung beans out of a plastic bag, dropped them one by one down the funnel, and watched idly as they spilled on the ground. Some spun around in the funnel, and he moved his fingers in circles, clockwise and counterclockwise, so that some of the beans spun a long time before falling through onto the ground. Bruce, although weary, found some relief in watching Howie, his faded and dusty patchwork shirt still the most cheerful thing in view, and his tricks with the beans, were, in the fading light, a little like a circus side show. At least they were a distraction from their situation.

"I must say, you're the only one I've met who could put the fun in *funnel*," Bruce joked lamely as he joined him at the campfire.

Howie grinned and began, gently, to beat a quiet little rhythm with the funnel against the hollow plastic cylinder. Where did the cylinder come from? Bruce tried to remember. It seemed so long ago. Yes. Howie would pour mung beans into a plastic bag in the soil, then, to measure how many beans, poured them back into the funnel, actually a "graduated cylinder" Howie had called it — a piece of scientific laboratory equipment, so strangely out of place now, and began to sing quietly to the rhythm.

> "The best for me is destiny.
> What destiny is chanced for me?
> What spins around must last fall down,
> Beans through a grate
> My date with fate.
> What chance for me with destiny?
> Whose beans do fall? Whose chance at all?
> What's best for me is what I see.

It was a pleasant, childlike tune that only Bruce heard. Then Howie grinned, put his funnel away, and lay down to sleep. He did not pick up the beans, Bruce noticed, but left them where they had fallen.

Joseph and Michael approached Bruce. He looked up as they neared. Michael appeared comfortable with Joseph. Memories of their time in school together flooded back and Bruce grudgingly admitted to himself that Joseph had been an eager and intelligent student who didn't always get his due because of money and class distinctions. One thing leads to another, he thought, and all those things led up to where they were today.

"We should get to a large baobab tree tomorrow," Michael said. "Joseph has arranged for Horst to be picked up there."

"Excellent," said Bruce and tried to give them both some kind of smile.

"'Spect we'll get there mid-day," Joseph said. "It'll be good to be rid of the bloody bastard."

"My thoughts, exactly," said Bruce as Michael looked off into the distance, smiling to himself.

"Today went well, Joseph," said Bruce. "As they say, couldn't have done it without you."

"I figure we got about twelve miles in. Should make it in another four days or so if we can keep that Rover going."

"Yeah, well that's the ten thousand dollar question, I guess."

Joseph and Bruce looked into the fire and Michael walked off to begin his guard duty. Bruce watched him go. Clearly, Michael felt responsible for the others. He was a person of this landscape, having grown up to know what were dangers and what were not. And he could not let these friends of his continue without his watching out for them. Joseph joined Michael. So, Bruce thought, Joseph also sees himself as a person of this land and wants to act as another of the protector of the group. Who would have thought, he wondered. Their small fire lingered and dwindled.

The rest of the group found blankets and places to sleep. Paul and Mary waited until it was dark and went off together to the edge of the palm trees.

Davie walked to the edge of their tiny oasis and stared out into the distance, then paced back and forth nervously. Elizabeth saw Davie pacing. What was he up to now? Was his craziness going to come to the surface, like the bare bones of the others of the group seemed to be doing? Was he going to become dangerous, just as he had seemed early in the trip — before he brought out his record player and began to sing?

CHAPTER 41

Davie's Choice

Air Attack
Wednesday

The machine does not isolate man from the great problems of nature but plunges him more deeply into them.

Antoine de Saint Exupéry, *Wind, Sand, and Stars*

Paul was awakened by a familiar droning sound. Drifting dreamlike, he felt himself flying, then sat up with a start — he was hearing an airplane. It was barely light out but he could see it appear from the west, heading toward them. Bruce was already up and hurrying toward the Land Rover. Paul rushed to the low slope by the stream, hiding behind a fallen palm. Then he looked to the edge of their camp and saw Michael and Joseph grabbing their rifles. He remembered he had seen the two of them as he was falling asleep standing guard for the rest.

The plane descended, turned, and headed at them from the northwest. The passenger door opened, and Paul saw the barrel of a gun and felt more than heard the rapid fire of an automatic weapon. The bullets tore at the soil, and a rapid series of metal *pings* told him that their last Land Rover had been hit. It did not explode — he heard the sound of dripping liquid but did not smell gasoline. The plane circled and came back. The gun fired into the palms. Twice more the plane circled, the last time almost at treetops. Then he saw Joseph aiming his rifle and heard shots. The plane dived suddenly toward the ground and crashed a few hundred yards beyond them. Davie, lying on the ground next to Elizabeth shook his head in wonder and told her it was a miracle that anybody could shoot down an airplane with a rifle. Johnny and Bruce were up and running toward the plane. It began to burn. No one came out of the pilot's seat, but a man in flames struggled out of the passenger door, still holding a weapon. Johnny shot him.

Everyone gathered and watched the plane burn. Bruce looked around. All the rest were there. No one was hurt. Joseph, Johnny, and Michael came over to him and they talked quietly. They agreed that it had to be poachers who had been able to track the team from the air. This meant that the poachers not only knew where they were, but didn't want to leave anybody alive who knew what they were doing and could report about it. Michael and Joseph agreed to take care of the bodies in the plane; he would take care of the Land Rover. Johnny said he would again go on the lookout to see if any other planes or vehicles might be on the attack, and he went off quickly with a rifle and his binoculars.

Bruce's head was spinning. Not only did his group suffer another attack, but now more deaths. And they were going to use up more valuable time and energy burying more dead. It seemed brutal of him, but he wanted to leave these bodies to rot and be eaten by vultures.

He was exhausted, but he felt he had to be in charge. Paul joined him and they went to look at the Land Rover. There were bullet holes in the front. Paul opened the hood and looked at the engine. The dripping Paul had heard was from the radiator. Bruce saw that it had been hit and was leaking — probably ruined. He realized if he had parked it facing in the opposite direction — the way they were going — the bullets would have hit the fuel tank and at least some of the group might have been killed or badly burned from the explosion.

Paul's help was settling Bruce down. Thinking more clearly, he told Paul that they could still get some use out of the Rover — run the engine until it overheated, stop to let it cool, run it some more, and do that over and over until the engine just froze up. But water was an issue and they needed it for human consumption.

Elizabeth had been watching Bruce and Paul. She joined them and suggested they just abandon it and take only what they could get into the Land Cruiser. Bruce, his mind still foggy, thought it over and agreed that would be best. He noticed Joseph to his side and realized Joseph was impressed with Elizabeth's clear thinking, and probably not too impressed with his.

Joseph wandered over to where Michael was preparing some sort of breakfast. He and Michael had reached the plane and realized the bodies had been incinerated with the burning of the plane. They set their sights to getting the team ready for the day's trek. Paul told them to pack only the bare necessities. When that was done, they ate a quick breakfast of oryx and crackers Michael laid out.

Elizabeth looked up to see Horst come out of his tent, limping, looking groggy, and using a walking stick to steady himself. She realized the pain pills she had been giving him must have let him sleep through the exchange of gunfire.

"Are we going to get out of here sometime today?" he asked Bruce, who was walking by.

"Jesus Christ, Horst," said Joseph, "Didn't you get it that we were just shot at from an airplane?"

"So, that was all the noise," Horst said, still barely awake.

Bruce ignored him but wanted to turn and knock him off his feet. Horst kept walking.

"You got it. What a genius," Joseph said mockingly.

"He's been drugged, guys. The pain pills. Take it easy," Elizabeth said as she placed herself between Joseph and Horst. She realized how angry and disgusted Joseph and Bruce — in fact all of them — were with Horst. She backed off and gave herself a chance to think of how to help the group survive this latest terrible event.

"Keep your nose out of this, Joseph," said Horst, still not understanding all that had happened. "Think about getting me out of this hell hole. That's what you were hired for."

Michael came up behind Joseph as he went for Horst. Joseph's temper, which was legendary among those who knew him, had barely been contained the last two days. In his mind Horst was healed enough to take a little abuse. After all, with his help, Horst would get out soon while the rest would likely have to walk through miles of dust. He got to Horst and knocked him off his walking stick and to the ground. But he felt Michael forcefully pulling him back.

Bruce, still in a kind of daze, looked on. More craziness, he thought, but he wanted to do what Joseph had done.

Facing away from Horst, Michael said to Joseph, "Not now. Not the place for anger. We've just got to get ourselves out." Joseph kicked a mound of dust toward Horst, then walked away from the group. Michael helped Horst off the ground and into a camp chair while Elizabeth brought him his breakfast of oryx and crackers.

"Very kind of you, Elizabeth," he said. "Thank God there's one person here who's got some sense." He stood and tried to give her a hug, but she was backing away and Horst saw Bruce was striding toward them. Michael gave Bruce a steely look, then turned his gaze to Davie, who seemed to want to tell them all something.

At Davie's request, Paul called the group together, except Johnny who was too far away. Davie cleared his throat and stood up, looking especially ill at ease. "Folks, I got somethin' to tell you," he said. "You guys might as well put down bread crumbs for them poachers to track you. We're just too visible — too big a group. I say we split up. They can't follow all of us. Whatever the rest of you think, I've decided it's time for me to go my own way."

Bruce objected. "Visible or not, I think it's best to stay together."

"Most times, yeah. But right now, no. I've seen enough with Horst's bullshit and Joseph and Bruce ready about any minute to give it to him — probably would if he weren't wounded. I plan to get outta here alive, an' fightin' among ourselves ain't the way. I've been seeing places I've been before and I've figured another route out. If

I'm guessin' right, it's shorter, but you couldn't take a vehicle on it. If one or two a you wanna come with me, that's okay." He looked at Mary longingly. Nobody volunteered. He shrugged. "Well, I know Tsavo, and Tsavo knows me. Bruce, jus' lemme have a gun and some food. I got a hatchet, some matches, an' a canteen. I'm goin' straight west till I hit the main road."

"We don't know where water is that way," Bruce reminded him. "We already went through this. Michael and I believe there are some more wells and some of those hidden caches of water. I don't know any water the way you're planning to go ..." But as he talked, Bruce handed Davie the things he asked for.

"You don't, but maybe I do. I'm sure I seen some of them water holes the poachers left straight west of here. Joseph knows a few others, I'll bet. I'll talk with him 'fore I leave. I'll find 'em. First I'm gonna walk downstream a while to get my footprints away from yours. Then I'll walk backward a ways, smoothin' my tracks with a palm frond."

"Your data," Paul said. "You'll have to leave it with me. It's part of our report, and you were paid for the work."

"Oh, sure." Davie dug in his pack and handed Mary a bound field notebook, saying he hoped she could read his writing. She opened it. The pages were stained with vulture droppings, but the columns of figures were printed elegantly, as if by some eighteenth-century hand. Each column was clearly labeled.

Paul looked over her shoulder. "I can read it better than m y own notes, Davie. Thanks very much." He shook Davie's hand and wished him a safe journey.

Davie looked at the ground, his long neck stretched out. "Take care of that pretty lady," he whispered to Paul. Then he walked over to Howie. "Thanks for the loan of this, Howie, but I don't need it right now, so I'm givin' it back." He handed him the yo-yo. "But hey, my man, don't forget, when we get back, you owe me a yo-yo."

Howie shook his hand. "You got it."

Davie dug around in his pack again and walked over to Mary. "My mom gave me this, but I really ain't got much use for it. So would ya take it from me as a — a — remembrance?" He held something out to her, and when he opened his palm she saw a perfect diamond on a fine golden strand.

"Davie — I can't. It's so sweet of you, but — it's your mother's. You should save it for the girl you marry."

He shook his head. "Not likely. Not in this life. Like you to have it. I know you haven't always thought the best a' me, but I ain't as bad as I sometimes seem. And, well, you're a princess, no doubt about it. Nobody'd look prettier'n you in this necklace. I'd be honored if you take it to remember me by. I may be a grave-diggin' vulture-lover, but down deep I like to think I'm like this here diamond that's been sittin' in my pack under all that dirty field gear. Diamond in the rough. Please."

Mary, touched, could not refuse. "Thank you, Davie. How lovely. And what a sweet thing you just said. I will remember you just as you are now, at this moment." She reached up and gave him a hug and a kiss on his cheek, stretching up on her toes to reach above his long neck to his whiskered face. "Please be careful, Davie. We'll see you in Nairobi."

"Maybe. When I get back, first thing I'm doin' is goin' home to Brooklyn, someplace safe, like Coney Island or Brighton Beach, hit the jazz clubs up in Harlem, listen to some good music. But I'll be thinkin' of you when I do. I'll lift a beer to you, Mary. You're a princess, you definitely are."

Bruce took Davie aside. "You know the route we're taking — following the riverbed and the roads, swinging to the south somewhat."

"Yeah, sure."

Joseph came up and put his arm around Davie's shoulder. "You and I both know Tsavo pretty well, Davie," Joseph said, "but let's compare notes. I think I know the path you're goin' to follow and I think there's some water along the way." The two sat down and talked, both drawing in the sandy soil rough maps of the route they were discussing.

Horst, getting up slowly and leaning on his walking stick, felt a sudden ache in his leg. He realized that Elizabeth's doctoring had kept him from infection and the swelling in his thigh had gone down. He was lucky the bullet went in a part of his quadriceps and exited the back of his leg, a clean hit, so to speak, but he knew he needed medical attention. More than that he needed a drink and he was almost down to the last of his store.

"Can we get this show on the road?" he called out to no one in particular. No one answered him.

"If you get to Voi, and we haven't, let them know at the Ranger station which way we're coming," Bruce said to Davie.

"You got it." He picked up his pack and, without looking back, waded into the water and headed west, downstream. He was soon out of sight.

Bruce turned back to the others. They looked tired, dejected. Really, they needed another day to rest, gather their strength for the long walk. He looked each of them over, thinking once again about who would make it and who might not. In balance, he decided that all of them had the capability to make it out, as long as they could find water and each had the will to go forward. Will was the crucial element. He had been in equally difficult situations and knew the strain even a few days of walking in Tsavo could cause. He was not concerned about food — they had plenty of ammunition and could shoot game, sparse as it was, and they had matches. In the worst case, they could drink the blood of the animals they shot. Like Davie, though, he knew many of the secret water holes. His main concern was water containers; they did not have enough.

They should probably walk at night, although nighttime was more dangerous — they could suffer an attack by lions or stumble across other dangerous animals. But they needed to move from where they were as soon as possible, since the poachers were successfully tracking them. Once the poachers learned their plane was shot down, they'd be coming again for the team — and with more vengeance. Bruce walked to where people were packing up gear. He reminded them that many people, including poachers and white hunters, had died trying to walk out of Tsavo through the area they were now entering, and that they needed to stay alert.

Bruce studied the geological map with Michael, Johnny, and Paul. Johnny listened and made occasional comments, but he maintained his carefree demeanor. Bruce knew that Johnny was totally at home in the bush and unworried about his own survival. Johnny would think some of the others lacked the strength of character to make it out, but he wouldn't consider that his business. Bruce also knew that Michael and Joseph would not consider this a terribly serious situation except for the danger from the poachers. Traveling in dry country had been part of their lives. It was the Americans that Bruce felt were the most vulnerable, especially Mary.

Joseph approached and Bruce asked him if he could point out on the map where the large baobab tree was. Joseph crouched down and looked briefly at the map, then pointed to the spot.

"I'd say 'bout 15 miles from here, maybe less," he said. "There's seasonal springs along the way but can't be sure they haven't dried up by now. We'll have to ration today."

Mary had come around behind Paul and heard the talk about water.

"There should be water in the baobab if it's as big as you've said, Joseph," she offered.

"I've heard a people gettin' water that way," said Joseph, "but I never have myself." The others turned to her.

"Me neither," Mary said, flattered with the attention being given her. "But I've read about it and those trees store a lot of water."

"Well, let's hope," said Bruce. "Now let's get going."

Mary suggested they stop at intervals and take notes on what they observed, so that they would have something to show for their long walk. Bruce agreed; more important than the observations, he knew, was that this would give the group a purpose other than survival.

Each carried a backpack with only the essentials. Paul, Elizabeth, Mary, and Howie had packed their field notebooks with their data, and Paul had Davie's field notebook as well. Bruce warned them about the dangers of carrying any added weight, but he understood the importance of the notebooks and did not push the issue. Of what value would the journey have been if they arrived back without these notebooks? If nothing else, Paul thought, Horst would be proved

right—actually measuring things did not matter. And rhetoric —
Horst's bullshit, Paul thought angrily as he stuffed things into his
pack — would win. It was decided that Paul would drive the Land
Cruiser for the first part of the day, with Horst in the back. With
their remaining gear now in the Cruiser, there was only room for
another person in the front seat. Elizabeth won the toss. Johnny,
Bruce, Joseph and Michael would walk with rifles ready in case of
attack.

By midmorning, the sun shone in their faces so brightly that
Mary could not see clearly where they were going. It was as if she
were struggling blind in a desert darkness. Paul had turned driving
over to Joseph, who said he'd drive Horst as long as no word was
spoken between the two. Paul whispered something to Mary and
dropped back to talk quietly with Bruce, asking whether it would
not be better to walk at night and rest during the day. "If we could
find some shade and water, yes," Bruce said, "but out here in the
open, we can only keep moving. As I said, if we can just do fifteen
miles a day, we'll be out in another four days."

By mid-day they came to the spot Joseph had thought would
have a spring, but the water had retreated to form a small puddle.
It still looked drinkable, so each quietly bent down to get what
little water they could into their containers and rested in the nearby
shade. Nothing to be said. Now they were focused on getting to the
baobab.

Mary tried to keep both Michael, ahead of her, in view, and the
Land Cruiser, but repeatedly turning to see it behind her made her
feel dizzy, lost in a fog of dust and light. Dreamlike, blindly, she
moved forward.

"You're doing great, Mary," a voice said.

With great effort she turned her head and saw that Howie was
alongside her, appearing out of nowhere. "I didn't know you were
next to me, Heck," she managed to say.

He smiled reassuringly. He looked untired. His soiled and sweaty
multicolored shirt shimmered in Mary's eyes. He whistled, then sang
a little song:

Rings on his fingers and bells in his nose,
He shall have music whenever he blows.

"That doesn't seem quite right to me," Mary murmured vaguely.

"It sounds all right to me," Howie replied.

"I didn't say it didn't sound right, I said it doesn't *seem* quite right."

"It's about a whale."

"There are whales here?"

"Mary, you know there are no whales in Tsavo."

"Well, then — ummh — whales don't have fingers, so they can't have rings on them."

"If they don't have fingers, how do they put the bells in their nose?"

"Heck, they don't have a nose."

"If they don't have a nose, how do they breathe?"

"Howie. . . !"

But Howie just gave her a pat on the back and was gone — she was too tired to turn to see where. She felt Horst's eyes on her. She looked to the side to see him starring out the window of the Land Cruiser. His pale blue eyes seemed to glow in the blinding light. Paul was suddenly next to her, offering her some water. Only enough to wet her mouth, but it felt wonderful. Paul looked past her to see Horst watching them. He put his arm around Mary, almost lifting her off the ground, and waited until the Land Cruiser was in front of them.

"That bastard," Paul said.

"No problem," said Mary. "He doesn't bother me."

She grabbed at her pendant and clutched it, as if it could give her strength.

The line of marchers snaked along. They trudged over the empty land, pale figures casting dark shadows in the blinding light, an uneven line staggering slowly southwestward, a miniature migration of a strange mammal rarely viewed by the soaring vultures that followed in their wake. If it were the Middle Ages, a bystander would think these were flagellants intentionally torturing themselves for their sins, carrying heavy burdens across a Biblical wilderness, lacking only whips and led by a strange Revelations — like beasts that spouted smoke and growled.

Elizabeth noticed that the countryside had become much drier and the soil extremely fine, as if it were a fine volcanic material. She wondered about it, but her mouth was too dry to talk about it with Bruce. The dust made her cough and she stopped briefly, so that Bruce got ahead of her. She saw that he threw up a fine cloud of dust as he walked, and when he was ten or twenty yards away he appeared through the dust as a ghostly gray figure. The desiccated grasses she walked over were covered with the same dust and were stunted, bunched, with bare soil covering as much ground or more than the grasses. The ground was reddish, and the dust a reddish gray, as if some catastrophe had spilled the blood of a million animals onto the land.

Bruce stopped to wait for her, and Paul caught up with her and gave her more water to drink. Howie coughed. The fine dust was getting into his mouth and throat. He took out a red bandanna and tied it around his neck, then pulled it up over his mouth and nose, outlaw-style.

They started out again and Mary walked onward in an almost dreamlike state, with the image of blood pouring onto the ground growing in her mind. As her feet touched the hot soil, she felt that the earth was emitting warmth from that blood and wondered again if she was becoming delirious from the heat. She was thankful for her broad-brimmed hat she was wearing, her cowboy hat, now tied under her chin with a red ribbon. Even hot and dusty and haggard with exhaustion, she managed to smile up at Paul when he looked at her.

"I'll never understand how anybody can look so pretty in a situation like this, Mary, but you do it," he said. Her smile widened. She put her arm in his and they walked together, holding each other for a short way, then broke away to make the going easier.

When they stopped briefly, Elizabeth saw that the dust cloud thickened with each person down the line, so that Michael, now last in line, was walking in a dry fog and was barely visible. They stopped under what shade they could find by half-dead shrubs, and each took a sip of water.

They rested in the late afternoon, some sleeping fitfully. Once Paul awoke and noticed that Howie was not there. Later, he saw Howie returning with a plastic bag of soil and some leaves, which he set down and examined carefully. Didn't Howie ever stop being curious? He wondered.

Paul and Mary lay a little bit away from the others, so they could talk by themselves. "Howie's a strange one, isn't he?" she said, rubbing her finger in the sandy soil and making a geometric design like a snowflake.

"Always has been," Paul said.

"I don't always understand him."

"Howie takes some getting used to. After working with him for years, I've gotten used to the way he does things."

"I suppose," Mary said, and changed the subject. "I'm gritty and hot and thirsty. I'd love to at least wash my face."

Paul looked at her and smiled sympathetically. Without her, he wondered if he would have the will to go on. But as long as she was there, he was going to keep going and get her home.

CHAPTER 42

Water from a Baobab

Thursday

Squeeze water out of a rock
And I make water come out of dry sand.
Squeeze water out of a rock
And I get water out of dry sand.
Oh, If you listen to my story, little girl,
I'll prove to you I'm a man.

Buddy Guy Blues

Mary saw it first. A lone baobab tree off in the distance, so far ahead it seemed to float above the ground, to shimmer and move. Was it really a tree, or just a mirage? She was even more light-headed from the heat, but stopped and pulled out her binoculars. The image continued to shimmer and move in waves through the lenses, but she was certain it was a real tree. She looked at her compass. It was to the right of the direction they were headed — about 30° away and a long walk. But they hadn't found water the whole day walking and it was late in the afternoon. The water it had might save them. She handed Paul the binoculars.

"These baobabs swell up when they have a lot of water," she said, "and get thinner in a drought. This one looks very big." Paul motioned to Joseph, driving the Land Cruiser behind him, and they headed for the tree. Horst sat up in the back of the vehicle, scanning the sky for a plane.

When they reached the baobab, Mary looked at its roots, trying to remember how deep-rooting they were and the best way to get at the water inside. Michael was beside her. And the others. She knew they were all parched, but were doing their best to let her have time to analyze the situation. She touched the bark — it felt incredibly solid and permanent, like a nature she had dreamed about but which did not seem to exist in Tsavo. The bark reminded her of an elephant's skin, the same color, the same toughness, yet one seemed permanent, unchanging, patient, silent; another Tsavo entity that seemed dynamic, mysterious, hard to understand, confusing. Which was real? The baobab or the elephant? Both? And which was real nature?

For a moment, Elizabeth thought the baobab moved, at least the strange limbs did and so did the trunk. Perhaps it shifted in a wind. It reminded her of an elephant, *the* elephant, that old elephant, Zam ani Baba. She remembered her first view of Tsavo from the Manyani Gate, and then her first weeks in the park — her first meeting with the elephants, her flight over Tsavo with Bruce, watching the vultures with Davie, almost being attacked by a lion when she got angry with Horst, meeting up with Baker, being shot at with arrows by the elephant people, as Michael had called them , meeting up with the two tourists, Deborah and Bob, who thought Tsavo a fine place for a Sunday drive until they were held up by poachers, the bomb that she and Davie had made, her conversations with Michael and Howie, and on and on.

Horst tottered away from the rest of the group, into the blinding sun, dug into his pack for his Scotch and took the last swig. It wasn't water, but it sure helped take his mind off his thirst. He was almost out of this place. It would be a small plane, just a two-seater Piper Cub that could land almost anywhere. He could leave this stupid bunch and let them find their own way out. He hoped it hadn't already come, it was so late in the day.

Let them use their science to find water and a way out. Let Joseph lead them to the road. To hell with them. He would be glad to be free of them all. And if none of them made it, whatever story he told would be taken as true and he would become a hero as the only survivor of this safari. For a moment he imagined himself before an applauding crowd.

Everyone but Horst was gathered around the tree. Their thirst palpably painful. They looked at the tree in wonder. Howie remembered that Mary had told them these were the widest trees in the world, and he suggested they all try to hold hands to see if they could reach around it; maybe they had discovered the biggest baobab in the world. It seemed a crazy thing to do to the rest of them, but Howie insisted, and this seemed to cheer them up — all but Horst who walked to the Land Cruiser and leaned against it, scanning the sky.

In the endless empty plain the seven of them stood against the tree and stretched out their arm s until each touched two others' hands. They reached about halfway around the tree. Bruce, at one end, made a hatchet mark where his left hand reached. Then they moved as one, like flat figures cut out of paper, still holding hands, so that Elizabeth, at the other end, touched Bruce's hatchet mark with her right hand. They nearly made around again on the second pass.

"Okay, we each reach about five or six feet, so five times seven's thirty-five, and done twice, we've reached seventy feet," Mary said. It was hard for her to talk; her tongue felt large in her dry mouth. "It's a world record!" The others cheered and clapped. Paul took out his notebook and wrote in it. Well, she had accomplished something, she thought. She looked at Joseph who she could see was impressed that at a moment fraught with peril she and the others could still find time to do their science.

"Now, how shall we cut into it?" Elizabeth asked. In response, Michael picked up the small hatchet that they had with them. They were so focused on the tree that they didn't notice the elephant moving slowly toward them. Bruce noticed and shouted to them, and they jumped away. It was Zamani Baba — could he be following them? The elephant charged, scattering them in all directions, and started to dig with his tusks into the tree, tearing it open, then eating the bark and drinking the water. Mary watched in amazement and dismay. The more water the elephant gouged from the tree, the thirstier she felt. She squatted on the ground, feeling faint. Was the elephant simply getting water for himself, or was he intentionally helping them? She couldn't tell.

Joseph watched the big elephant with an empty feeling. Here he was, about as close as he'd ever been to that biggest of the big — in front of one of his life goals, one of his strongest desires, to be able kill this elephant and walk away with the biggest, heaviest, ivory tusks that anybody would have ever seen. But of course he couldn't do that now that he had joined this group. He looked at them one by one, thoughts racing through his mind about how each would react if he did what he had so often desired. He picked up his rifle and aimed it at Zamani Baba, imagining the elephant arching back from the bullet burying itself in its head, then reeling and toppling over.

Elizabeth was suddenly at his side. He pointed the rifle down at the soil. "Relax, Double-E, I'm not doin' nothin'. Just a little imagining. Couldn't help it. Thinkin' about them poachers comin' across this guy. Probably wouldn't even notice he was the biggest of the big, the oldest of the old. Been fascinated by him all my adult life, yuh know. Wonderful to get this close to him." He turned around and walked away.

Zamani Baba, having drunk his fill, backed away from the baobab, but did not move off.

"And if you were here by yourself, Joseph?" Bruce asked, following him.

"Yeah. Well, that's the question, ain't it?" he answered. "Tell you what I think. Now that I've been with you guys this long and gotten to like most of you, and you and most of the others treatin' me right, well," he paused. "I probably could never shoot him, now."

Bruce looked him straight in the eye.

"But you never know what you're goin' to do in some crazy situation before you're there, do you, Bruce?" He looked down at the ground, feeling a little ashamed. "Yep. You guys are the best. And I'll get you all out of here. Yes I will."

Elizabeth saw Bruce talking with Joseph and wondered if he'd ever get over his fascination with the big bull. In their fascination, and in some other ways the two men seemed alike.

"How far did we make it today?" Elizabeth asked Joseph.

"'About thirteen," Joseph replied, still watching Zamani Baba, "not a bad day, considerin'."

Finally, the elephant backed away from the tree and turned to look at each of them. He looked at Mary — she was sure he was looking at her — then moved slowly away from the baobab, trumpeted, and moved off.

Michael went over to the torn baobab and looked at it. "There's plenty of water left for us," he said. Mary joined him, and soon all of them were sucking on pieces of the wet bark and filling their small containers. Horst hobbled up.

"Anyone have any idea where my plane is?" he said after taking a long drink. He looked directly at Joseph, who was drinking deeply from his canteen, ignoring Horst.

"Nice, Joseph, nice. Totally shirking your duty. Should have known you couldn't be trusted. Where's the goddamned plane?"

Joseph stood and moved toward Horst, who made a feeble attempt at moving away. Paul reluctantly got up and stood between them.

"I know Joseph called your people, Horst. I was there. Maybe we were too late in getting here. And there's probably another hour before dusk. They could be coming."

When they had slaked their thirst and were feeling a great deal better Elizabeth asked the others if the elephant had just come to get himself a drink, or did he actually mean to help them, too? But no one answered; they were all too exhausted to respond.

Beyond the baobab, the ground angled up to a low rise. Without a word or signal, they put down their packs and collapsed on the ground, except for Elizabeth and Howie. They stood looking at the hill and the surrounding countryside, then went off to one side to talk quietly while the others rested.

"Howie, this is the best time you'll ever get to use what you know about soils to find more water," she said. "I'm going to use what I can tell from the topography to see if we can find some H-two-O not too deep below the surface."

For a moment, Howie was distracted by a secretary bird scurrying busily along. It didn't seem to fit in this dry country, and it only glanced at Howie briefly and, seeing him, rushed away. Howie puzzled about this until Elizabeth touched his arm and looked at him questioningly.

"Yep. Something's gotta be watering this baobab. Must be some sort of drainage off that rise," Howie said. "Let's go see." He handed her Davie's folding shovel, then picked up a small Y-shaped branch that had fallen from the baobab. Bruce caught up with them, carrying his rifle. He let the two Americans lead so he could keep an eye on them. Although they walked slowly in the heat, they looked remarkably good, he thought, tougher than he had expected. They seemed unaware of him, talking to each other. Howie bent down and felt the soil. Elizabeth stopped and viewed the terrain with what Bruce knew was a practiced eye. She turned around 360° slowly, then took her binoculars and looked up the rise and down it. She hunkered down and spoke softly to Howie, who was still stirring the soil. About halfway up the rise, they stood for a long time, so Bruce joined them, but he did not speak or interfere. He was trying to remember whether poachers had any hidden caches of water nearby.

Bruce was all too aware of how visible they were. And he supposed they had to be if the pilot was going to find them. Damn Horst all to hell. He couldn't wait for the sun to go down. It looked like it would be another hour or so until dark.

As they neared the top of the rise, they saw Mary and Michael approaching from another direction, Mary looking at the ground. She stopped and pointed to a different color in the soil. Elizabeth and Howie joined her. Howie's Y-shaped stick pointed down. Elizabeth pushed him away and gave him a look as if he were a child playing in her garden. She brushed the soil and started to dig. It was so hot that the shovel burned her hands, and she tired after a few shovelfuls. Bruce was instantly at her side, taking the shovel from her and digging.

Johnny, who had just caught up with them, took turns digging, stopping every so often to push his fine blond hair out of his eyes. Michael pitched in, too, and then Joseph, and they dug quickly. Not far below the surface, the soil was damp. When the shovel reached just about an arm's length below the surface water seeped in until there was about two inches of water at the bottom of the hole, just enough to get water into a cup without getting any of the soil in it too. Joseph widened the hole. They were all so thirsty they didn't wait to make it any deeper. Mary lay down on the ground and began to dip a metal cup in the water and drink several cupfuls.

Joseph carefully put his radio on the ground near the hole, borrowed the cup from Mary, and like her lay down and filled his cup several times and drank his fill. The bat-eared fox that followed him dropped into the hole and drank rapidly from it and was out in a flash, running by the radio. He sniffed at it and picked it up in his teeth and ran off toward the brush. Joseph ran after it. "Hey! Get back here!" he shouted. Then a jackal rushed out of the brush — Joseph was sure it was side-striped jackal — and attacked the fox, grabbed the radio and bit it.

"Damned animal, always stealing stuff from campsites," he said as he chased it. The jackal stopped and bit hard on the radio again and Joseph heard a crack. With Joseph almost on top of him, the jackal dropped the radio and ran off. Joseph picked up the radio and saw that there were some holes and cracks in the cover going inside and the radio no longer worked.

"Damn it all to hell. Now we're without a goddamned radio."

Bruce just looked at Joseph chasing the fox and then the jackal, a helpless feeling rising up. He needed to keep his mind on the possible. Bruce gently put a tin of water up to Elizabeth's mouth. She drank gratefully, already thirsty again in the heat. When she'd drunk her fill, Bruce took her arm and lifted her up off the ground. He walked her away from the strong sun, sat her down in the shade of the baobab and gave her a dry cracker to eat.

He had turned to go back and help dig some more when he was startled to see a Thomson's gazelle. He motioned to Michael, and the two of them approached the animal slowly. Michael brought his spear to his shoulder, but Bruce shot the animal first and brought it down. Together they butchered the gazelle, then dug a small pit and built a tiny fire where they were to make camp, making sure that no smoke could be seen from it. Using small sticks as skewers, they cooked little cubes of meat. Soon the smell of meat cooking made them ravenous. Mary punched Paul playfully when she heard his stomach rumbling.

Night had fallen before they finished eating. Horst had tried to make the meal unpleasant, but his complaints had been largely ignored as everyone was famished and intent on eating with little or no conversation.

"Not our problem," Paul had said. "You're getting the prime seat in the only vehicle."

"You're lucky there's water here," Bruce noted. "If we have to leave you, we'll set you up with food and water to last a couple of days. Unless, of course, you want to continue with us."

"Totally unacceptable," Horst grumbled.

"What — the water or the food?" Joseph laughed.

Horst ignored him and hobbled to the Land Cruiser, where he had decided he would sleep.

Paul sat on the crest of the rise looking out over the plains in the moonlight. He felt that at last he had come to understand Tsavo. He saw its plains through Elizabeth's eyes as a changing landscape, building up, eroding, subjected to many forces, even that of the elephants. And through his understanding, and through what he had experienced since they'd crossed the Manyani Gate, he felt a new kind of connection with this dry landscape. He reached down and rubbed soil between his fingers, touching the landscape the way Howie seemed to, as one person touches another — perhaps a mutual sensation. He rubbed his hand against the rough soil and rocks, once again sifting the soil between his fingers. Though his life seemed fragile, more so than it had ever seemed before, he felt alive and at peace. From Tsavo and from Mary he was arriving at some kind of peace with the plains, with this wildest country. He, Mary, and the plains. W hat did it matter if he made it back now to the road? Perhaps it no longer mattered. Perhaps he had achieved all that he would ever need or want. A time to die. Or continue an existence in this circle of relationships, this walking lifeboatful, this moving desert island. Tsavo no longer looked dry or deserted.

Mary came up the slope and sat down next to him. They talked quietly. Elizabeth joined them, then Howie. The setting sun seemed to have thrown off stars that decorated the heavens. Elizabeth looked out over the moonlit landscape. "Confusing, isn't it?" she said quietly.

"What is?" Paul asked.

"I thought I understood what went into creating this landscape — huge floating plates of the continents colliding, building the land up as they broke upon each other. Rain and wind and, yes, even elephants, tearing the land down. But I don't know. Somehow I feel connected, as if it were alive."

Paul nodded. "When I first looked out over Tsavo, I saw only dusty vistas that I didn't understand. Now I feel, as you say, sort of connected."

"You're feeling better about yourself is what you're saying, and so you think you feel better about this dust and dryness, this open emptiness. I guess it's the same with me."

"A sea of sand," Howie said, sifting it through his fingers.

Paul looked up at the brightening stars and out over the darkening earth and wondered. He looked at Mary, sitting peacefully, a dreamy look in her eyes. He looked to Howie, but Howie too was looking far into the distance.

CHAPTER 43

Horst's Airplane

Friday Morning

Alas oh death, what has ailed thee
That now you could have taken me
Instead you took my lady sweet?
Who was so fair, so fresh, so free
So good that men might all could see
Geoffrey Chaucer

The Book of the Duchess (loosely translated)

They slept long and soundly, awakened just at dawn by noise. Mary thought she heard engine sounds. She sat up with a start — perhaps they were saved! Paul put one hand gently over her mouth and put a finger to his lips, then motioned for her to stay down. He, Bruce, Johnny, and Michael crawled up a slope near their camp. Elizabeth followed, crawling as they did.

They looked out at the cleared area a distance from the baobab and saw Joseph helping Horst to the clearing's edge. Horst had his sport jacket on and Joseph was carrying a small briefcase.

The noise of the airplane was getting louder.

"That's a J-3 Piper Cub," Johnny said very quietly.

"Aha! Horst's ticket out of here," Paul said.

The plane landed and Paul and Michael hurried over to help Joseph get Horst into the plane, the engine still running. Once Horst's briefcase was handed up, the door closed and the J-3 Cub taxied down to the end of the clearing. Paul noticed that this very small two-seater was quickly in the air but then it climbed slowly, near its maximum weight with Horst and the pilot, just clearing the trees at the far end of the clearing.

"Hurray," Joseph shouted. "Goodbye you S-O-B." The bat-eared fox that had befriended Joseph scampered across the opening and stopped near Joseph. The others joined him, walking together to the far end of the clearing so they could best watch the J-3 with Horst fly into the distance.

Paul heard the sound of another airplane, as did the others, and they ran for cover, certain that it was one of the planes the poachers were flying, likely searching for them. He said quietly, to nobody in particular, "But why? We could do them no harm now."

"The bastards don't want anybody knowin' what they doing and tellin' the world about it," Joseph said. "Better get goin'. No time to waste." After this second plane had disappeared, Joseph said, "Tell you what. It's a short walk to a place I know pretty well. Should have water and a protected place to camp."

"Better get going now, then" Paul said. "Let's fill every container we can find."

"You're right, on that," said Joseph. "Still got 'bout 40 miles to go. My Cruiser's got enough to get us another 10, 15 miles. Then we'll have to store it."

They packed quickly and Michael, Bruce and Johnny led the way, each turning occasionally to scan the skies, their rifles ready. Joseph followed in the Land Cruiser, with Mary, Elizabeth and Howie riding.

After a few hours, Mary got out of the Land Cruiser and was walking near Paul. Joseph raised his hand and pointed to one of the artesian wells with trees growing near it. She felt greatly relieved. It was so good to see green. She saw again the pair of crowned hornbills, had to be the same ones she saw the other day, maybe yesterday. *Her* hornbills, she was certain.

"I have to go visit with them, Paul," she said, "They're my friends. Like family almost and they are a great charm to me." She hurried over to the tree where they had settled, taking her a small distance from the others. She reached the bottom of the tree and called out to the hornbills, then started to climb up the tree's broad branches. So intent was she on the birds that she failed to notice a leopard lying silently above her in the same tree. It descended and attacked her, throwing her off the tree onto the ground. Johnny raised his rifle and shot the leopard, wounding it. It turned toward Johnny, who shot it again. Now badly wounded, it limped away into the bush, leaving Mary behind.

Paul rushed to Mary, certain she was all right, because Johnny had shot the animal before it could do her any harm. Elizabeth and Howie immediately came to him and Mary. Seeing that she was not moving, Paul's heart stopped. He thought at first she was just temporarily stunned, or had fallen or fainted. He put his arm under her shoulders and raised her up gently. She looked peaceful, and he saw no blood, but she didn't move and wasn't conscious. Hunkering down, Elizabeth smoothed her hair back and realized that her head was at an odd angle. She looked closely. In the fall, Mary had landed on her head and had broken her neck and there was no doubt about it, she was dead. Howie believed that he saw the freckles that had always decorated her face so charmingly begin to fade. It was like the fading of a rainbow trout just landed whose bright iridescent colors quickly paled to dull gray.

Paul felt weak. He sank beside her. The crowned hornbills rose into the air, circling higher and higher, crying their mournful cry, and then disappeared.

Paul held Mary's body across his lap. Perhaps, he thought bitterly, Horst had been right. They could have made a quick decision, gone back home, told people what they thought, and Mary would be alive. But they hadn't. They'd all decided to do things the right way, to pursue their science as far as they could, poachers or not. Mary had insisted on it, too. Paul picked up her bare arm below her short-sleeved shirt and kissed it, caressing the still soft, warm skin. It still felt healthy, robust, alive, the skin of an arm that could hold and love, had loved, had loved him.

They had been surrounded by death on the plains, but this death Paul could not accept. He hugged her body while it was still soft and pliant, knowing that this was a last caress. It was too much for him. He had no tears for this; they were for a more ordinary event. His mind went dull, blank, and he barely noticed when Bruce touched his shoulder. He looked around to find that everyone had gathered around Mary's body. Michael bent down and touched her gently, then took a lovely purple stone from his pocket and put it on her chest and said something in Maasai that Paul did not understand.

Paul realized that Howie and Elizabeth were moving Mary's body away. He wanted to scream out at this final separation, but no sound came. Already her body was beyond his touch. She was at that moment lost to him forever. He saw, as through a dusty glass, Elizabeth was bending down, feeling once more Mary's pulse, opening her eyelids. Howie then took a dried herb from his pocket and laying it gently beside her, then stood up and spoke quietly to someone. Paul did not hear him. His world had gone silent. Bruce was speaking to him silently, first trying gently to get him to stand, and then, failing this, sitting down beside him. Johnny was there too, lips forming words without sound. No one spoke, or at least Paul heard no speaking. Slowly, very slowly, he seemed to come back to the world of dusty plains, the world of birds calling, an animal coughing a warning call, sunlight burning down on him. He became keenly aware of Bruce sitting next to him with a strong arm around his shoulders. There was nothing to say, and Bruce therefore said nothing, only providing a human presence to guide Paul through what Bruce knew would be a terrible transition. Behind Bruce, unseen by Paul, stood Johnny, Michael, and Howie, who was holding Elizabeth. They looked on in silence, almost in awe, as if at a wonderful painting of two men, one comforting the other.

For Bruce, the goal remained strong within him to get the group out of Tsavo, to Nairobi and back to the States, where they would send off their report. This goal had been Paul's too until a few moments ago. Bruce had to bring Paul's mind back into focus quickly, because danger lay all around them. The poachers could not be far off, and agitated elephant survivors were nearby. Bruce was concerned that Paul might not be able to function for a while, perhaps for days, at a time when everyone had to be entirely alert. He knew that it was now up to him, Johnny, Michael, and Elizabeth to work together to get their report to the States. Bruce spoke softly to Paul, telling him what they would have to do to find a way back. Then Bruce got up and went with Michael to patrol the perimeter of their camp, watching out for the poachers. Johnny and Howie stayed with the rest, guns ready. Elizabeth, trained in emergency medical aid, suppressed her feelings and focused on the tasks at hand, the first of which was what to do with Mary's body. They could not carry it out before serious decay set in. So they had to bury it. But where and how?

They decided that Mary's body should be buried where it could be readily located, in something close to a casket, so that eventually it could be flown back to the States. Elizabeth scanned the landscape. "Please, let us find a pretty place, with some green," she said. They picked out a slope of sandy and gravelly soil with a sweeping view of sky and plains. Howie poked the soil with a long metal rod and found it soft as far as the rod would reach. They fashioned a sort of coffin from several backpacks, good enough, they hoped, to protect Mary's body until it could be returned to America. Elizabeth went to Mary's body and quietly removed the necklace with the pendant, and the diamond on a gold chain that Davie had given Mary, and put them carefully in her own pocket.

CHAPTER 44

A Makeshift Grave

Friday Afternoon

We make woe wanton with this fond delay; once more adieu,
the rest let sorry say.

Shakespeare, *Richard II*

I have wrestled with death. It is the most unexciting contest
you can imagine. It takes place in an impalpable greyness,
with nothing underfoot, with nothing around, without
spectators, without clamour, without glory, without the great
desire of victory, without the great fear of defeat, in a sickly
atmosphere of tepid scepticism, without much belief in your
own right, and still less in that of your adversary. If such
is the form of ultimate wisdom, then life is a greater riddle
than some of us think it to be.

Joseph Conrad, *Heart of Darkness*

Elizabeth and Howie stayed with Paul. Elizabeth held his hand and no one talked. Bruce came over and spoke with them quietly, saying that he and Johnny were going to walk around the perimeter of the camping place they had found to make sure no poachers or dangerous animals were near, and that Joseph and Michael would stay nearby, leaving them in quiet. Elizabeth suggested to Howie that he might want to take a break and go for a short walk; she and he could take turns being with Paul.

As Howie turned and walked away, he saw a figure in the distance coming toward them, a man on horseback, riding alone. Howie studied him through field glasses and saw that he had a rifle mounted on one side of his saddle and what looked like a long sword on the other. He was white and dressed in leather. Howie watched him approach. He guessed it must be the old man on horseback Elizabeth had seen and told them all about. A dry wind came up, stirring the soil between the old man and Howie. When the man and his horse came within a hundred yards, Howie went down to meet him. Up close, he could see that the man was dressed in what looked to be an old British military uniform, including an officer's hat, not only an incongruous outfit but hot for the climate.

"Good afternoon to you," said the man. Taking off a riding glove, he extended his hand. Howie shook hands, looking the strange figure over. "Out for a long ride to see Tsavo once again," the man explained. "I've lived here off and on since the thirties. Watched the place change. Still make the trip occasionally. And what might bring you here?" he asked Howie, looking at him from what seemed to Howie a long distance. Howie felt for the first time improperly dressed, too casual for the visitor.

"Howie's the name. We came here to do a scientific study of Tsavo's elephants."

"I just saw one of your group, I believe," the man said. "Tall, thin young man with a bit of an accent."

"That could have been Davie. So he made it out?"

"Well, he was quite thirsty and looked almost dead, but he made it to the gate. Said he was part of some scientific group and asked me to check on you chaps."

Howie nodded sadly. "That would be us."

"Can't abide you science chaps myself," the man said. "I watch the game, I hunt the game, have trophies. I love the bush and the animals. Don't see the sense in studying them, just let them be and shoot a few now and again."

"We've had a serious mishap," Howie said. "One of our party has been killed."

"Some beginner with a gun misfire, was it?"

"No, an accident, a leopard — a leopard and an accident, I guess. Just killed one of our group."

"I hope it isn't a girl named Mary. Your friend made a point of telling me to look out for her."

"It *was* Davie then," Howie sighed, "and the woman we're burying is the very one he was worried about."

"That's a shame, I'm sad to hear it." The man abruptly reined his horse to the side and headed off into the horizon.

"Well, see ya …." Howie said but he doubted the old man heard him. He disappeared into the barren plain and Howie watched the dust settle in his wake.

Going back to the others, he found Elizabeth had secured Mary's body in the makeshift coffin of backpacks and tent material. Johnny and Bruce carefully lifted the body and moved it to the grave that had been dug. Howie and Elizabeth propped Paul up as they walked. Michael stood guard, turning constantly to scan the skies and brittle landscape.

Bruce led the group over to the grave, and they gathered around as Howie began to sing.

> A'rovin' on a winter's night
> And a'drinkin' good old wine,
> A'thinkin' about that pretty little girl
> Who stole that heart of mine.
> I'll love you till the seas run dry
> Or till the rocks melt in the sun.
> I'll love you till the day I die,
> Though you will never be my own."

The words fell onto the sand, without echo, and there was silence. Tsavo had accepted the song and the singing. They placed Mary's body in the grave and Johnny took the small shovel and gently scattered some soil over it. Each of the others did the same, except Paul, who stood numbly.

Then Joseph turned toward the sun and said "I gave my heart to know wisdom, and madness and folly: For in wisdom is much grief," he stopped, trying to remember the words. "Increasing knowledge, increasing sorrow." He paused. "Sorrow's better than laughter, 'cause it makes the heart better."

He paused, and turned away from the sun and toward the others. "Just a little of the Bible that I remembered. Now, in your own way, let each of us pray for Mary."

"There will be a proper service when we get her back," Elizabeth said faintly.

The group seemed struck dumb; they stared down at the makeshift coffin.

Elizabeth walked away by herself and sat down on the ground and cried. Time passed unmeasured.

After a while, Bruce brought the group together and spoke softly. Clearly, they needed some time to rest. They decided they needed to stay in the cover of brush and trees of their camp for the rest of this day and probably the next if they were going to walk at night.

Johnny went for a walk around the periphery of where they were camping, checking once again for any sign of poachers and dangerous wildlife. On the way, he saw an impala and shot it. He bled and gutted the animal, and kept the best edible parts for them.

When he brought the meat back to the group, Joseph stood up suddenly, saying, "Got an idea." He walked over to his Land Cruiser and came back with an unopened bottle of gin and some paper cups, and proceeded, in silence, to put out a cupful for each of the others.

They discussed the strange man on horseback.

"He said he likes to shoot game for trophies," Howie put in, "and he said he saw Davie at the gate. He made it! I forgot to tell you with all that's been going on."

"Well, bless his heart. He *is* a survivor," said Elizabeth.

"Hallelujah!" saluted Johnny, toasting with his cup and downing his the gin. "The first to get back. Gotta hand it to him. That guy has grit."

"The old man said Davie was half dead but still told him to look out for Mary," Howie said, a catch in his voice.

No one could talk for a while.

"The locals will tell you he's minister of death," Joseph said, sipping the gin.

"Old wives tales," Johnny responded. "People love those kind of stories."

"He's a jerk, if you ask me," Bruce said, suddenly sitting up. "Riding around Tsavo on that damned horse. He is known for killing alright – for sport. Heard he has all sorts of heads mounted in his excuse for a house. Nothing more than a rundown shack, stuffed with animal heads."

"There was something about him," Howie ventured. "He was there and sort of not there at the same time."

"He gives me the creeps," Elizabeth said.

As night approached Johnny built a small fire. They ate impala and drank more gin.

Howie suggested they sing in honor of Mary.

"Sing what?" Elizabeth asks. The entire situation was getting beyond her. Nothing was making sense.

"Sing that song again you sang when that old man was here," Bruce said. And Howie did, and sang a few more. Johnny was able to pick up the tunes and added some harmony.

"I'll teach you an old folk song or two," Howie said, and he began to sing.

> *There is a bird in yonder tree,*
> *Some say he's blind and cannot see,*
> *And I wish it had been the same with me,*
> *When first I met your company.*
>
> *I wish, I wish, but it's all in vain*
> *I wish I was a sweet maid again*
> *But a maid again I never shall be*
> *Till apples grow on an orange tree*

Go dig my grave long, wide and deep.
Put a marble stone at my head and feet
Above it all put a turtle white dove
To show for the world I died for love.

Somehow this sad song helped them all, putting to a lovely melody the deep sadness they all were feeling.

"One more, Heck," Elizabeth asked, "One more."

Feel like a broke down engine,
Ain't got no drivin' wheel
Feel like a broke down engine, Momma
Ain't got no drivin' wheel
You been down and lonesome
And know how a poor man feel

Lordy Lord, Lordy Lordy Lord
Lordy Lord, Lordy Lordy Lord

Went down to my praying ground
and fell on bended knees
I went down to my praying ground
and fell on bended knees
I ain't camped no religion
But give back my good gal please

And again, although none of them could explain it, Howie's strange lyrics helped each of them through their grief.

Each lay down as best they could. A half moon rose, somehow seeming suitable to their time and sadness. They slept fitfully and on waking decided to take the day to rest, and gather themselves so they would feel stronger when they left.

They rested a good while, then slowly gathered in a group. "What the hell did we come here for anyway?" Elizabeth asked. "Supposed to do science and help the damned world about elephants. And what did we really get done? Got one of my very best friends ever killed. Did the same for that kindly old Cecile. Some big favor we did him."

"Mary so loved being out here, you know. And loved doing all those measurements. Kept the neatest notebooks ever," Howie said. "Made friends with that pair of birds, the hornbills. Like family, they were, she said."

"Yeah, and they're the ones got her killed," Elizabeth said. "I say again, so what the hell did we get out of it?"

"Maybe the world she came to know she wouldn't trade if she could be talkin' to you right now," Howie replied. "Hell, Cecile too. 'Member how he just loved each animal? You don't get it Double-E. Maybe if you were Cecile, well dyin' the way he did might be the most meaningful thing to him."

"Don't believe it."

"'Course you don't. That isn't you. And never will be."

Elizabeth looked hurt and tears welled up in her eyes.

"But Liz, you said yourself Tsavo changed the way you thought about your own life's work. About how geology changed the world," Bruce said, "And you completely changed the way I thought about this place." He paused, "'Remember when we flew over it, and the time we sat up on that strange hill."

"Isenberg," Elizabeth said.

"Whatever. You changed my way of looking at Tsavo from two-dimensions to three! And I've been out here most of my life trying to figure this place out."

"But at what a cost."

"I'm not saying that I can add up Mary's death against what I learned from you and the others, like it was some kind of, I don't know, money thing. I'm just saying that some very wonderful things happened on this trip as well."

"He means getting together with you, period." Howie put in.

Elizabeth smiled. "Oh that," she said, and took Bruce's hand and looked him warmly in the eye.

"Mary was something else," Joseph said, sipping his gin. "'Member how she got us to that baobab and knew we could get water out of it when we really needed it? You know, she probably saved our lives."

Elizabeth looked at Joseph and smiled.

"And what a looker, too," Joseph said, turning to Howie and blushing.

"I agree, you got it wrong. Thinking about it wrong," said Johnny. "Being out here isn't some kind of damned academic thing, Double-E. Hell, I learn things all the time. But I have a hell of a good time too."

"Damned risk-taker," Michael said, surprising the others with his first swearing.

"Damned fun-lover, you mean. Hell, if you don't take chances, what this crazy life worth?" Johnny answered. "Can't you people have a little fun? Jesus, Double-E, you ought to take up flying. Get up there and soar with the vultures. See if you can outdo them."

"One of your buddies got killed doin' that," Joseph put in.

"Yes. But I don't think he would regret it if he could look back. Traded soaring with the birds for some dull job in an office in Voi, he did."

"You'd do the same?"

"You're asking Mr. Risk-taker number one of them all," Michael said.

"Don't even need to ask," Bruce put in.

"Well, you're right up there with him, I'd say," Howie put in.

"Me?"

"Come on Bruce. You and having to touch that damned elephant. Don't call that risk taking?"

"Not understanding me."

"Oh no, Bruce, Just the other way round. I get here right down to the heart," Howie pounded his chest with his fist. "It's the damned wildness you wanted. Wanted to touch it, touch that elephant. Nah, not want. Can't live without. Brought you back from Bermuda, didn't it?"

Bruce said nothing.

Howie shook his head. "You see, friends. That's your Bruce. Shuts up any time you get close to telling him what it is, what he is."

"Then, what's all this with you, Howie, with your beans in your funnel, watching them spill out onto the ground?"

"Got to play with the meaning of life, Brucey," Howie said. "Fool around with stuff, whatever. I ain't so literal as you. I don't have'ta love that big jumbo, but you do," Howie continued. "Little safer too." Howie looked at Paul, who had been silent. "Mr. silent scientist, all by himself," Howie said, walking over and patting Paul warming on the shoulder. "Got the love of his life outa this trip. Got to know Tsavo like few people ever do. And kept telling me this was just gonna be a fun trip."

Bruce looked at Howie. "Yo-yo's the answer to the world, to life, to everything. That what you're saying?"

"Not saying it isn't," Howie replied.

"There you go again."

"Ain't goin' nowhere," Howie said under his breath, smiling.

Howie sat on the ground next to Paul. Elizabeth came over as well and took Paul's hand.

"It's alright, Paul, for you to be silent. Hell, cry a little why not?" she gave him a hug. She and Howie sat close to Paul. Elizabeth rubbed his back.

"She's not so bad, you know," Joseph said quietly to Bruce. "You got the right girl all right." Joseph looked into the distance. The bat-eared fox came out of the brush and sat down next to Joseph. "Only friend I got," Joseph said very quietly to no one.

"You've saved us, you know, Joseph," said Bruce. "Hell, I never would of thought you were worth a thing." Joseph looked surprised, then nodded.

They still had about half of the containers they'd filled at the baobab tree, Joseph thought. They had made good time that day before Mary died — close to ten miles. Two nights' walking would get them out if they could make 15 miles a night, and there should be water on the way. The moon was waxing, so they would have more light at night.

They'd used backpacks to bury Mary so they had to assure their data was secure in something else. Bruce did a survey of the team's journals, gathering them together. Joseph found an old duffle bag in his Land Cruiser and Bruce carefully placed all the journals inside and wrapped it tight and bound it with a rope. He fastened another rope around it so it could function as a sort of backpack. Now that they would be walking the last distance out, they'd need to figure out a way to carry what food and water they had. Michael stretched out tents and began to rip the material. Soon he had fashioned bags that could be carried by each member of the team. Johnny took tenting rope and made loops so all could carry water bottles around their waists.

Joseph found a place to park his Land Cruiser, closed it up tight, and started piling branches around it to assure it could not be spotted by air or land. Soon Johnny was helping him, and then Elizabeth and Bruce.

Howie stayed close to Paul. Elizabeth tried to help as well, but the irrationality of everything that was happening was getting her down. Bruce realized this and kept close to her.

That afternoon, they gathered and ate the last of the impala. They were all hungry, but no one mentioned it. They knew that was the least of their problems. Two more nights and they'd be out.

At dusk, they got themselves ready to leave and began their walk through the night.

CHAPTER 45

Howie and the Arrows

Saturday Night

Science itself is now the only field through which the dimension of mythology can be again revealed.

Joseph Campbell, *The Masks of God: Primitive Mythology*

The moon had not risen and the group was finding its way in darkness. Paul had lost track of day and night and had little idea where he was or where he was going. Elizabeth and Howie stayed with him, guiding him as if he were blind.

Bruce had told them the rest of their trek would be through some of the driest of the park's countryside. They would need to drink a little regularly but should try to ration their water. They stayed close to each other as they walked. After a few hours the moon cast a faint glow on the land and Joseph kept his compass handy to keep them on track. Both he and Bruce knew of a watertank Sheldrick had built and Joseph estimated it would be close to ten miles from their camp.

Bruce called Johnny, Joseph, and Michael to his side as they walked, and they discussed their situation. They had confidence in themselves and in Elizabeth, but all had doubts about Paul.

"And Howie?" Johnny asked.

"Howie won't fail. He and this land are one," Michael said.

"Anyway, I suppose he's just too weird to die like a normal person," Johnny said. "He'll probably dance and sing his way to the road."

Bruce was not sure about Howie.

"Leave him to me and Elizabeth," Johnny said. "We'll get him there. He's got spirit. He's tougher than he seems."

As the night wore on, people began stumbling over impediments in their path they didn't see or hadn't expected. Bruce called frequent stops to gather the group and encourage them. Joseph took out a flashlight he had saved from his Land Cruiser and turned it on so that Elizabeth and Howie could see their way better, knowing that the others, used to Tsavo, would do better than the Americans in the darkness. Once in a while Joseph would shine the flashlight ahead.

"Joseph, I just saw a pair of eyes, reflected in the flashlight's beam," she whispered. "What the heck is that?"

In the darkness, Joseph smiled to himself. "It's okay, Double-E. That's just a bush baby. If it was daylight, you would see he's one of the cutest little creatures you'll ever see out here or anywhere, matter of fact."

A little later, Elizabeth heard a lion roaring. It seemed to be very near. It roared again, seeming to be even closer. Bruce came to her side. "I hope it's not one of the famous man-eater lions of Tsavo," she said, shivering.

"Long gone, Liz," Bruce said. "Don't worry. Right around you are some of the best hunters in all of east Africa. Nobody's better than Michael. And Joseph's damned good, too.

Hearing Elizabeth, Michael dropped back and walked on her other side. "To become a Maasai man, I had to kill one of those lions without a gun," he said to her. "Remember that. We'll get you through. Just take care of Paul."

She was relieved for a while, but then she began to hear strange snorting kinds of sounds, coming from different directions. "Warning calls from different animals," Michael whispered to her.

"Goddamned lions probably coming right for us," she whispered back. Something flew past her right over her head, she couldn't tell what in the darkness.

"Bloody bat," Joseph said.

"Jesus, Howie, doesn't any of this scare you? You aren't saying anything."

"Too scared to talk, I guess," he said. "What the hell. Throw of the dice is what's gonna happen." He reached around and patted her on her shoulder. Paul, silent, kept moving.

Joseph turned his flashlight entirely around, but saw nothing dangerous, maybe a hyrax in a tree they passed, a few gazelles off to his right. The bat-eared fox he had fed was suddenly at his heels, as if he felt safer among this group of strange creatures. Bruce held up his hand, just barely visible in the pale moonlight, motioning everybody to stop. In the silence, Michael and Joseph searched the area around them, Bruce keeping guard over Elizabeth, Howie, and Paul. Elizabeth was exhausted. She wanted to lie on the ground with Paul on one side and Howie on the other for comfort.

Bruce let the group rest for a while, then motioned them to move on. He seemed far from her, intent on leading, telling people what to do, urging them on, when all they wanted to do was lie down and sleep. Suddenly, some small animals ran past her, an entire group.

"Just mongoose," Joseph said. "Won't bother you."

Just when she felt the night would never end, she realized that the eastern sky was lightening and a tiny light on the horizon seemed to get bigger with each step. She saw Bruce looking through his binoculars, seeking landmarks. The old concrete tank that Sheldrick, Tsavo's first head ranger, had built when he was first working at the park shimmered in the distance.

"There it is," he announced, relieved more than he cared to admit. They were all nearly out of water. They reached the water tank as the sun cleared the horizon. They drank, then filled every container they could, washed themselves, and rested. Through the binoculars they could just make out the Lugard Hills. Joseph knew there was a nearly year-round spring there. If they could only get that far, but Bruce knew the sun would bring heat within an hour.

He made the call. Better to stay in the cover nearby bushes provided, with water available, and rest. If they had a good night, they'd be close. They'd have only a few miles to go in the daylight to Voi — hopefully close enough that the poachers wouldn't take a chance at another attack.

They rested during the day, sleeping fitfully at best, then set out again at nightfall, Elizabeth and Johnny leading Paul as if guiding a blind man. Howie, nearby, came over to Paul often to check on him and touch him and speak to him softly, saying things the others could not hear. Paul shook his head or nodded in answer but did not speak.

After an uncounted number of hours, they found themselves following a narrow game trail among dense shrubs. The moon was bigger than the night before. Elizabeth had forgotten how dramatically the moon changed in its waxing and waning. They actually could see a little better than the night before. They could see vague shadows of the dry, dusty shrubs that crackled whenever they brushed against them.

At dawn they came to a rise and struggled over it, their thirst palpable. Below the rise was a clump of rushes and sedges, bright green, almost blindingly green after so many hours of moon-lit gray-green shrubland. Several boulders surrounded reeds and sedges and were stained with moisture and mud. Behind the boulders was a gnarled, half-dead tree, its bark worn away by elephants rubbing against it. Elephant tracks trampled the vegetation surrounding a small spring. At first, Elizabeth wondered if it was a mirage. But she saw the others hurry to the pretty trickle of water. They knelt down and slapped the clear water against their faces and, cleaning their sandy hands as best they could, scooped up water into their mouths. Beyond them was a marshy area, fed by the spring. None mentioned the hunger that gnawed at them. They had not eaten in more than a day.

Joseph said they'd probably done another eight miles or so and had about six to go. They filled their water bottles. It was clear they needed to keep going. They'd make it to Voi by noon if they could keep their pace.

They walked on in silence on a game trail through the marshland. The sun was high when Bruce heard a quiet sound like a wind and saw an arrow fly through the shrubs. More arrows followed. He realized suddenly where they were. They were retracing their own path of weeks before.

"Quick — down!" he said. "We're back where we were attacked by the Waliangulu — poison arrows." Bruce took out his gun and fired, but he didn't think he hit anything.

Joseph, crouched down next to him, fired his gun. "Dealt with them a lot. Pretty dangerous. Lost some buddies to them."

Howie turned to look, and an arrow struck him in the shoulder. The others, rushing for cover, didn't notice him sinking to the ground. Four small men, one carrying a small bow, crept out of the shrubs, picked him up, and carried him off, leaving his baseball cap and his pack, and a small pool of blood.

Bruce waited and listened for a long time, then crept back to where he had last seen Howie. Johnny and Michael joined him. Michael found Howie's hat, Johnny his pack. Bruce saw a little blood on it and pointed it out to Michael. Elizabeth emerged from hiding, leading Paul, and Bruce called them over.

"Where's Howie?" Elizabeth asked.

"They must have hit him with an arrow and then taken him," Bruce told her.

Horrified, her hand flew to her mouth. "Is he dead?"

"I don't know. Like I told you when we first came through here on the way in — these Waliangulu have stunning arrows and killing arrows. He may be immobilized like a fly in a spider web, or he may be dead, or maybe they're keeping him so he can tell them stories, over and over."

"If he's alive, we have to save him," she insisted, vehemently.

"We can't. We can die trying or go on. Those Waliangulu are dangerous. And we're vulnerable. No food left and not a lot of water." But Elizabeth wouldn't hear of leaving without Howie. And she didn't care if they were visible to poachers. This was something they had to do. In the end, Bruce agreed and Michael said he'd stay back with Paul while Johnny, Bruce, Joseph and Elizabeth went searching as best they could. They came back near sundown without finding anything. They had gone through most of their water supply.

"We'll rest here for a few hours," Bruce said.

They moved back from where Howie was taken, not wanting to think about what might happen to him. Paul sat down. Elizabeth sat by him and held him, looking up at Bruce, who stood with Michael and Johnny, their heads bowed. Joseph was looking into the distance, a tear running down his cheek.

"We've only got about three miles, I figure," he said. "Just three goddam miles."

After a silence, Bruce spoke softly. "Look, we don't know if he's dead, but we can hope he's not. Let's say a prayer for him. He's one of the oddest people I've met, but one of the best."

"Heck did nothing but good in his own way," Elizabeth said. "He never hurt a soul. If the world were all Howies, it would be a peaceful place."

"Crazy, but peaceful," Johnny said.

"Nice kind a crazy," added Joseph.

"May his gods, whatever and whoever they are, grant him what he wishes," said Bruce.

Michael was looking to the distance. "He's not dead. That is what I believe," he said.

"Why'd they take him?" Elizabeth asked.

"They felt his magic. Powerful. What you would call a medicine man, I believe," Michael said.

"You mean they'll treat him like some kind of god?"

Michael looked down at her sympathetically, but said nothing.

"Maybe. In this world, it's possible," Bruce said.

Paul stood up. "Maybe my best friend, certainly my oldest, and definitely my strangest. He understood more than he could say. I hope he lives." It was the first coherent thing Paul had said in several days. As one, they sat upon the ground and mourned their losses. One by one they curled up in their blankets on the hard ground. They slept until after midnight when Joseph woke them. The moon was high and lit the ground in a ghostly way. They took sips from their water bottles and walked on.

CHAPTER 46

The Road to Voi

Monday

The elephant herd moved quietly in the early morning. They ambled slowly, more or less as one group but with much individuality doing its own thing, a timeless, lumbering, native choreography.

Some were pulling at dry leaves from bushes with their trunks; others digging wilted grasses from the hard soil. The great matriarch held her trunk to the sky, catching a scent of dampness. She turned to walk toward it. Others silently followed, a meandering line of her descendants.

The sun slowly emerged as a red ball on the eastern horizon. Soon the herd reached a small spring. The matriarch pulled water up and sprayed it over a young elephant near her as she watched two young bulls on the outskirts of the herd rise up against each other, tusks intertwined in a playful confrontation.

Weaverbirds rose from a nearby bush. A crowned hornbill emerged from its nest in a hollow of a tree. A rock hyrax scurried to the spring, looking up to make sure the way was clear of the matriarch and others. Time passed.

The tip of the matriarch's trunk suddenly pointed to the sky and then to her right. Her ears had picked up a scent — very feint — but similar to what she had sensed in the past. She moved from the spring and looked over a rise to see a line of humans walking haltingly across the plain, some falling and being picked up, some with those strange sticks that could kill, pointed into the air. One was making hollow small sounds to the others, maybe sounds of alarm and fear, and the old matriarch did not want to be near it. She saw others in the herd had stopped what they were doing and were also watching these creatures on two legs. She turned slowly, lifted her head and trunk, trumpeted, and led the herd away.

* * *

In the light from a rising sun, Paul saw it first, a glittering, glancing glow, as light cascaded down the sands, the road. It was not long after they had passed an elephant herd, when he, like the others, had been too tired, thirsty, and hungry to even mention it to the others. Now dust devils divided his view. Ahead, beyond, ridged by the road, was the green earth outside Tsavo, the reality of what seemed now-long-ago. Parched, his perceptions pallid, he imagined a boundary, a hollow wall he was within, an outside that was beyond. He staggered, stared, and stopped. Had he reached the road? Had he survived?

Elizabeth took his hand. "Sit down before you fall down, for God's sake," she said. She took out her canteen and held it to his lips. He heard Elizabeth and Bruce speaking above him. Then ahead Bruce battled beyond the park's barrier, the railroad tracks, and the road. Would he wander with them as well?

"Shall we carry him?" Joseph asked.

"No, no. He'll be all right. Let him sit. Bruce has gone to flag down any passing vehicle. Put his hat back on. Fan his f ace. Give him a hug. He'll come to."

They sat on the ground, one on each side of Paul, propping him up to something of a sitting position.

"Did you see those elephants?" Joseph asked

"Yeah, pretty cool," was all Elizabeth could manage. Paul seemed to come around some and managed to hold himself up. Elizabeth fanned his face with her hat.

"Funny to see them so close to the road."

"I saw one of those cute little mammals you talked about.

"Ah … the rock hyrax."

"Yeah … it seemed to be communing with the elephants … "

Paul thought he saw Howie spinning his toy, but he looked again and it was Michael marching over the tracks.

"Is there water nearby?" It was Elizabeth.

"Don't know."

"Better be."

"Michael'll find it. Best to get him up now. We'll carry him over if we have to."

Arms lifted him from behind. "Come on, buddy, you're there," a voice said. The track and trail, rail and road, approached. Might he make it? Over and out. No, those were the wrong words. Over and up? Out and beyond? Stretching, he touched the rail, hot, glittering, slippery, silvery. He slid slowly. Sadly.

"Geez, Paul, we're here. Walk." He walked, wandering. A bird hovered overhead, a vulture, or was it one of the elegant eagles gliding easily, slowly sideways?

He was down, face first onto the asphalt.

"There," Bruce's voice huffed, lifting him.

Paul came to himself. Elizabeth was looking at him queerly.

"I'm all right," he said. "I'm all right."

"No, you're not, but you're safe."

Bruce patted him on the shoulder. "Have a sit, Paul. We're flagging down a vehicle. Be in Voi soon."

"Good. We'll have a beer," Paul said, bending and rubbing his leg.

But the road was empty for a long time. A small plane was approaching them. Elizabeth and Paul fell to the ground, crawling toward any cover they could find. Bruce and Johnny fell and aimed their rifles toward the aircraft. Joseph kneeled down as well and Michael looked to the sky.

"It's okay," Joseph said, standing. "That's a tourist plane. I know it. Not to worry."

The rest stood and walked on.

Paul was parched. He began again to lose track of where he was. He thought he saw elephants. Something brushed by his face and he waved it away. He was sure it was a bird, a hornbill. He heard African doves calling. And then . . . the sound of a motor. A battered bus came down the highway from Nairobi, and stopped. Before boarding it, Paul turned and looked into Tsavo. The last rays of the sun lit up the land beyond the highway and railroad as if it were another world in another time. In his past he had thought he had fit into that landscape, but now he had no thoughts. Elizabeth paused and looked over the plains, wondering again who really fit in there. Then she looked at Bruce and smiled.

Bruce checked around him, patted Johnny on the shoulder, and they pushed Paul onto the bus. Michael and Joseph followed, carrying the group's rifles and Michael's spear. Other passengers gave them plenty of room, noting the weapons and makeshift water bottles attached to their belts. Dust rose from them as they found seats.

The smell of sweat and stuffy air, of diesel fuel, chickens and overripe fruits, swept over Elizabeth. She helped Paul into a seat and sat down next to him, holding his hand. Johnny and Bruce sat together. Michael, barely fitting, sat across from them, knees drawn up, still holding his long spear and rifle. Johnny gave a smile and a wink to a pretty girl sitting just ahead of him. Joseph watched, amused, thinking how lucky they all were. He pushed thoughts of Howie from his mind. The gears ground and whined, the engine pushed brown smoke in through the window, and the road began to flow past them. Looking out, he saw the bat eared fox running next to the bus.

CHAPTER 47

On the Veranda

Sunday, October 28, evening

We shall not cease from exploration,
And the end of all our exploring
Will be to arrive where we started
And know the place for the first time

T. S. Eliot

lizabeth, Bruce, Paul, and Johnny sat quietly on the veranda at the Norfolk Hotel in Nairobi. They had showered and put on clean clothes, and now they were meeting for dinner. It was not yet twilight; people chatted in small groups. Elizabeth heard the sound of someone raking one of the sandy walks that led from the veranda to the guest cottages — rhythmic, calming, civilized, almost a yoga mantra.

A waiter walked through the crowd ringing a bell and carrying a small blackboard on a wooden pole with a message for a guest written in chalk. It was a message for Johnny, who rose and hurried out past the rows of wooden tables. In spite of the crowds of people and the droning hubbub of their conversations, the veranda had an orderliness. a kind of symmetry that Elizabeth would not have noticed before; in fact, compared to a resort hotel on Lake Michigan near her Chicago home, this veranda would have seemed chaotic to her a few months ago.

It was the same comfortable veranda they had sat on that evening — how long ago? — the night before their trip to Mombasa on the Indian Ocean coast and then to Tsavo. That evening Howie had joked, Mary had talked dreamily, and the four American scientists had huddled together, planning the trip and discussing the new things and new experiences they might face, with great excitement about the wildlife they would soon see.

The memory of Mary's enthusiasm for the adventure brought tears to Elizabeth's eyes. Bruce silently took her hand, caressing it. She turned to him and asked whether there was some small chance that Howie at least was still alive, held captive by the Waliangulu. Bruce smiled sympathetically. "With Howie there's always a chance. He could be captivating them now with a yo-yo made from elephant ivory. Having a dickens of a time, what with the waugh and woof of the context, as Howie himself might have put it."

"In the end, it looks like Howie was right," Elizabeth said. "Might as well search for elephants with a book of random numbers, and try to understand Tsavo that way too."

Paul disagreed, saying that wasn't what Howie believed and wouldn't have concluded. "How you search for the truth, and what the truth is are two different things," he said.

Michael had gone back to his village and hadn't been heard from for two weeks. Elizabeth missed him; she wanted to talk more with him about the differences between Tsavo and America and between Maasai and Western cultures.

Bruce put his arm gently around her shoulders and gave her a hug. She hugged back. She wasn't sure she had found the truth about Tsavo, but she had found Bruce. And now, to her own surprise more than anyone else's, they were going to marry and begin the life together in a pleasing house just outside of Nairobi. It was the last thing she would have guessed would happen to her when she accepted Paul's invitation to come along with a bunch of ecologists as a geological adviser — just a pleasant diversion, she had thought, from her ordinary life.

Johnny returned to their table with a newspaper. "Here's something to amuse you," he said, handing the paper to Elizabeth. There was a small headline over a short article.

AMERICAN SCIENTIST SAVES OUR ELEPHANTS

It was an article about Horst. He had just won another prize for his work, this time . . . for his work in Africa.

The article read: "World-renowned scientist Dr. Horst Grobbin says Tsavo's elephants will be saved if the rest of the world cares enough. On a recent fact-finding trip, Dr. Grobben concluded that Tsavo's elephant herd, although down, was not out, and was undergoing a revival. Data collected by Dr. Horst's team, just returned from the field, proved this." There was a photograph of Horst holding up a report. Elizabeth read the rest of the article, looked at Paul, who seemed distracted and did not respond, and passed the newspaper without a word to Bruce. Bruce read it and passed it back to Johnny. "I always said you can never beat his type. Butter side up, that's him."

"I've got another one for you," Johnny," Elizabeth said. "You'll never believe it. I went to the university library here and looked up Baker Kingsley in *Marquis's Who's Who*. I copied the entry. Here it is." She read from a piece of paper.

"'Kingsley, Baker. Botanist. Member, National Academy of Sciences — '"

"What!"

"Ummm . . . several plant species named after him. Let's see . . . 'Perhaps best known for discovering a chemical in a tropical rain-forest plant that serves as a growth hormone and has been used in cases of dwarfism.' Here's an interesting bit. Member of the Marine Corps, 1968 to 1972. Heavily decorated for action in Vietnam. Purple heart, et cetera."

The rest were incredulous. "That can't be the same Baker Kingsley," Paul said. "The Baker Kingsley we met is a really weird guy gallivanting all over Tsavo in a jam-packed VW bug all by himself. Weird like Howie. But different weird. He *is* a botanist, though."

"Vietnam, huh?" said Bruce. "That would explain the sharp shooting."

"Also, some people think he suffered from battle fatigue. Here's a quote in an article about him. Let's see. . . oh, yes, right here. 'After the war, I realized what life was really worth — how precious it was. I decided to give up the game of science and make a science of games.'"

"That'll give Horst a run for his money," Bruce said.

"And here's another one that'll blow your socks off, " Elizabeth said. "Word at the museum is that a crazy American expert on African vultures was heading to California at the request of the Audubon Society to help save the condor."

"Davie?"

"None other."

"But why didn't Davie try to contact us, to tell us he made it out?" Elizabeth asked, and then answered her own question. "He'll never get over Mary, will he?" she said. "He couldn't have brought himself to contact us even if he had wanted to."

She was quiet for a while.

"Penny for your thoughts," Bruce said.

"I was just thinking. You know, in the end, Davie was right. When he took us to see that big bull elephant on our first day in Tsavo, he said we'd thank him for it, that it was something we'd tell our grandchildren about. As crazy as it seemed at the time, he was probably right."

"Well, I'm glad he made it out and I wish him the best," Paul said.

"And finds a girl who can stand him and his smells, and civilizes him some," Elizabeth added. "But not too much — not so it takes the music out of him, just so he cleans up good." The rest laughed.

Elizabeth wondered aloud about Zamani Baba — where he might be, and whether the poachers had killed him.

"Nah. We'll know from the grapevine when he's killed. The poacher who gets those tusks won't be able to keep from bragging about it," Johnny said. "He isn't dead yet."

She asked Bruce whether he had gotten over whatever it was he had sought in Tsavo — she was still not entirely clear what that was, rational knowledge or spiritual awakening or something else.

Bruce was silent for what seemed to be a long time, looking out beyond the veranda. "No, I don't think so," he said finally. "It will take centuries more of science before anyone could."

"Could what?"

"Understand that big bull and Tsavo in a way that would make sense for both our Western rationality and our human spirits. That's what I did learn."

"And until then?"

"We'll just be wanderers, forever searching, forever missing the mark, more like busybody secretary birds scurrying about than ancient elephants grazing peacefully, at ease in their world. Wayfarers marching across a desert landscape, just the way we were on our way out of Tsavo, desperately seeking safety. The result? We run away and trample over exactly that which we seek, and we have just two choices. Truth and death, or safety and survival."

"I see it differently," Johnny said. "You see the path as dark, but I see us soaring in my airplane, high above all your problems, happy in the never-ending search, like you and Paul and I were when we counted elephants from the air. You've become so dour and depressed that you think any adventure — and any adventurer — will be as sour as you've become. Don't lay your personal troubles on the rest of the world. Especially not now that you have this lovely lady as your companion." He leaned over and gave Elizabeth a peck on the check.

Elizabeth smiled at Johnny, surprised that this playboy of the wildlife crowd could think so clearly and talk so philosophically. He had certainly hidden it well during their time in Tsavo.

"Don't let it get to you, Bruce. The future's Paul anyway — the next generation, free of our prejudices, and I hope free of the Horsts of the world — that is, if Paul ever gets ahold of himself." He put a hand on Paul's arm and looked into his eyes. "Cheer up, old son," he said. "You and I will go soaring in my new Cessna, anytime you want, next week maybe."

Paul gave him a slight smile. "I've been thinking about Mary again. What could be the meaning of her life, cut so short? Not thinking about much else, to tell the truth. Mary, the perfect observer, devoted to data, ever the empiricist. Science begins with observation, but the beauty of what is observed just isn't enough," Paul's voice trailed off.

The group was quiet for a while, lost in their own thoughts

Nearby, three American women sat down and began to chat about a safari they had just been on, loudly enough so that Elizabeth and the others could not help overhearing them.

"Oh, and those little tree creatures — what are they called?"

"Hyraxes, baby hyraxes."

"Oh, right. So cute! They reminded me of little Yodas — you know, from Star Wars."

Another group of tourists, each wearing a colored pin identifying him or her as a member of an elite and expensive guided tour, came out onto the veranda. They chose a table near Elizabeth and sat down, continuing to talk and laugh loudly. The men ordered beer, and the women white wine. As they munched on snacks, they talked excitedly about their forthcoming trip.

"Do you really think we'll see a leopard?" one of the women asked. "I'd so love to see one. How exciting!"

"I've seen at least one each time I've done the trip," one of the men answered. "Always up a tree feeding on a kill."

"Oh, how really exciting!" the woman exclaimed again. "And elephants. So marvelous." She turned to Elizabeth. "You look like you just returned from a safari. I'll bet you had a grand adventure. I'll bet you saw elephants!" she gushed. "Tell us about it — what was the famous wilderness really like? As grand as they say?"

"We've just returned from a scientific expedition in Tsavo," Elizabeth replied calmly.

"And did you collect any animals — live ones, I mean — to take back?" the woman asked.

"I'd say it was more that the animals collected us," Elizabeth answered.

"I do hope to bring something back. Just between us — us Americans, I mean—the last time I was here I took a rock hyrax back home."

"No!" said one of her companions. "How did you ever get it?"

"That part's a secret, but I will tell you that I put it into a cat carrier, and that's what I told them it was. And nobody asked any questions." She turned to Elizabeth. "You're a scientist. What do you think about my doing that? I mean, I'm just one person but I have a lot of curiosity. *Scientific* curiosity. So I thought it was okay. I mean, not everybody should do that. But it was just me. And I just had to take it home, it was so adorable." She winked. "Speaking strictly scientifically."

"I never heard s-e-l-f-i-s-h-l-y pronounced that way," Elizabeth replied. "But since you asked what I think—"

"Did I?" said the woman, clearly already regretting it.

"You certainly did," her companion said.

"Well, I'll tell you what I think," Elizabeth said. "First of all, if you're asking whether it matters if you take one bush baby away from the entire population, the answer is no, it doesn't — if you're the only one to do it. As for bringing it into the United States without its undergoing quarantine, that could pose a problem. A lot of serious pests have been brought into North America by well-meaning people. So, yes, that would be a bad thing to do." Elizabeth was beginning to lose control. "Now, if you're asking me whether it's okay for someone to believe they are somehow special and therefore have some kind of special right —"

Bruce grabbed her arm and interrupted. "What she means is that it probably wasn't the best idea, and we certainly hope you won't try such a thing again. You won't, will you, dear?" He looked the woman straight in the eye, and Elizabeth saw that the stupid creature was entranced by his gaze.

"I'm a big-game hunter and guide, so I've taken many people out into the parks here. We always discourage that kind of thing. It is hard to resist, though, isn't it? Especially bush babies, they're so appealing. But surely you didn't catch it yourself, did you?"

The woman giggled. "Well, I'm certainly not going to tell *you*. You might shoot me!"

"There, there, dear," Bruce said. "You just go and have a good time, and leave the animals here this time, won't you?" He looked her straight in the eye without smiling.

She nodded obediently and held out her hand. "So much fun to meet you. A real live big-game hunter, like Robert Redford. You even look like him. What a lucky girl you are," she said, turning to Elizabeth. Bruce took one look at Elizabeth's expression and tightened his grip on her arm. Her face was starting to get a certain angry look that he'd learned didn't bode well. Fortunately, the other group left shortly..

"Stupid bitch," Elizabeth said. "Stupid goddamned bitch. We went through all this to save the parks for people like her? Well, shit on that!"

Bruce sat back and smiled at her admiringly.

"And why the hell are you grinning at me?" she said. "When I get pissed off, you grin at me. You think this is funny?"

He laughed. "Ah, Liz, there's no other woman like you. You're as tough as any man I've seen, but the madder you get, the prettier you are. Believe me, I'm not laughing because I think you're silly. I'm laughing from sheer pleasure."

"Well said, old man, "Johnny said admiringly. "No woman could stay mad after that."

"You're patronizing me," she said, but she smiled, and it was clear that Johnny was right. Bruce did respect her, she knew that. He was a survivor, and so was she. He was rational and practical, and so was she. Or, at least both of them were becoming more so — more than when she'd started the trip, and maybe with a little help from each other they'd improve even more.

Of a sudden, the air seemed to change. There was a bustle of activity. Elizabeth looked toward the door. All of it seemed to swirl around a large figure coming to them in an oversized flapping Hawaiian shirt. All at the table were up and moving toward him.

"Howie!" Elizabeth exclaimed, the first to reach him. The others waited until their bear hug was over, then each took a turn embracing him, laughing and talking of their happiness in seeing him. He was slimmer than he had been — burnt from the sun with scabs from insect bites — but his smile was radiant.

"Here, sit down," said Bruce, waving toward a waiter. "Round of drinks here!"

"So, the rangers tracked down the Waliangulu people, made a night raid and gotcha? We'd heard that something like that was in the works, but had no idea it worked," Johnny said.

"That's about it," said Howie, grinning broadly. "Actually, it was Joseph that led them to me."

"So what was it like being with those Waliangulu? They hurt you at all?" Paul asked.

"Not a bit. But their food left something to be desired. And they were moving constantly. But, tell the truth, they sure know how to survive Tsavo. Better'n us."

"You're amazing," said Elizabeth. "There's no one like you, Heck."

"No one close," Bruce said, smiling widely.

"I'll have stories for you later," said Howie. "Now I just want to soak in some civilization."

The waiter arrived with drinks.

Paul seemed to come alive with Howie next to him.

"Heck, I just had a great idea, now that you've turned up. In fact, you've turned up just at the right time,," he said.

"How's that?"

"Got another project. Turned out that the organization Horst worked for fired him. Asked me to lead a new project. I wanted to do it, but then I thought about getting a team together on my own.

Wasn't sure I wanted to be with a bunch of strangers. And I couldn't think of anybody who knew about soils that I could work easily with. Now I realized you've got to come along. You're the man I was looking for, and it would be great to have a friend along as well. In fact, I believe I couldn't do it without you."

"On no, not another one of your wonderful safaris just to have a good time and see a lot of wildlife out here in Africa," Howie laughed.

"Nope. North America."

"And there I was with the Waliangulu, lots of time to think. Thought you'd have given up on this science stuff.

"Not yet. Can't get it right every time

"What is it, this new project?"

"Got to say yes before I tell you."

Howie looked at Paul, then at each of the others one at a time.

"Think I should trust this guy?"

"Come on Heck," Paul said, a grin widening on his face.

"Okay, yes, I'll go with you. 'Long as it's in North America. What the hell is it?"

"Gonna do the first scientifically sound count of polar bears in north Ontario – Canada – that is.

Nobody's done that before."

"Oh shit," Howie said.

"Don't worry. There's nineteen subpopulations, but we're only going to count one," Paul said, tipping his glass to Howie.

"Like I said, oh shit." Howie took a long pull on his drink.

"You agreed. As I said, can't do it without you. You'll have plenty of time to cool off, lose that sunburn."

They all were laughing, toasting Paul and Howie's next project when suddenly Joseph was striding toward them. He pulled Howie up from his chair into a bear hug. He seemed too full of emotion to talk.

"I'm good, Joseph. I'm fine," said Howie, but thanks again for saving me.

"Hell, by the time I found you, you were just about half Waliangulu. Probably would have had a happy life with 'em."

"'Cept for their food choices, yeah, maybe. Roll of the dice. Rather be here."

Bruce found another chair at a nearby table. "Here you go, Joseph."

Paul stood and motioned for the waiter.

"Sir – we'll have another round here and we've got a another in our party. Don't forget him."

EPILOGUE

On the Tsavo Plains

Spring, 1980

On the Tsavo plains, within an emptiness beyond his eyesight, near a baobab broken open, the ancient elephant stood. He lowered his trunk, pulled sand into his nostrils, and, raising his trunk high, blew the sand over his head, neck and back. The blinding sun blazed upon his back. He moved slowly, stopped, and picked up a long, shiny object, like a straight stick but with a sharp and large bulge at the end. He rolled it in his trunk and put it into his mouth. He walked slowly, carrying it around, the way he carried elephant bones. It smelled of those two-legged creatures he had seen so many times, especially like the pale female, the small one. Even though Mary's body had been recovered and flown back to the States, some scents from her remained. By a rock under a tree, he picked up a soft rectangle of a shiny substance. Sniffing it, he shuffled away, up a small rise and looked down on the raised soil, peering at it as if through bifocals, then meandered in a slow circle around the raised earth. He dropped the soft, shiny object and turned.

A pack of hyenas came toward him, seeking, smelling. One slunk by him and started to paw at the ground. Zamani Baba turned and charged, picking the hyena up in his trunk, cutting into it with his tusks. He tossed it high into the air, and when it fell to earth he charged and trampled it. Then he let out a loud trumpeting, a mournful sound that carried across the open grasslands. In a nearby tree, a crowned hornbill, busily putting mud into a hollow, flew up, circled, cried its own mournful call, and fluttered back to its tree. A pair of weaverbirds hunted for nest materials. One picked up some golden strands, thinner than the stems of a vine, and flew away. The other picked up a small seed with the shape of a cross on it, flew in a circle, changed its mind and poked the seed into the ground, then flew away, following its mate.

The ancient bull moved on, chewing on dried leaves from scattered shrubs along its way. Far off a dust cloud rose in the west, lit by the setting sun. The big bull lifted his head to look, but what he saw with an elephant's eyesight we will never know. No other animals approached as the darkness descended.

Long after, on a clear fall day, Bruce and Paul drove from Nairobi south to the Manyani Gate. They parked their car and stepped out to look at the countryside, the small box Elizabeth had given Paul still in his pocket, unopened. The land to the horizon was the golden brown of a lion's fur stretched out to dry. At the end of the furry, shrub-filled landscape, the horizon formed a straight line like a part cut by a knife blade into the lion's skin. In the midday light, the sky was a blinding blue, too bright to be real, whitened by dust blown up from the almost treeless landscape.

They wandered eastward, separating, each with his own thoughts. Bruce looked into the distance and was silent. What he thought we will never know. Paul strode to the top of a small rise, took out the box and opened it. He realized it contained the seeds Baker had given to Mary and the necklace she wore and loved given to her by her aunt. He scattered the seeds, then went to the rock by the tree where the big elephant had found something. Paul put the necklace back into its box, dug a shallow grave-like hole and buried the box forever there.